PRAISE FOR DEMOCRACY HACKED

'The world is belatedly waking up to some frightening realities about the intersection of digital technologies and the health of democracies. Martin Moore's book is a sharp wake-up call – ambitious in its sweep and urgent in its important message.'

Alan Rusbridger, author of *Breaking News*

'*Democracy Hacked* gets beyond the headlines – a compelling, informed and highly readable account of how democracy is being disrupted by the tech revolution, and what can be done to get us back on track. One of the best expositions I've read yet of what is the biggest political challenge of our generation.'

Jamie Bartlett, author of *The People Vs Tech* and *The Dark Net*

'Enormously wide-ranging and deeply researched, this is the definitive account of how digital technology has changed the entire political landscape, with profound consequences for democracy. From Brexit to Trump, and from Estonia to the Philippines, Martin Moore uncovers the real stories behind the fake ones. You'll discover that the truth is often stranger than fiction and that the future is more open than you think.'

David Runciman, author of *How Democracy Ends*

'Eye-opening… An important, timely, and clearly written look at a crucial subject.'

Booklist

'Moore demonstrates how data has affected elections across the world, in the Philippines, Turkey, India, Iran, Britain and beyond… Engrossing, instructive, and urgently necessary.'

Kirkus

ABOUT THE AUTHOR

Martin Moore is director of the Centre for the Study of Media, Communication and Power, and a senior lecturer in the Department of Political Economy at King's College London. He was previously founding director of the Media Standards Trust (2006–2015) where he won a Knight News Challenge award and a *Prospect* Think Tank award. He writes extensively on the news media and public policy, and lives on a farm in Oxfordshire.

DEMOCRACY
HACKED

How Technology is
Destabilising
Global Politics

Martin Moore

ONEWORLD

A Oneworld Book

First published by Oneworld Publications Ltd, 2018

This paperback edition published 2019

Copyright © Martin Moore 2018

ISBN 978-1-78607-575-8
eISBN 978-1-78607-409-6

Typeset by Hewer Text UK Ltd, Edinburgh
Printed and bound in Great Britain by Clays Ltd, Elcograf S.p.A.

Oneworld Publications Ltd
10 Bloomsbury Street
London WC1B 3SR
England

Stay up to date with the latest books,
special offers, and exclusive content from
Oneworld with our newsletter

Sign up on our website
oneworld-publications.com

To Jojo

CONTENTS

INTRODUCTION

There is a washed-out old colour photograph, taken in autumn 1974, of my family sitting in an orange Triumph convertible. I am sitting in the back seat, aged four, wearing a Davy Crockett hat, looking chilly and a little grumpy. My dad and my elder sister are squeezed in the back with me, while my baby brother is sitting on my mum's lap in the front passenger seat. Stuck on the door of the car is my dad's campaign poster for the upcoming general election. It was his second as a candidate – his first having been only seven months earlier – and we were out leafleting, door-knocking and canvassing constituents. I cannot imagine I was much help but, over the course of the campaign, my dad was determined to knock on every door in the constituency. When – or rather if – someone opened it, he would make his pitch and hear what they wanted from a candidate. The script, if you could call it that, was his own, and the only help and direction he received from central office was a national campaign guide, containing a list of general policy statements from the party.

That world is coming to an end. This is not meant as a sort of 'The End is Nigh' sandwich board slogan. But the democracy of long-established, rigidly hierarchical, centrist parties is collapsing. The idea that we should entrust the job of informing people about news and politics to an exclusive group of news outlets is disappearing. The concept of sporadic political representation through occasional elections is losing its legitimacy. And, the idea that we could ignore politics most of the time – and be ignored in return – is fading into a sepia past.

Almost half a century on, political campaigning is virtually unrecognizable. Official campaigns are powered centrally by mountains of voter data, run through complex algorithmic models, and used to micro-target messages to the most sought-after voters. You are no longer an anonymous resident of 43 Belvedere Avenue. You are known by hundreds of 'data points' that capture what you buy, what you earn, what you read, what you watch, who you know and what you care about. Merge this with campaign survey data and a candidate will know whether to lavish you with attention, appeal to you for a donation, or perhaps even discourage you from going out to vote. Unofficial campaigns – those fought by wealthy individuals and organizations, by pressure groups and by us, the great unwashed public – have changed even more. We all now have access to such an arsenal of digital tools that we can take up arms and fight for our own message on the same battlefield.

Already, Donald Trump's victory in 2016 has been written off by some as a peculiar confluence of circumstances, a freak black-swan event that will not be repeated. But political surprises are becoming the norm. Before the election of Donald Trump there was Narendra Modi's Indian landslide in 2014, Rodrigo Duterte's shock win in the Philippines in May 2016 and the Brexit vote a month later. After Trump there was Emmanuel Macron's ascension in 2017, Jeremy Corbyn's double-digit swing in the UK election the same year and M5S's rise to dominance in Italy in 2018. You might say there are good material reasons for people's anger at the political establishment and frustration with the neo-liberal global financial order. Or that these surprises are an ongoing response to the global economic rupture of 2008, and the twin spectres of climate change and mass migration. But there has been similar anger and frustration before, with much more predictable political outcomes. No, these political surprises – and there will be more – cannot be understood without recognizing the fundamental transformation of our communications environment.

The revolution in digital communications – the collapse of news media and the rise of dominant tech platforms like Google, Facebook and Twitter – is buffeting our elections, capsizing conventional candidates and drowning centrist parties. More than that, it is restructuring our politics, undermining existing institutions and remaking the role of the citizen. It is creating openings for those who previously had none, space in which to sidestep norms, rules and established practices, and opportunities for gaming and distortion. If we are to have any chance of determining the type of political system that will emerge from this maelstrom, then we need to start by trying to understand it.

The political upheavals of 2011 were the first proper sign of the scale of disruption, though democratic governments drew the wrong conclusions from them. Across North Africa and the Middle East, citizens used digital tools like Facebook and Twitter to incubate protest and coordinate collective action against authoritarian and autocratic governments. Watching these revolutions unfold, democratic governments, and those running the digital platforms, congratulated themselves. Their mistake was to assume that their tools were inherently democratizing, when technology was simply enabling new ways of pursuing political ends. Those who saw how politically powerful these platforms could be, and used digital tools to pursue their political aims, benefited disproportionately. It did not matter if these aims were democratic, autocratic or anarchistic.

Authoritarian governments, scared to death by what happened that year, took a very different lesson from the Arab Spring, and sought to tame and domesticate the net. In Russia, Vladimir Putin's government looked to impose digital sovereignty, requiring that all personal data of Russian citizens be held within Russia, and forcing all blogs with a readership of over three thousand visitors a day (not much bigger than a decent Instagram account) to register as regulated media organizations. In Iran, President Rouhani set about building a national internet, complete with its own government-approved domestic sites, the first stage of which was completed by the end of 2017. The Chinese government already had the Great Firewall and Great Shield to police the net, but extended and deepened its methods of control, experimenting with even more invasive systems like Social Credit.

The year 2016 should have been our wake-up call. Our old democratic systems are just as prone to being gamed. This is not a partisan political point, though some will undoubtedly interpret it as such. What became clear in 2016 was that those who consciously sought to upend the status quo, and who used digital tools to do so, had far greater success than they would have had at any other point over the previous half century. This is why the three types of 'hackers' who successfully distorted the 2016 US election – individuals, plutocrats and foreign states – ought to be seen not as anomalies, but as models for what is coming next. Seeing them as models allows us to understand how they did what they did, what helped them do it, and how others can do the same, whether this means deploying memetic warfare tools, amassing vast voter data sets, developing sophisticated behavioural targeting methods, or poisoning the democratic well with false information. These methods, like the digital ecosystem generally, are not unique to any particular political persuasion, though they work better for those at the extremes than those in the centre, for those wanting to transgress political principles and conventions, and for those willing to ignore ethical norms.

None of the hackers could have done what they did had politics not migrated online. We get our political information online, we join and like political campaigns online, we donate to political causes online, we sign online petitions, and some of us even vote online. We have already seen "the first campaign in the UK to put almost all [of its] money into digital communication", according to the director of the UK's official Vote Leave campaign after the 2016 Brexit referendum. It is rare now to find a political consultancy that does not sell itself on its data, digital and social media skills. Cambridge Analytica achieved global infamy for the amount of digital personal data it collected and used to target voters, but it was hardly unique.

These models might have remained distinct to the US, except for the fact that politics has not only migrated online, but onto a handful of transnational digital platforms. Techniques and tools pioneered in America can as easily be tried in Britain, Germany, India, Malaysia or Brazil. Though each country's political context is different, the same communications platforms are dominant in almost all. Amongst these, three stand pre-eminent: Facebook (and its subsidiaries WhatsApp, Instagram and Messenger), Alphabet (notably Google and YouTube) and Twitter. Together these have become the virtual *public sphere*, though a world away from the one imagined by the German philosopher Jürgen Habermas when he first popularized the term.

Of the three, Facebook became the platform of choice for political campaigners. It is not hard to see why. By 2018 Facebook had well over two billion active users and in some countries had become almost synonymous with the internet. Across South and East Asia, for example – in Thailand, Taiwan, Sri Lanka, Singapore, Malaysia, Myanmar, Laos and Indonesia – more than eight out of ten people on the internet were also on Facebook.

Democratic systems had begun to feel its full force in 2012, when Facebook turned itself into the world's most powerful propaganda machine. This was not due to any Machiavellian master plan, or because Mark Zuckerberg entertained ambitions to be US president. It was more banal than that. Facebook needed to justify its valuation and fund its ambition to connect the world. To do this it leveraged its most valuable assets – reach, attention and personal information – to produce the tools that would allow commercial advertisers to target their customers with unprecedented accuracy and efficiency. It was not the social media platform's intention that these same tools should be used by political parties, activists, extremists or those determined to sow political chaos. Like the scientists who developed nuclear fission without predicting the frightening breadth of destructive uses to which it would later be put, the engineers at Facebook just built the most effective advertising service they could.

Anyway, those engineers might argue, it was not Facebook that first developed the surveillance-based, behaviour-driven advertising model that powered content and communication on the net. It was Google. Since 2000, Google had carefully constructed the largest, fastest, most sophisticated, most automated and most ludicrously complicated advertising superstructure ever known. The whole thing was built so as to minimize human involvement and maximize the latent power of algorithms and the market. So fantastically interlinked was it that an ad could target someone wherever they were in the world, almost wherever they were on the web, with the message most likely to make them click, at the lowest possible cost. Looked at from the perspective of an advertiser, this sounds fabulous. Looked at from the perspective of democracy, where a propagandist of any persuasion can reach the most susceptible (or vulnerable) voter at the most opportunistic moment with the message most likely to provoke a reaction, it is not quite so appealing. The system was so open and frictionless that it couldn't easily distinguish between an ad selling facial cream and an ad selling fascism.

The faster and more virtual our political communication and information systems have become, the more weightless they have become, constantly flitting to keep up with our wayward attention. As we consume information and news more quickly, skimming Twitter, dipping into Instagram, leaping in and out of

WhatsApp, so we lose track of what has substance and what does not. At the same time, in the background, our stolid, flawed, necessary mechanisms for reporting the news and separating the weighty from the weightless have shrunk and withered.

As democratic governments started to gauge the extent of political disruption caused by digital platforms in the years after 2016, they floundered in trying to find ways in which to respond. Some hoped that the market would act as a self-correcting mechanism. Others decided it was time for the state to step in and take greater control of the net. The real question is, where will democracies go next? Based on their reactions so far, they look like they will splinter in three directions: towards *platform democracy*; towards *surveillance democracy*; and towards a re-formed – 'rehacked' – *digital democracy*. In the first, digital platforms will become even more powerful than they currently are, such that they become gateways not just to commercial services, but to public services like healthcare, education and transport. In this scenario, switching digital platform in the future could have a greater effect on citizens' lives than changing their elected government. In the second scenario, the state will ascribe far more power to itself, such that it has much greater ability to watch, nudge and direct its citizens. Necessarily, in this model, many of the freedoms that citizens currently enjoy will be much more constrained. Both these directions – towards an etiolated government or towards an over-powerful state – have long been seen as innate frailties of democracy. Way back in 1861, at the start of the US Civil War, Abraham Lincoln asked Congress whether there was "in all republics, this inherent, and fatal weakness". "Must a government," Lincoln said, "of necessity, be too strong for the liberties of its own people, or too weak to maintain its own existence?" The digital communications revolution, and the rise of the tech giants, makes this question urgent once again.

There is a third direction, which is towards a rehacked democracy for the digital age. Those that want to head in this direction will need to rethink what democracy – "perhaps the most promiscuous word in the world of public affairs" – really means, and what aspects of it need protecting. Having figured this out, they will need to radically reform their current political systems and redistribute power in a way that many incumbents will not like. This will mean electing political leaders who have foresight, bravery and acumen.

We are at what communications scholar Robert McChesney has called a "critical juncture". A growing number of people are recognizing that our democratic political systems are no longer working as they should. Equally, we are coming to realize that the digital platforms we thought were supporting and enhancing these systems are actually undermining and reshaping them. Democratic governments and policy makers have come late to this realization, prompted by mounting evidence of political abuse of the platforms. Yet, as they learn about this abuse, so, despite their limited understanding, they rush collectively to respond. "A little learning", the poet Alexander Pope wrote in 1709, "is a dang'rous thing: / Drink deep, or taste not the Pierian spring." So it is with government responses at this critical juncture. Some sniff the dangers of digital disruption and hare off in the wrong direction. Others invest further responsibility in the platforms themselves, trusting them to figure out how to fix politics in the digital sphere. Going in either of these directions will hasten the demise of liberal democracy and usher in a new political era: an era that may be more efficient and convenient, but will also be less tolerant, less forgiving and less free. We can take a different path, where we allow democracy to evolve such that it benefits from digital technology but is not directed by it, and where we renew people's faith in the efficacy of democratic political systems, but only if we act now.

Part 1
HACKERS

1

INDIVIDUALS: THE FREEXTREMIST MODEL

> Bollocks to the rules! We're strong – we hunt! If there's a beast,
> we'll hunt it down! We'll close in and beat and beat and beat—!
> William Golding, *Lord of the Flies*

In the weeks before the elections to the Bundestag in September 2017, a group of German extremists were conspiring online to raise support for the far-right Alternative für Deutschland (AfD) and to suppress votes for its mainstream opponents. More than five thousand of them were members of a private, anonymous internet chat channel called Reconquista Germania. There they discussed how to use technology to coordinate their activities, how to hijack the agenda on social media, to mob established politicians, to attack mainstream media, to synchronize social networking raids, and to nurture the normalization of hateful and prejudicial language and images in political debate.

When they were ready, at the beginning of September 2017, the group announced publicly that it was "opening the meme war against the half-breeds in parliament".[1] "Blitzkrieg Against the Old Parties!" one of the members screamed online. Another called for the storming of the offices of the German news outlet *Der Spiegel*. On a separate internet channel, called #Infokrieg or Infowar, there were chatrooms devoted to developing extremist political propaganda and discussing strategies to game Twitter. In parallel, on an online imageboard on the website 4chan, German users were building up a library of inflammatory images with slogans ready to spread across social media. In one section of the German subforum called 'meme jihad', *Buzzfeed* reported, members posted links to YouTube videos explaining how to make extremist content go viral.[2] Some of these images used Japanese anime, and many included Pepe the Frog, while others deliberately referenced Nazi and anti-Semitic imagery. Elsewhere on the same website, researchers at the Institute for Strategic Dialogue (ISD) found, members shared "psychological operations resources", for use during the 2017 German election campaign, "such as a 'step by step how to manipulate narratives' that links to GCHQ online deception and disruption playbooks".[3]

Despite their limited numbers, these extremists were able to have a distorting and damaging impact on the German election. They took down an aspiring politician, raised 'patriotic videos' to the top of YouTube's plays, and repeatedly gamed social media. "In the two-week run-up to the election," the ISD discovered, "not a single day passed when #AfD was not in the top two trending hashtags in Germany." The aim was not just to mobilize the far right, but to militarize political discourse online, smother other voices and stifle turnout for the mainstream parties. In early September, before these groups became highly active, the AfD was lying fifth in the polls. At the election itself it came third, winning 13.3% of the vote, exceeding most polls and expectations, and enabling a far-right party to enter the Bundestag for the first time since 1961.

If this was unique, then we could probably ignore it and assume that it will not happen next time, or elsewhere. But the strategies and techniques had been used before September 2017 and have been used since. They have become part of a toolkit used by ideologues, mercenaries and political footsoldiers to try to hack democratic politics and elections. Though the toolkit has been enthusiastically and energetically adopted by the far right, it is not particular to one country, nor to one specific political ideology. Indeed, many of the methods are straightforward and accessible to anyone with the time and inclination. How did we get here? How do we find ourselves in a place where democratic processes and norms have degenerated into open conflict across digital platforms? A place where political campaigners trade psy-ops manuals, discuss open source intelligence techniques and talk about memetic warfare; where people produce bot armies in their bedrooms; and where online campaigners race to 'own the political narrative', or to flood the digital public sphere with their hyper-partisan perspective.

To understand where we have got to, we have to trace the thread back before the election cycles of 2016–17, before the development of social media, before even the invention of the World Wide Web. Follow the trail back and you discover that being able to navigate round existing societal norms and values, coordinate collective action at speed, and undermining existing power structures, was baked into the original structures of the internet. Of course, back then there was no sense that doing this was political – in the real-world sense. It was just how you did things on the net. Cyberspace was separate from the real world – the 'meatspace'. In cyberspace, decisions were made differently; communities were self-governing and made up their own rules; nation states and corporations held little sway. Few of the early settlers in cyberspace anticipated that the virtual population would soon rival or even exceed that in the real world. Few thought that the practices and beliefs that governed their communities would harden into ideologies. And it would have been anathema for them to think that these online communities would ever start fighting one another, or that these battles could spill over into mainstream politics, or – heaven forbid – that democratic systems could be upended as a result. Indeed, those who bought into the ideals of cyberspace – the engineers, the idealists and the digital homesteaders back in the 1980s world of the DeLorean and Space Invaders – were characterized by their digital optimism. The future they conceived was a utopia.

★

In November 1984, in an old military base by the Rodeo Lagoon just north of San Francisco, 150 hackers got together for a three-day conference organized by Stewart Brand and Kevin Kelly. It had been over a decade since Brand published the last edition of the iconic Whole Earth Catalog in 1971, and he had just embarked on a new project to catalogue the burgeoning world of computer software. The original Whole Earth Catalog, pulled together by Brand from offices in Menlo Park between 1968 and 1971, was a hotchpotch of counter-cultural how-tos coupled with a dash of consumerism and tech utopianism, all bound together in an over-sized print volume. It managed to mash together everything from fixing a Volkswagen to growing your own marijuana, from finding a deerskin jacket to using the new Hewlett-Packard calculator. It was like an early version of the hyperlinked web but in print. Or, as Apple's founder Steve Jobs said in 2011, "It was sort of like Google in paperback form."

For someone who has had such a profound influence on the modern world, Stewart Brand is remarkably little known outside Silicon Valley. Three times, in three decades, Brand managed to draw together seemingly disparate cultural threads and cohere the voice of a new generation: in the late 1960s with his Whole Earth Catalog, in the 1980s through the hackers' conference and the Whole Earth 'Lectronic Link, and in the 1990s with *Wired* magazine (again organized with Kevin Kelly). Brand encapsulated, both in who he was and in what he did, the seemingly contradictory "Californian Ideology" – as defined by Richard Barbrook and

Andy Cameron back in 1995 – of the marriage of the freewheeling alternative generation with tech innovation and free-market entrepreneurialism.[4]

When Brand organized the first-ever hackers' conference in 1984, he was seeing how the ideals he had managed to connect in the Whole Earth Catalog transferred to the world of computers. He was exploring whether the spirit of the 1960s Merry Pranksters that he had captured in print was reflected in the ethics and sensibilities of the growing community of entrepreneurial computer geeks. In particular, he was seeing if these hackers embraced the "Hacker Ethic" that was described in a new book by Steven Levy.[5] Levy, who was at the conference himself – nervously watching participants leaf through his freshly printed book – had identified six ethics, from "Access to computers . . . should be unlimited and total" through to "Computers can change your life for the better." All of them struck a chord. But the one that best captured the ideology of the hackers, that melded the individual geeks into a wider collective, and that would prove the most revolutionary, was the second, that "All information should be free." As Fred Turner writes in *From Counterculture to Cyberculture*, "Like the mystical energy that was supposed to circulate through the communes of the back-to-the-land movement, binding its members to one another, information was to circulate openly through the community of hackers, simultaneously freeing them to act as individuals and binding them in a community of like minds."[6] 'Information', as Levy described it, refers to code, and 'free' to its flow through the computing system, rather than to its cost. Indeed, some of the hackers at the conference emphasized that 'free' did not mean they could not charge for their work. Brand tried to make this distinction when he said to the participants that "on the one hand information wants to be expensive, because it's so valuable . . . On the other hand, information wants to be free, because the cost of getting it out is getting lower and lower all the time." Yet, as happens with powerful ideas, this distinction soon got lost, leaving the belief that 'all information should be free' as the first catechism of internet citizens, or netizens.

While the hacker community was emerging in the 1970s and early 1980s, John Perry Barlow was writing lyrics for the Grateful Dead, and running the Bar Cross Land and Livestock Company in Wyoming. You would not have thought that, in between writing songs and cattle ranching, Barlow would become an early migrant to cyberspace. And had it not been for Steward Brand, he probably would not have done. But, following the hackers' conference Brand and Larry Brilliant set up the Whole Earth 'Lectronic Link or WELL. The WELL was essentially an early text-based bulletin board, where subscribers could post topics and others could respond. While Brilliant sorted out the technology, Brand gathered together the community. Given his munificent social network this turned out to be an eclectic mix of hackers, journalists, writers, musicians and lyricists. Much like the communes of the 1960s, Brand wanted this community to be open, uninhibited and self-governing. Barlow, who joined the Grateful Dead's David Gans on the WELL in 1987, was immediately captivated by it. Cyberspace, Barlow thought, was a new, unexplored territory, an 'electronic frontier'. Here he had the chance to experience "the noble, essentially human, act of plunging off into unassayed wilderness", of going west to find gold and glory: something his parents and grandparents had done in the physical world, but which had so far been denied to his generation. Now, "another frontier yawns before us," he wrote excitedly. "This frontier, the Virtual World, offers opportunities and perils like none before. Entering it, we are engaging what will likely prove the most transforming technological event since the capture of fire."

So taken was Barlow by this idea of cyberspace as an unexplored land where he and fellow adventurers could go forth and settle, that he took strong exception when the old world intruded into the new. In 1990, when a small games book publisher was almost put out of business after the US Secret Service raided its offices and accessed its emails in search of a document (which was not there), Barlow and two others from the WELL formed the Electronic Frontier Foundation – to protect civil liberties in cyberspace. When, six years later, the US government tried to introduce a law that would punish the exchange of 'obscene or indecent' communications amongst those under eighteen, Barlow penned his infamous Declaration of the Independence of Cyberspace. "Governments of the Industrial World, you weary giants of flesh and steel, I come from Cyberspace, the new home of Mind," Barlow wrote in Jeffersonian tones. "On behalf of the future, I ask you of the past to leave us alone. You are not welcome among us. You have no sovereignty where we gather."[7] Despite its gravitas, Barlow dashed it off over the course of a night in Davos, in the midst of the World Economic Forum, in between dances with graduate students.[8] He published it online from Switzerland and, even in that pre-social-media era, it went viral. Even at this early stage in its evolution, the idea that the net was a new world that would be run by its inhabitants according to different rules than the old was magnetic and irresistible. So powerful was it that it gave birth to the second catechism of the net – that the inhabitants of cyberspace should be sovereign in their own land.

Not long after Barlow presented his declaration there was, just as he had predicted, an internet gold rush. Digital entrepreneurs, bloggers and prospectors rushed to settle this new-found land. Amongst the shopkeepers, self-promoters and innovators were pioneers wanting to set up new communities. Some of these took their lead from the early bulletin boards of the 1980s and 1990s, though each individual community was defined by the personal proclivities of its founder, and by whoever chose to settle there. Some sites evolved from the text-based format of bulletin boards into early weblogs like Memepool (1998); others distinguished themselves by letting people post images and text, like Fark (1999) and Something Awful (1999). One, set up a few years later in the summer of 2003 by Chris 'moot' Poole and called 4chan, looked similarly basic and homespun, though it had some distinctive characteristics. Characteristics which would, later, come to make all the difference.

★

It is impossible to explain the subsequent political impact of the 4chan community and the methods they devised without understanding how the site works. The architecture of the site and the way it functions are integral both to the way it was politicized and to its subsequent political impact.

4chan is an imageboard. This means that, to add something to the site, you have to post an image (or a video), beside which you can add comments. Others can then respond to your post with a comment, or another image and comment. There are no other ways to respond. You cannot, for example, like a post as on Facebook, or upvote it as on Reddit, or retweet it as on Twitter. If no-one responds, then your post quickly – very quickly – sinks down the page (and subsequent pages). A 2011 academic study found that most threads stayed on the home page for only five seconds, and on the site for less than five minutes.[9] When posts disappear, they are gone. Occasionally, memorable threads are captured on another site – Encyclopedia Dramatica – but there is no official archive (something originally done to save server space). Your post only rises again if someone responds, bumping it back up to the top of the board. Posts are anonymous – not pseudonymous but properly anonymous. There is a space where posters can add a name but few do, preferring to be allocated a random alphanumeric ID for that particular thread, plus the default name given to each user – 'Anonymous'. If they participate in a new thread they will receive a new ID. When the site started there was one board called /b/, for random posts. This was, and remained for most of 4chan's first decade, "the beating heart of the website".[10]

The evolutionary biologist Richard Dawkins invented the term 'meme' in 1976. It was, he wrote, information that spread through human culture like a virus, "as genes spread through the gene pool". As they spread they evolve and mutate. Indeed, the term itself evolved to refer to images – often accompanied by text – that spread, or went viral, online. The structure of 4chan was fantastically well suited to the production of these sorts of memes. Images posted to the site evolved or died. Memes were judged purely on the basis of their content, not context (since there was none), or author (since this was unknown). Those that were successful replicated. "The joke", Chris Poole told an interviewer in 2009, "is that a 4chan post is a repost of a repost of a repost . . . it's survival of the fittest. Ideas that are carried over to the next day are worth repeating."[11] Uninhibited by their real-life persona or by societal norms, users could experiment freely. Since no-one could own a meme, their production and adaptation was inherently collaborative – it was a genuine hivemind. This structure, as long as it was coupled with a large enough community, was bound to create viral content. And the community, which began as twenty of Poole's friends, had grown to 3.2 million users by 2008, and 9 million by 2011. Many users meant many posts, and frenetic image evolution. In 2010, MIT computer scientist Michael Bernstein and his colleagues discovered, 4chan users were adding 400,000 posts per day. Four in ten of these received no reply at all, and the median lifespan of a thread was under four minutes. It became, in Poole's words, a "meme factory". According to Whitney Phillips, who has studied online trolling since 2008, between 2003 – when 4chan was founded – and 2011, every meme created on the internet (or at least amplified) emerged from 4chan's /b/ board or those around it.[12] Global phenomena like lolcats and Rickrolling (a link that leads to Rick Astley singing 'Never Gonna Give You Up') emerged from 4chan, as did lucrative commercial businesses like ICanHasCheezburger and 9GAG. In some ways the structure of 4chan fitted perfectly with the model of Silicon Valley innovation – experiment, test, evolve. Or, to steal Facebook's original guiding ethos, move fast and break things. Similarly, this method resulted in memes that were tailor-made for the social media attention economy – guaranteed to engage people and to trigger a response. Still, had 4chan simply been a meme factory, its political influence would have been limited. It was the site's culture, coupled with its meme production, that gave it its destructive power.

*

Founding stories are central to the establishment of culture. Google's Sergey Brin and Larry Page are brilliant nerdy engineers, and Google is known as a company of brilliant, nerdy engineers. Twitter was hacked together by a bunch of chaotic, sleep-deprived twenty-somethings in San Francisco, who could not even decide what its purpose was. A decade after its invention it still had not really figured it out. 4chan was no different. Chris Poole – who looks a little like a cross between Ferris Bueller and his gangly friend Cameron Frye – was fifteen years old in 2003, living at home, and spending much of his time on the internet. Poole was a fan of Japanese anime and posted regularly to a site called Something Awful (the Anime Death Tentacle Rape Whorehouse subforum). Following his curiosity, he came across a popular Japanese imageboard – 2chan – whose speed and creativity surpassed anything in the US at that time. So, Poole says, he took 2chan's code and used it to build 4chan. He built something that he knew he – and presumably others like him – would like. He was not interested in leading the community, but participating in it. It turns out there were many users like him out there, who were not offended by things like Anime Death Tentacle Rape Whorehouses.

The culture of 4chan is toxic, and deliberately so. The need to shock in order to get noticed, the disinhibition created by anonymity, and the predominance of competitive young males on the site, quickly led to a culture that was self-consciously offensive, taboo-breaking and transgressive. Since anyone could post to the site and every poster was anonymous, the only way to create a distinctive community was through attitude and behaviour. The offensiveness, particularly towards women, Jews, the LGBT community and non-whites, sent a very clear message that, if you were offended by misogyny, anti-Semitism, homophobia or racism, then you were not welcome. This also explains their use of terms like 'fag' to describe people ('newfags', 'oldfags', 'Britfags'), and frequent references to raping and killing. Users argue that the language was used for effect, and should not be taken seriously. Those that do take it seriously, they argue, do not know 'Poe's law' of the internet. This states "that it is difficult to distinguish extremism from satire of extremism in online discussions unless the author clearly indicates his/her intent".[13] Or, to put it another way, devoid of context the language could just as likely be meant ironically as seriously. It is, 4channers would say, just for the lulz.

'The lulz' (an adaptation of 'lol') is the term most often used to describe the culture of the 4chan community (and its progenitors). It also explains why this toxic subculture did not remain in some isolated corner of the web but came to spread, and eventually to infect, almost the whole online public sphere. 'The lulz' translates better into German or British idiom than American. In German the word *Schadenfreude* is the best comparator – taking pleasure in someone else's distress. In English, it is 'just having a laugh' at someone's expense. At 4chan it meant throwing bricks at someone outside the 4chan community, then collectively enjoying the anguished or angry reaction. The more damaging the attack and the more emotive the reaction, the greater the lulz. This is by definition a destructive and nihilistic form of pleasure, but again, the structure of the site helps explain it. When you tot up how few community bonds tied 4chan users together, and how dissociated they were from one another in real life, then you start to understand why collective destruction became an essential glue. Have you ever conspired with a group of others to do something you know is against the rules or breaks social conventions? Most of us have, at least once. If you have, then you will know that, once the deed is done, you are complicit with your co-conspirators and share a common bond, even if you hardly know one another.

In pursuit of the lulz, the 4chan community developed a series of methods and techniques that were both highly effective and scalable. They would coordinate raids on other communities, flooding a YouTube video with comments or pictures, mobbing someone on Twitter, or gaming the votes on an online post – what became known as 'brigading'. They would get hold of deeply personal information from someone's Facebook profile or MySpace account and then send it to all their contacts or just publish it on the web – known as 'doxxing'. In one well-known early raid a 4channer found a high school student on MySpace who had not made her photos private – including some pictures of her naked.[14] They then doxxed her – took all her naked photos, posted them all over her MySpace account and sent them to everyone in her address book, her teachers at school and her parents. For the lulz. Techniques, such as how to DDoS, were posted on 4chan boards so that members could join in collective attacks. DDoS, or Distributed Denial of Service, is what happens when huge numbers of requests are made to a server so it temporarily collapses the system. A 4chan user would suggest a target website and, if other users agreed it ought to be attacked, then they would jump into an IRC channel (essentially a group instant messaging window) and plan how to hit it. Users also took great pleasure in gaming online systems. In 2009 the 4chan community gamed the top twenty-one places on the *Time* 100 Reader Poll, with Chris Poole as the winner. In each case, they found that working collectively they could cause havoc and then step back and laugh. As an Anonymous meme later said, "Because none of us is as cruel as all of us."

Up until 2007 most of these raids were at a small scale: individuals attacked on a whim, teenage pranks pulled on people or organizations that 4channers took against (to whom they would send unwanted pizzas, taxis or all-black faxes, or make prank calls). Occasionally the community would club together to do a good deed (such as sending flowers or crowdsourcing donations). Two things shifted the community and its methods to a much bigger stage: mainstream media and the Church of Scientology. On 27 July 2007 Fox News published a report in which the anonymous users of 4chan were described as "hackers on steroids" and an "Internet Hate Machine". As Whitney Phillips shows in her careful analysis of the role of mainstream media in building up the reputation of Anonymous, this and similar later coverage delighted those on 4chan. Infamy was exactly what the users wanted. TV coverage advertised their work, brought newbies to the community and credited channers with magical powers to manipulate the net. The more that mainstream media sensationalized 4chan and claimed it was the source of all evil, the more the community laughed at the inflated and melodramatic claims made about them while embracing their growing reputation.

The raid on the Church of Scientology began like many previous ones. On 15 January 2008, at 7:37 p.m., a 4chan user posted an image of the Scientology logo and titled it simply 'Scientology raid?'. The catalyst was the church's attempts to censor an embarrassing video featuring Tom Cruise, leaked by a member of the church and published on the Gawker website. Despite scepticism amongst some 4chan members, the proposed raid quickly gained support. Given the scale of the operation, word was put out beyond the site – to other chan imageboards. The collective adopted the name that 4chan users were given automatically, 'Anonymous'. The aim was to build a small army of raiders who could launch DDoS attacks on Scientology websites. What was most striking about the raid, and this is symptomatic of many attacks, was the accessibility of the weapons. Most of those participating, the journalist Parmy Olson found, were using an openly available online service that was designed to help stress-test websites. "Only a few Anonymous supporters were skilled hackers," Olson writes. "Many more were simply young Internet users who felt like doing something other than wasting time on 4chan or 7chan."[15] Within a fortnight, there were participants in over 140 different chans across forty-two countries. 'Project Chanology', as it was dubbed, spilt out of the internet and onto the streets, with protests outside Scientology centres in over a hundred cities worldwide. These continued sporadically through 2008 until eventually tailing off. Project Chanology showed how, if you wanted to instigate coordinated digital disruption, it was not hard to do – particularly through synchronized collective action. "If we can destroy Scientology," the original poster wrote over-excitedly, "we can destroy whatever we like!"

In the year following Project Chanology Fox News's Bill O'Reilly called the site "far left". This misunderstood the culture and motives of 4chan and its ilk. The community was not far left, indeed was not political in any traditional sense. Most of those who went to the site went for its dark entertainment value or to participate in malicious pranks. Yet the community did become highly politicized, first between 2008 and 2011, then after 2013. This politicization was partly a consequence of 4chan's structure. Research scientist Jessica Beyer, who studied four online communities for her book *Expect Us*, found that other communities – though their members were demographically similar – were not nearly so easily politicized as 4chan. Beyer ascribes this to the anonymity of 4chan, the relative lack of moderation (the site's 'janitors' were generally ignored), and the lack of small or intimate spaces. There is nowhere you can go for a one-to-one conversation, or a small group chat (without jumping off-site to a chat channel). The result was that when someone suggested a raid or something similar, if enough other people liked the idea, then they would join in – adopting particular techniques and roles depending on the activity. "If target and purpose did not resonate with enough people," Beyer writes, "nothing happened." Censorship – as with the Tom Cruise video – breached the first hacker ethic, that information should be free, and immediately resonated with the community as a consequence. It was political, but not in the traditional sense of 'left' versus 'right'.

The belief that 'all information should be free' also motivated Operation Payback, an operation that began as revenge for attacks on The Pirate Bay, a file-sharing site, in 2010 and morphed into retribution on behalf of WikiLeaks. WikiLeaks, and its founder Julian Assange in particular, captured the spirit of Anonymous hackers, even if Assange had not emerged from 4chan. "Julian Assange deifies everything we hold dear," an Operation Payback poster wrote. "He despises and fights censorship constantly [and] is probably the most successful troll of all time."[16] Taking revenge on the payment companies that stopped taking donations for WikiLeaks, the chan collective launched DDoS attacks on MasterCard, Visa and PayPal, bringing down the first two websites and slowing the third. After that, the 'hacktivism' spiralled and splintered. Various publications declared 2011 to be 'the year of the hack'. It was the year Anonymous became not just a US but a global phenomenon. The amorphous group was credited with helping Tunisians and Egyptians overthrow their governments in the Arab Spring, with taking down Sony's PlayStation Network, and with helping to lay the foundations of the Occupy movement. Parts of the mainstream liberal press started to write about it in fond terms, as a sort of digital Robin Hood. *The Atlantic* was even able to talk about "the mysterious, even mystifying allure of the 21st-century hacker".[17] Anthropologist Gabriella Coleman, who spent years researching Anonymous, came to admire these 'tricksters' and their antics: "This admiration stems from the fact that criminality reveals the limits of the state's monopoly on violence and the rule of law."[18]

This was a long way from the nihilistic, apolitical, toxic reputation 4chan had back in 2008. Rather than doing raids for the lulz, the 'moralfags' of Anonymous – as the hacktivists were known on 4chan – were doing them for a cause. They were no longer in it for the entertainment, they had become committed. Back on 4chan itself, the established members were not happy. Partly as a consequence of the success of Anonymous, its parent site was growing ever more popular and attracting lots of 'noobs' (new users). In August 2012, it had over twenty-two million unique visitors.[19] Old-timers "were constantly railing against the flood of 'newfags' and 'summerfags'", Whitney Phillips writes. 'The cancer', as they referred to recent arrivals, was taking over. 4chan's content – in terms of memes – was more popular still. 9GAG, which aggregated funny (and less offensive) memes from 4chan and around the web, claimed sixty-five million monthly visitors that summer.[20]

The flight of Anonymous from 4chan to Occupy and other radical causes, combined with the influx of newcomers to the site and the normalization of memes, provoked a reactionary lurch. Those left behind on 4chan reacted against the causefags, the noobs and the cute Advice Animals. They hunkered down and became more protective of their territory, more aggressive towards outsiders, more intransigent. These users, while sympathetic to the first tenet of netizens – *all information should be free* – were increasingly motivated by the second – *here we are sovereign*. Unsurprisingly, given the character of 4chan and its pursuit of pleasure at the expense of others, sovereignty was expressed as intolerance of the 'other'. The 'other' could be black people, or gay people, or Jews, or Muslims, or women. Discriminatory language had been inherent to 4chan since its earliest days, but language was hardening into ideology. A reactionary style merged into reactionary politics. This could be seen in the rise of 4chan's /pol/ board (short for 'politically incorrect') over /b/ (for random posts).

As 4chan lurched even further away from the centre, some of its members started other sites, copying the structure and approach of 4chan, yet still more extreme. "I had always been into 4chan, as I am at heart a troll," the self-proclaimed neo-Nazi Andrew Anglin later wrote. "This [2011–12] is about the time /new/ was going full-Nazi [/new/ preceded /pol/], and so I got into Hitler, and realized that through this type of nationalist system, alienation could be replaced with community in a real sense, while the authoritarianism would allow for technology to develop in a direction that was beneficial rather than destructive to the people."[21] In July 2013, Anglin set up the *Daily Stormer*, a far-right site named after *Der Stürmer*, a Nazi propaganda paper from the interwar period. Like 4chan, the site enabled users to post images anonymously, and Anglin set up 'Memetic Monday' to encourage members to develop right-wing propaganda memes (learning from 4chan's 'Caturday', which spawned lolcats). Also like 4chan, Anglin organized raids on other communities or individuals, appealing to his site's members – or 'Stormers' as he called them – to launch coordinated attacks. In 2014 he mobilized them to mob the British MP Luciana Berger, after a white supremacist who had attacked her was sentenced to four weeks in prison. The site even provided a user guide for abusers and a cache of anti-Semitic images.[22] That week, Berger received over four hundred abusive messages on Twitter. In October 2013 another 4chan user, Fredrick Brennan, launched 8chan, as a 'Free Speech Friendly 4chan Alternative'.[23]

Yet despite the reactionary turn, there was no sign – at this point – that users would participate in mainstream politics; and certainly no indication that they would swing their weight, as a community, behind a candidate from one of the two main parties in the 2016 US election. Indeed, though the political attitudes of chan members became more pronounced at this time, this only served to illustrate how disparate those attitudes were. Some users came out as neo-Nazis, others as ethno-nationalists, others as paleo-conservatives, as neo-reactionaries, as techno-libertarians, as national anarchists, or as survivalists. A whole other set of members – who may or may not have overlapped with the first – have been labelled 'the Manosphere', which includes men's rights activists, pick-up artists, anti-feminists, incels (for 'involuntary celibates') and 'men going their own way'.[24] Some members of these communities may well have become involved in the 2016 US election campaign of their own accord, but it is unlikely the chan collective would have mobilized at the scale and the extent that it did without being coaxed into the campaign.

★

It was in 2014 that Steve Bannon's Breitbart website started to woo these communities in order to encourage them to participate in the forthcoming election campaign in earnest. In one sense it is not surprising that Bannon and Breitbart should see these communities, and their techniques, as useful to their cause. They were committed – as their founder Andrew Breitbart had set out – to destroying the political and media establishment. What better way to take down the establishment than by enlisting the most destructive people and techniques on the net? Those at 4chan and its progeny had shown themselves to be enormously effective at producing powerful images that spread on social media, and at coordinating attacks on those they did not like. Both powers could be extremely effective during an election campaign. Yet, in another respect, the recruitment of these communities and their techniques to a democratic campaign is astonishing. These were groups that defined themselves by their prejudice and aggression – some explicitly described themselves as far-right neo-Nazi extremists. They were not interested in constructive dialogue or democratic process; they were motivated by how much havoc, disruption and distress they could cause. The only coherent ideological beliefs that linked these nihilistic communities together – beyond 'the lulz' – were that information should be free and that – online – they should be sovereign. Yet it was these beliefs that Bannon's Breitbart would use to enlist them in the forthcoming US election campaign.

Steve Bannon had first become intrigued by the power of these communities back in 2007. Back then, he told journalist and writer Joshua Green, he had been brought in to help run an online business that sold virtual items to multi-player gamers – like those on *World of Warcraft* – for real money.[25] The gamers hated companies like this and did all they could to force them out. The enterprise itself tanked, but Green writes that "Bannon was captivated by what he had discovered by trying to build the business . . . an underworld he hadn't known existed that was populated by millions of intense young men" whose collective power could destroy businesses. Prior to 2012, Breitbart would have struggled to enrol these users in its cause. It was only after Anonymous grew beyond the limits of 4chan (and after some of those involved were prosecuted by the FBI) that this subculture became more reactionary, partly in response to the normalization of aspects of trolling, and in defence of their sovereignty ('sovereignty' meaning anything from white supremacy to gaming to men's rights). Even then, it was far from inevitable that they would mobilize in support of any particular party or candidate. As a 4chan board – 'invasions' (/i/) – had memorably told users back in 2008, "We are not your personal army, we will not raid your ex or some random person without a lulzy motivation."

Before 2014 Breitbart virtually ignored 4chan and community sites like Reddit. Yet, in the autumn of that year, it saw an opportunity to draw members of these communities into its political crusade. This opportunity was #Gamergate. Given that #Gamergate subsequently became, in Buzzfeed's words, a "diffuse, hydra-headed internet phenomenon", it would require a doctoral thesis to describe it fully.[26] Distilled to its bare bones, disparate online users from 4chan and the gaming community convinced themselves that videogame journalism was unethical, and then used this belief to justify brutal and persistent online attacks – including multiple rape and death threats – against female journalists and game developers.[27] It might have remained a nasty but relatively self-contained episode had Breitbart – and subsequently Bannon and the Trump campaign – not sought to channel the anger and vitriol of the gamers towards political ends. Breitbart did this by presenting the battle as a front in a much larger cultural war, and framing channers as freedom fighters, defending their territory against unwanted outsiders and the suffocating dictates of the establishment. It leveraged, in other words, the only two political beliefs that held these subcultures together – information freedom and sovereignty. The left, as caricatured by Breitbart, was anti-freedom (expressed as 'political correctness') and anti-sovereignty (by being pro-immigration, pro-minorities and pro-gender equality).

It was Breitbart's freshly recruited firestarter, Milo Yiannopoulos, who in September 2014 leapt into the online #Gamergate wars and sought to become the champion of the gamer movement. To do this Yiannopoulos inverted the narrative. Instead of pointing to harassment, doxxing and mobbing by the activist gamers, he painted them as the victims of "an army of sociopathic feminist programmers and campaigners, abetted by achingly politically correct American tech bloggers".[28] He claimed that death threats sent to women online "aren't all they're cracked up to be", that hateful and violent tweets at women were simply "ungallant", and that campaigners were whipping up "death threat hysteria". Yiannopoulos's deliberately offensive and provocative articles consciously politicized #Gamergate, portraying it as symptomatic of a much bigger cultural phenomenon, where a corrupt establishment mainstream was seeking to kill off a free, self-governing online community. He stoked the anger so much that the online battles escalated, to the point where even Chris Poole, 4chan's founder, decided he had to ban #Gamergate debate from the site. The anger simply migrated to 8chan, where posts jumped from a hundred per hour to four thousand per hour.[29]

Yiannopoulos's support for the #Gamergaters in 2014 was, however, just a prelude to an even more blatant appeal by Breitbart to 4chan, 8chan and Reddit. On 27 October 2015, Breitbart launched a new section, or vertical, called Breitbart Tech. Its launch was equivalent to a manifesto for the members of these communities. "Readers", Yiannopoulos said in a launch video, "are sick of getting called trolls, harassers, misogynists, abusers, all because they don't agree with the opinions of journalists ... we'll stick up for channers when they want to stay anonymous, Redditors against overbearing moderators. We'll stick up for gamers against anyone stupid enough to take them on." This was followed by an invitation from Yiannopoulos to those on 4chan, 8chan and Reddit, and in online gaming, not just to become Breitbart readers, but to become part of a movement: "Join me ... as we take on the big tech companies, the government, VCs [venture capitalists], social justice warriors, and anybody else who wants to get between you, free speech and the truth." This was not a bid to get regular readers to tech news; this was an invitation to join the culture wars, on Breitbart's side. In case Yiannopoulos's invitation was not well enough signposted, the launch article was illustrated with a cartoon by a cult 4chan cartoonist, Ben Garrison. And, in another bid to mobilize channers against the left, a separate piece presented progressives as the enemies of anonymity. "Centres of anonymous culture, such as reddit [*sic*], 8chan and 4chan, are the subject of particularly fearful narratives," Yiannopoulos and his colleague Allum Bokhari wrote. Progressive writers and critics, they claimed, see anonymous commenters as "dangerous evildoers in need of punishment". Extraordinarily, they compared the "anonymous dissenters of today" with the authors of the Federalist Papers – including Alexander Hamilton, James Madison and John Jay (who originally wrote under pseudonyms).[30]

On the day Breitbart Tech launched, the lead story on the main site was an exclusive interview with Donald Trump. Having coaxed the channers, the Redditors and the gamers to the site, Breitbart wanted to make clear which presidential candidate was on their side. "With the exception of Mrs Clinton and her email scandal," the introduction to the interview began, "few presidential candidates of either party have been moved during their campaigns to discuss technology at length. That changes today, as Donald Trump gives an exclusive interview to Breitbart Tech about hacking, cyber-warfare and artificial intelligence." At the top of the piece Trump was drawn, like Schwarzenegger's Terminator, as a cyborg, complete with a Make America Great Again cap. From this point on, Breitbart presented itself as a friend and ally of the chans, the Redditors and the gamers. It was, it claimed, working with them to defend free speech fundamentalism and anonymity against any attempts by progressives on the left to take them away.

The framing of this as a fight for freedom against dark forces of control was not accidental. Breitbart was not recruiting volunteers for a traditional election campaign; it was drafting in footsoldiers to a culture war, one that would come to a head in November 2016. To mobilize this dispersed collection of lulzy malcontents it had to give them some coherence, and it did this by creating a common enemy. It also had to convince them that this enemy represented a direct threat to their world. You are in danger,

Breitbart warned: if you do not take up arms then you will be overrun by normies, noobs, social justice warriors and politically correct feminazis who will destroy your world and take over your freedoms. It presented the forthcoming election campaign, not as an opportunity to debate and discuss the policies and promises of parties and candidates, but as a war. The enemy in this war was 'the left', and, since the left had successfully overtaken the main-stream, this meant a battle to overturn the mainstream. "The reason I fought in the meme war," a frequent poster to /pol/ and 8chan told *Politico*'s Ben Schreckinger, "is that as Andrew Breitbart said we are at literal war with the left. There is an ideological Cold War going on right now and the victor will determine the fate of Western Civilization."[31]

Presenting the upcoming US election campaign as a war ration-alized the adoption of methods and tactics that, though brutally effective, were anathema to the democratic process. It meant encouraging an online army to develop political memes that created hyper-partisan, distorted or false narratives, that distracted and obscured substantive debate, that sought to demoralize constit-uencies and depress voter turnout, and that trashed candidates and critics. The channers, Redditors and gamers hacked opinion polls, raided opposing communities, doxxed journalists, harassed critics, gamed social media and baited mainstream media. They used digital tools and platforms to do to politics what Silicon Valley had already done to the economy and society, to cause disruption. On behalf of the Breitbart/Trump campaign they turned the US elec-tion into an ongoing guerrilla war in which participants assumed bad faith in others, and respect for social norms disappeared. And it was Breitbart, Steve Bannon and Donald Trump who drew these communities to their cause and who made these methods central to their campaign. In so doing they not only vandalized the demo-cratic process but – given their electoral success – provided a model that other campaigns could mimic.

Those involved in the Trump insurgency were aware that some of these methods were better suited to conflict situations than to democratic campaigns. Jeff Giesea is not a soldier or a professional propagandist. He has spent most of his career to date in Silicon Valley, working with tech billionaire Peter Thiel at Thiel Capital Management, investing in and selling internet start-ups. But in 2014 he became convinced that Western civilization was under threat and decided he wanted to do something about it. Based on his knowledge of social media, Giesea was aware of the power of memes, especially as a means of conflict propaganda. In a 2015 article for the journal *Defence Strategic Communications*, titled 'It's Time to Embrace Memetic Warfare', Giesea wrote that "for many of us in the social media world, it seems obvious that more aggressive communication tactics and broader warfare through trolling and memes is a necessary, inexpensive, and easy way to help destroy the appeal and morale of our common enemies". The stumbling blocks to using memes were, Giesea argued, conceptual and practical. Conceptually, people needed to understand that memetic warfare could "be viewed as a 'digital native' version of psychological warfare" and used to win the battle of narratives and ideas. Practically, it needed investment and software. Although Giesea was talking about using memes against ISIS/Daesh, he would later help apply this approach much closer to home. In 2016, working with men's rights 'alt-lite' activist Mike Cernovich and other Trump supporters, he set up MAGA3X, a pro-Trump mobilization campaign built on memes and flash mobs. Amongst other tools for Trump campaigners, MAGA3X provided a 'meme generator' that simplified the 4chan process for those less technically savvy, a 'demotivational poster maker' to discourage people from supporting other candidates, and a bank of emblematic images to which you just needed to add a caption.[32]

Enabling Trump supporters to participate in memetic warfare was complementary to the production of political memes by those steeped in meme generation at 4chan and 8chan. While it is extremely difficult to measure the production and dissemination of specific memes from the chans, given the ephemerality of posts and the way in which they mutate and spread, there is evidence that Chris Poole's 'meme factory' produced an enormous number of political memes, and that some of them were the most viral – and influential – of the campaign. This evidence comes from four sources: from the claims of the chans themselves; from an academic study that collected more than eight million 4chan posts in mid-2016; from the number of people who viewed and shared memes as compared to other political content; and from contemporary reports and analysis by news organizations.

Victory has a thousand fathers, John F. Kennedy said, and Trump's election win was no different. "We actually elected a meme as president," one 4channer posted the evening of the election.[33] Another wrote, "I don't think it's possible for an image to convey the level of smug I feel right now" (illustrating this with an image of Pepe the Frog). Soon many on 4chan were referring to the 'First Great Meme War', adapting images from the First World War. Members of 4chan were far from alone in claiming credit for winning Trump the election. This ignores the plethora of other factors that led to his victory, and obscures the fact that the chan subcultures' influence was more negative than positive. Yet it is true that they generated a huge number of original political images during the campaign. The academic study 'Keks, Cucks and God Emperor Trump', which collected 4chan posts from June to August 2016, found over one million unique images posted to /pol/. The majority of these images, the study found, "were either original content or sourced from outside /pol/". Some of the most infamous memes have also been tracked back to 4chan or 8chan, including Pepe the Frog, You Can't Stump the Trump, and an image of Hillary Clinton with the Star of David.[34]

One of the reasons it is difficult to trace these and other memes is due to how they were spread via social media. If the memes had stayed in the subcultural depths, then they would have had little influence on the electorate at large. Equally, the electorate at large were unlikely to tweet or share memes directly from 4chan. They therefore had to be laundered via major social media platforms and news sites. This was done via a network of Trump supporters on social media who could be relied upon to share the memes with their large followings – people such as Mike Cernovich, Anthime Gionet (also known as Baked Alaska), Jack Posobiec and Paul Joseph Watson – as well as through fake Twitter and Facebook accounts.[35] Memes were also posted to public Facebook pages like GodEmperorTrump and on some news sites' Facebook pages, like Breitbart's. One meme, which read "Remember that time Republicans rioted, beat innocent Democratic voters, destroyed property, and torched American flags? Me neither", was shared over 500,000 times from Breitbart's Facebook page. So popular were these images that, in the case of Breitbart, they far outstripped links to articles. A study by the Tow Center at Columbia University found that while "images made up just 5 percent of Breitbart's total posts in 2016 ... they accounted for half of the page's most-shared posts".[36] Just as with lolcats and Advice Animals before them, these images – each a discrete piece of propaganda – success-fully "hacked people's attention", in social media scholar danah boyd's phrase, and provoked a reaction. Only this time, rather than to prompt a smile or a chuckle, it was to ridicule a political candi-date or vilify the opposition.

Another route from the chans to the mainstream was via Reddit, the self-styled 'front page of the internet'. Reddit was the eighth most popular site in the US in November 2016 and, for seven out of ten of its users, a regular source of news.[37] In 2016 the channers managed to game it. They did this via one of the forums, or subreddits, on the site, called the_donald. This subreddit was created shortly after Donald Trump announced his candidacy in June 2015. It was, for its first six months, a pretty subdued space in which a few hundred users could share pro-Trump news. Then, in December 2015, it was discovered by users from 4chan's /pol/. "/pol/ found us and has given us a tremendous amount of energy and some fantastic content," the_donald's moderator told journalist Jason Koebler, who spent months tracking the subreddit.[38] These users, and those they brought with them, grew the subreddit's number of subscribers to forty thousand by the end of February 2016. In Reddit terms this is a small community. Many subreddits have millions of subscribers. Yet, through a combination of frenetic activity and coordination of votes for posts on the forum, the_donald's members were regularly able to push their stories to Reddit's front page (four times in February alone). To put this in perspective, given that Reddit users tend to start on the site's front page, that is equivalent to about five million people a day. By comparison, during the same period the *New York Times* website was receiving less than three million unique visitors per day. The subreddit the_donald, and by extension the channers, had hacked the 'front page of the internet'. In June, Reddit altered the way the site worked in order "to prevent any one community from dominating the listing".[39] Yet by this time the subreddit had over 170,000 subscribers, and in July 2016 Donald Trump himself joined the site for a question and answer session.

The the_donald subreddit served lots of useful purposes. It was a channel through which to launder memes, where they could be more easily picked up and shared by regular users without the seedy connotations of sharing something from 4chan or 8chan. It could be a source of propaganda and rebuttals for the Trump campaign. Trump staffers told *Politico* that they monitored Reddit daily for images, videos and trends, passing the most powerful on to the social media director or others in the team.[40] It could be used, like 4chan and 8chan themselves, as a space in which to coordinate collective action, whether this was upvoting posts on Reddit, poring over email leaks or gaming online opinion polls. It was here that Redditors swarmed over the twenty thousand pages of John Podesta emails in October 2016, carefully separating them into twenty-two parts, desperately searching for anything incriminating, and posting whatever they found.[41] This included the false assertions that the Clinton campaign was running a paedophile ring out of a pizza restaurant, that the Democratic National Committee had pre-planned the Trump sexual assault revelations, and that the election would be rigged.[42] It was also here where, in combination with 4chan, they coordinated the distortion of online opinion polls on the first Clinton–Trump presidential debates.[43] Links to online polls were posted on Reddit and 4chan and users urged to "get voting". They then flooded the polls with manual and automated votes so that Donald Trump 'won' the debate according to *Time*, CNBC, *Fortune*, *The Hill* and others. By contrast, a CNN telephone poll of 521 viewers found Trump lost by a wide margin, and a Public Policy Polling survey of 1,002 debate watchers found he lost by 51 per cent to 40.[44] Still, this did not stop Trump tweeting an image of ten online polls – all of which he 'won' – and writing, "Such a great honor. Final debate polls are in and the MOVEMENT wins!"[45]

The online movement used other techniques that had been popular since the early days of 4chan, such as raids on other online communities, and harassing and doxxing those they took against. In their analysis of 4chan activity during the summer of 2016, Gabriel Emile Hine and his fellow researchers found evidence to suggest that "/pol/ users *are* performing raids in an attempt to disrupt the community of YouTube users [their italics]." They discovered this by looking at how peaks of commenting activity on YouTube synchronized with threads posted on /pol/. Previously, raids had been organized via IRC channels – and still could be, but in 2016 there were also accessible mainstream alternatives like Periscope.[46]

On the evening of 17 October, the names and addresses of fifty journalists who were alleged to be anti-Trump were posted on 8chan, along with the comment that the anonymous poster did not "condone sending wave after wave of fast food, holy books, gay porn catalogs, bricks, emergency plumbers, locksmiths, transgender escorts, or freeze-dried bear shit to anyone's home".[47] Journalists found themselves targeted by Trump supporters throughout the campaign. Research by the Anti-Defamation League discovered that at least eight hundred journalists received anti-Semitic tweets between August 2015 and July 2016.[48]

The aim of many of these activities was to attract attention – whether positive or negative did not matter. Attracting attention, particularly when this led to mainstream media coverage, meant capturing the campaign agenda. And mainstream media invariably took the bait. Major news outlets regularly published outraged stories about offensive memes, the harassment of journalists or the attempts to game social media. In one sense this was inevitable given that the behaviour fitted within the criteria of what has, since Galton and Ruge's twelve-point list published in 1965, long been considered newsworthy (such as unexpectedness, unpredictability and scarcity).[49] This newsworthiness was significantly enhanced when the Trump campaign, or Donald Trump himself, amplified their efforts. Trump tweeted the distorted debate polls, the Hillary Star of David image, Pepe the Frog and the You Can't Stump the Trump video. Yet, just as with Fox News's coverage of 4chan in 2007, media outrage played directly into the hands of the chan collective, who whooped with glee every time mainstream news outlets publicized their exploits. The *coup de grâce*, from their perspective, was when Hillary Clinton herself delivered a speech in Nevada in August 2016, in which she said that Trump "traffics in dark conspiracy theories drawn from the pages of supermarket tabloids and the far reaches of the internet" and her campaign posted 'an explainer' of Pepe the Frog.[50]

There is not, nor will there ever be, conclusive evidence that the chan collective influenced the outcome of the US election on 8 November 2016. We can, however, point to some of their effects on the campaign and the way it was communicated. The collective produced some of the most memorable and viral political propaganda of 2015–16, much of it in the form of memes that spread far beyond the confines of 4chan and Reddit. Many of these memes were intended to demonize and ridicule people, to provoke visceral outrage or anger, or simply to capture media attention. Some were demonstrably false, calculatingly vicious or explicitly bigoted. Others were more ambiguous – deliberately designed to inflame a response in those who interpreted them as racist, anti-Semitic or misogynist. Others promoted wild conspiracy theories, invariably blaming the establishment.

Throughout the campaign this disparate, anonymized collective used methods and techniques they had honed over the previous decade. Few of these were rocket science. They relied on coordinated responses by multiple users, done at speed and spread via multiple mainstream social media channels – from Reddit to Twitter to Facebook to YouTube. In their study of media manipulation and disinformation online, Alice Marwick and Rebecca Lewis refer to these as "organized brigades" and "networked and agile groups".[51] As seen at Reddit, a relatively small number of users can have a significant distorting effect.

The dispersed chan community managed to give a false impression of popular sentiment and support for candidates, particularly Trump – both in the debates, and through the manipulation of hashtags (such as #HillarysHealth), likes and searches (see, for example, how a call to arms during the GOP debate of February 2016 led 'Is Ted Cruz the Zodiac killer' to trend on Google).[52] Perhaps most significantly, these users generated chaos, confusion and fear, and wrenched open the window of acceptable political discourse. And yet, only a few years before the election it was far from clear that these users would have any such impact. Certainly, the chans became more reactionary after 2011, but at that point there were still no signs that they would get so involved in mainstream politics. Indeed, there was anger amongst many of the members that Anonymous had become so mainstream and 'causeish'. They became increasingly politicized during 2013 and 2014, especially during #Gamergate, but that politicization was then channelled by Breitbart against progressives and 'the left'. Without the digital tools available to them, and the techniques of collective coordination they had developed, they would have remained a dispersed minority subculture. With these tools and techniques, combined with the delivery mechanism of social media, they were able to wreak havoc on the democratic process. They then exported these methods overseas.

Initial attempts to use similar techniques abroad floundered. Some of those – particularly on the hard right – who helped sow chaos and discord during the Trump campaign tried but failed to do the same in France the following spring. They failed chiefly because of a lack of cultural awareness. Non-French 4channers, for example, invented a false rumour that En Marche! candidate Emmanuel Macron was having an affair with his wife's daughter, not taking into account that the French have always been blasé about their politicians' personal lives. They created a version of the Front National's Marine Le Pen as Pepe the Frog, not recognizing that calling a French person a frog has long been an anti-French insult. Then, in the days before the vote itself, when far-right users in the US and around the world tried to promote the Macron email leaks, they did not factor in the French media's custom of avoiding political news in the forty-eight hours before an election. On top of which, Americans trying to promote French nationalistic sentiment (much of it written in English) were never likely to be a success.

The far right had more success in Germany, where their activities appeared to be led by Germans themselves – through

Reconquista Germania, for example. As described at the beginning of this chapter, this group used Discord channels, YouTube videos and fake social media accounts to plan and execute coordinated action to promote the AfD. Yet dig beneath the surface and the similarity of the techniques, the language and the images to those of non-German chan users quickly becomes apparent. This includes the use of memes and their dissemination (including specific figures and styles), the coordinated raids, and the creation and synchronization of Twitter accounts. A video, posted on 4chan's Kraut /pol/ and described as compulsory viewing, included extracts from Saul Alinsky's *Rules for Radicals* – the same rules Andrew Breitbart urged right-wing insurgents in the US to adopt. When *Buzzfeed* messaged the controller of an AfD chan Twitter account, the anonymous activist replied with a line that could have come straight out of the Bannon/Breitbart stable: "You have to keep in mind that Germany is not free," the controller wrote. "The lying media is trying to perpetuate their ideas of cultural Marxism and to further the genocide of whites."[53] Extensive work by the campaigning organization Hope not Hate, including a year-long infiltration of the alternative right, found extensive coordination and shared learning between European countries and with the US. The month after the German election, in October 2017, Austrians were shocked to discover a meme-led smear campaign on Facebook against the leader of the Austrian People's Party, Sebastian Kurz. The images, allegedly posted by members of the opposition Social Democrats' campaign team, sought to ridicule Kurz and link him to conspiracy theories. The smears failed and Kurz subsequently became chancellor.

The online activities were also spilling into the real world. Martin Sellner, leader of the 'new right' Identitarian Movement in Austria, built an app to "visualize, organize and unite the silent majority" who were unhappy about immigration. Patriot Peer let its members see those around them who were also using the app, and enabled them to join events and rallies and to compete with other users to earn points and become a "top Patriot". The app's aim, Sellner said in a YouTube video introducing it, was "to disrupt the firewall of political correctness and end the isolation of the silent majority". His dream was "an ocean of green dots [representing Patriots] covering the west". "There will never be an election again", the infamous neo-Nazi hacker Andrew 'weev' Auernheimer wrote after the US election, "in which trolling, hacking, and extreme far-right politics do not play a role."

The alternative right enthusiastically adopted and disseminated these methods, but its members were not the only ones using them. The alt-right took and adapted techniques used previously by the hacker collective Anonymous, techniques which had been associated with left-wing radicalism in 2010–11. Religious extremists too used these and similar techniques. Equally, by late 2016, political conflict online had spread far beyond the far right and across the social media platforms. British MPs said that the UK election of 2017 was the worst that they had experienced in terms of abuse. "We had abuse like nobody had seen before," the MP Ian Lavery told the Committee on Standards in Public Life. "It is torrid; this abuse is 24/7. It is not something that you can walk away from. When you go home, it is there with you and your kids. This abuse is constant."[54] This included "tangible issues of death threats, obscenity, defamation and slander, criminal damage, homophobia, sexism, anti-Semitism and menacing abuse".[55] Democratic elections and political events the world over were becoming synonymous with pitched battles between partisan groups, cyber-muggings and flame wars. Political campaigning online, in other words, was looking less like democratic deliberation and more like information warfare.

This deliberate transgression and destruction of democratic norms in the digital sphere has been driven forward by those who prize freedom and sovereignty online above all else. For this reason, you might call these people free extremists, or freextremists for short. Yet freedom, even in the most libertarian societies, has never been absolute. Nowhere is it legitimate, for example, to harm others in the pursuit of freedom – except in the context of war. This is presumably why many freextremists justify their behaviour by claiming they are in a virtual conflict with those who have different values than they do and who seek to inhibit their free-doms. Yet the consequence of this is an uninhibited, aggressive, violent and hyper-partisan online space, where democratic proc-esses of debate, respect, civility and compromise are collateral damage.

When the original hackers and prospectors set out to explore cyberspace and to set up communities there, it did not occur to them to replicate the structures and protections of democracy from the real world. Cyberspace had no national borders, so why recreate national political systems? Cyberspace was infinite so there ought to be plenty of room for everyone. Equally, why set any parameters on speech? Why not let truth and falsehood grap-ple in a free and open encounter, as the poet John Milton so memorably wrote in *Areopagitica* in 1644? As long as information was shared freely, and as long as the "weary giants of flesh and steel" left cyberspace's frontierspeople alone, then this new world would, they thought, take care of itself.

2
PLUTOCRATS: THE MERCER MODEL

> The battle for the survival of man as a responsible being in the
> Communications Era is not to be won where the communica-
> tion originates, but where it arrives.
>
> Umberto Eco, *Travels in Hyperreality*

In the last days of August 2017, a 203-foot super-yacht cruised into
Lake Union, Seattle, and docked for over a week. Its presence elic-
ited sporadic protests, including from a protest boat – the *Endeavour*
– which sported an inflatable 'Donald Trump chicken'. There was
no sign of the owner of the super-yacht himself. The *Sea Owl*, as the
yacht is called, was only completed in 2013, built in the Netherlands
to detailed and exacting specifications. Despite its considerable size
it was built chiefly for the owner and his family, plus a crew of eighteen. It had many of the usual amenities of a super-yacht: jacuzzi, lift,
cinema, Steinway baby grand piano. But there were also lots of individual touches: frescoed walls, a pirate-themed bedroom, a Dale
Chihuly chandelier and, painted on the ceiling of the library,
Newton's *Philosophiae Naturalis Principia Mathematica*.[1] The onboard
security system, the Dutch boat builder told *Yachting* magazine, "is
possibly the most elaborate ever built into a yacht".[2] This included
fingerprint recognition key pads and at least two safe rooms with
reinforced steel doors. The owner, Robert Mercer, made it clear to
the boatyard that the yacht's privacy and security were paramount.

Describing the Mercer super-yacht is not just an exercise in gawking at the rich and famous. It tells you that Robert Mercer qualifies as a plutocrat; it shows how important privacy and security are to him; and it sets in stark relief how little we know about the man who owns it. You can discover more about the *Sea Owl* in a few searches on the internet than you can about Robert Mercer in months of investigation. Mercer does not give interviews; he does not make public statements; he does not give speeches (save for one in 2014 when he accepted an award for services to computing – which is quoted in almost every article about him). He has never served in public office, or stood for election. He has not written about his political views, and there is no record of how he votes. There are, in other words, very few data points about him (the irony of which will become apparent later).[3] Yet through his patronage, he has managed to distort the public sphere, subvert democratic accountability and destabilize democratic legitimacy. On top of which, he has come up with a model that other plutocrats can copy.

Mercer's career has been dominated by two pursuits: computer programming and financial investment. Born in San Jose, California, in the summer of 1946, Robert Mercer was entranced by computers from the moment he learnt about them. As a teenager, before he even had access to a machine, he wrote computer programs with pen and paper. After completing a degree in physics and mathematics, he went on to do a PhD in the relatively new discipline of computer science in 1972. Along with other pioneering computer scientists, he then joined IBM, where he stayed for the next twenty-one years. His work there, particularly on computational linguistics, has been described as "revolutionary". In 1993 he was recruited by Renaissance Technologies, a hedge fund that deliberately eschews typical approaches to financial investment. Rather than use human intelligence and experience to decide where to invest, RenTech (as it is known in the industry) uses machine intelligence and big data. It gathers enormous amounts of information from across the world and develops computer programs that can mine this information for unexpected patterns and for potential investment opportunities. Its employees rarely come from banking or financial backgrounds, but rather are physicists, biologists and engineers. The nonconformist approach has worked staggeringly well. RenTech has made fortunes many times over by identifying opportunities from the data that others have missed and then leveraging them. Mercer became joint chief executive of RenTech in 2010, stepping down in 2017.

The little we know about Mercer's politics comes from what friends and colleagues have said, from the political company he keeps, and from his political investments.[4] From what friends and colleagues have said, Mercer comes across as a sort of angry libertarian anarchist. Patrick Caddell, who worked for Mercer, told *New Yorker* writer Jane Mayer that he "is a libertarian – he despises the Republican establishment . . . He thinks the leaders are corrupt crooks, and that they've ruined the country." "Bob and Rebekah Mercer [his middle daughter] harbour a deep and abiding enmity towards the political establishment," Kenneth Vogel and Ben Schreckinger wrote in their 2016 *Politico* piece. "They want to blow things up and start from scratch," an unnamed Mercer co-worker told them. Most seem to agree that they are, as Vicky Ward's cogent and compelling 2017 investigation is titled, the 'blow-it-all-up billionaires'. The political conferences or functions where Mercer has been spotted (but has said nothing on the record) range from those arranged by the Koch brothers and their network of right-wing funders, to those denying climate change, and those arguing for a return to the gold standard (a particular penchant of Mercer's, who seems to see no justification for central banks).

Robert Mercer and his politically active daughter Rebekah appear to be, in sum, anti-government, anti-establishment, anti-mainstream media, anti-tax, climate change deniers. If these were simply personal views, and the Mercers' influence on the political system was the same as everybody else's, then good luck to them. Or, had they pursued their political goals through democratic means – like seeking election, or participating in grassroots activism, then it would have represented no danger to the democratic process. Yet Robert Mercer chose neither to act like a private citizen, nor to seek election, nor to agitate from the ground up. Instead, he chose to use his phenomenal understanding of big data and his considerable wealth to do everything he could to explode the political system.

Mercer is far from the first billionaire to try to warp democratic politics to his own ends. Charles and David Koch, conservative libertarians who own most of the second largest private company in America, Koch Industries, spent decades using their tremendous wealth to shift American politics to the right.[5] So what is different about Mercer? And why should democracies – and not just the US – worry about what he managed to achieve in 2016? The difference is the manner in which Mercer sought to achieve his aims. Instead of supporting a party or candidate, or even funding his own candidacy, Mercer appeared to use his wealth chiefly to sabotage the existing political system. Again, this in itself is not entirely new. Yet Mercer made his political investments at just the moment when data and digital platforms were opening up new opportunities in politics. These opportunities enabled him to navigate within the limits of the law around the legal, regulatory and principled protections that democracies have built up to defend themselves against the undue influence of powerful, unelected individuals. There is no reason why other plutocrats, adopting a similar approach, could not do likewise.

Mercer is no political savant – he has invested in his fair share of oddball candidates and bizarre schemes (funding the collection of large quantities of urine to prolong life, for example). But his particular skills and his timing were such that he was able to transform the US political environment, and in so doing, expose fundamental weaknesses in digital democracy. The way he approached his political goals aligned closely with the way he approached financial investments. Rather than invest in a single individual or issue, Mercer invested in a range of different projects. These projects, though separate, were complementary. Like any good hedge fund manager he built up, in other words, a portfolio of investments. Yet, unlike a financial portfolio, Mercer was looking for a political return.

There were two lines of investment that Mercer made that had a major influence on the political process in 2016; the first was in digital media, the second was in professional data-driven campaigning. In media, he made his most important investment in 2011. It was an investment in the vision of an individual whose character – in terms of his flamboyance and extroversion – could not have been more different than Mercer's. What they shared was a hatred of the existing political and media establishments and an urge to destroy them.

★

Andrew Breitbart was not born a political animal. After a comfortable upper-middle-class childhood in Brentwood, California, brought up in a non-political household, he was, he wrote later, "a default liberal". It was not until his twenties that he was converted, by talk radio, into a reactionary, libertarian conservative. From that point onwards, like many late converts, Breitbart was evangelical. Everything, for Breitbart, became political. Gender was political, generation was political, ethnicity was political. But most of all, he saw culture as political. Not only that, but it had been taken over by what he called the 'Democrat-Media Complex'. For Breitbart, "art, humor, song, theater, television, film, dance" had, by the late twentieth century, all become instruments of left-wing propaganda. He explains how this left-wing takeover happened in his highly readable, if slightly dyspeptic, 2010 autobiography, *Righteous Indignation*. In it, Breitbart somehow manages to trace a line from Rousseau to Marx to Gramsci to Lukács and on to the Frankfurt school, a collection of intellectuals and academics that formed in Germany between the two world wars. The Frankfurt school, he seemed to believe, was America's ruin. Having fled Hitler's Germany, these academics – Max Horkheimer, Theodor Adorno and Herbert Marcuse amongst them – relocated to the West Coast and, Breitbart argues, immediately embarked on an insidious plan to undermine America and the American way of life, in order to prepare the ground for communism. They dressed up their plan as 'Critical Theory' and toured the country in the 1950s and 1960s, converting masses of impressionable young students who then went on to power the 1960s counter-cultural revolution, and subsequently to populate the upper reaches of the media, academia and government. It is quite a theory, and relies on many historical and cognitive leaps, but once constructed, it gave Andrew Breitbart – and those who followed in his footsteps – a framework in which to justify their subsequent actions and worldview. Its historical and theoretical scope – however tenuous and self-serving – allowed them to write off the whole contemporary media system as corrupt.

In the same way as Breitbart saw everything as political, so he saw politics as a pitched battle. Politics and warfare were virtually synonymous to him. And it was a battle that he thought the right was losing – but not because its beliefs were incorrect. No, the right was losing because it had not adopted the Machiavellian tactics of the left, and because it was limiting its activities to the political sphere. To win, the right had to take the fight beyond politics to culture, and had to learn to use the techniques of the left to defend itself. Winning this war on the battleground of traditional media would be impossible since traditional media had, in Breitbart's worldview, been captured by leftist cultural Marxists (strange as this may seem to readers of, say, the *Wall Street Journal*). The right therefore had to find new territory on which to fight its war. This is why, for Breitbart, the internet – and the dominant tech platforms – presented such an opportunity. This new land had yet to be conquered. The right's goal, he believed, should be to occupy the new territory and, in the process, bring about the destruction of legacy media. "We have the power to unravel the Complex," Breitbart wrote, "and destroy the Institutional Left. It won't be easy. It will take time and effort, and there will be false starts and roadblocks, but we'll do it because we have to do it." Breitbart's ideas may sound kooky and marginal but, thanks to his chutzpah and Robert Mercer's money, they were soon to occupy the mainstream.

In the summer of 2009, twenty-year-old journalism student Hannah Giles and twenty-five-year-old conservative activist James O'Keefe visited various US offices of ACORN, a non-profit organization that advocated on issues like affordable housing and voter registration on behalf of people on low incomes. Giles pretended to be a prostitute and O'Keefe her pimp.[6] Together they asked ACORN staff about how they could game the system for their benefit – including using their house as a brothel. Unbeknownst to the staff, the pair were wearing hidden cameras. The whole escapade was a sting, designed to catch ACORN workers on camera offering advice that was either illegal or unethical. While they failed to capture anything illegal, the pair filmed staff giving advice that was clearly compromising. As part of a carefully planned media strategy, Andrew Breitbart gave the edited videos to Fox News, staging their release over the course of a week, and simultaneously publishing transcripts and audio on one of his eponymous Breitbart websites, all promoted heavily on social media.[7] To push the story beyond the right-wing media ecosystem and keep it in the news cycle, Breitbart and Fox then claimed mainstream media were ignoring it and were attacking the young people who had engineered the sting (both claims based on highly subjective readings of the evidence).

Within days of the videos being published the House of Representatives passed the Defund ACORN Act. "ACORN has violated serious federal laws," Republican representative Eric Cantor said, "and today, the House voted to ensure that taxpayer dollars would no longer be used to fund this corrupt organization."[8] ACORN lost its federal funding contracts as well as many of its private contracts and, in November 2010, filed for bankruptcy. An organization established in 1970, with offices in seventy-five cities and with 400,000 family members, was effectively destroyed over the course of a fortnight in September 2009. A subsequent independent investigation by a law firm, while critical of ACORN governance and accountability, found that "there is no evidence that action, illegal or otherwise, was taken by any ACORN employee."[9]

Not only did the ACORN 'scoop' give the Breitbart sites national exposure, it validated their founder's convictions and modus operandi. The 'Institutional Left' could be taken down by using a virile mix of exposé, entertainment and outrage. The recipe: find a weak spot in an institution to which you are opposed – in this case the junior ACORN employees. Compile evidence that supports a particular partisan perspective – here, misuse of taxpayer dollars. Frame it in a way that provokes outrage in the audience – for example, that the protagonists (Giles and O'Keefe) were white and most of the villains (the staff of ACORN) black women, stimulating a furious reaction from the left and counter-reaction from the right. Package it so that it conforms with the grammar of journalistic investigations – hidden cameras, grainy and jumpy footage, narrated by the lead protagonist. Publish the edited footage as a big reveal amidst much fanfare, then promote it as hard as you can. Finally, so the story damages both the institution itself and legacy media, claim that any large media outlets not covering the story – or not leading on the story – are deliberately ignoring it for partisan reasons. Not only was this method effective, it was cheap. James O'Keefe said the whole ACORN operation cost less than $2,000, "the cost of a rental car and gas money, and food".[10] Andrew Breitbart had figured out how, in the new social media environment, news could be made into a political weapon with the power to destroy civil society's institutions and undermine trust in mainstream media at the same time.

Of course, Breitbart was far from the first to use stings as a way of producing news. The British tabloid press had been engineering them for years. In 1991 Rupert Murdoch's *News of the World* employed Mazher Mahmood, who dressed up as a 'fake sheikh' to trap unwitting celebrities, football coaches and politicians into saying incriminating things on film. He worked for News International and its successor for over two decades before being jailed in 2016 for conspiring to pervert the course of justice. Neither the Murdoch method nor the Breitbart method is journalism as taught in journalism schools. It is not about approaching a story with an open mind, or aspiring to the principle of objectivity. No, this alternative method of journalism is more akin to a lawyer preparing a case for the prosecution – searching for evidence that supports their case and, as importantly, undermines their adversary. It is journalism that starts and ends with a political objective.

The difference with Breitbart, and with its ACORN scoop, was timing. By late 2009 social media had gone mainstream. Twitter, launched in 2006, had almost eighteen million users by late 2009 – including most mainstream media journalists. Facebook had over 300 million active profiles, up from 50 million two years before. YouTube, bought by Google less than three years earlier, was serving over twelve billion videos in the US every month.[11]

Therefore, when Andrew Breitbart published the transcripts, audio, video and news reports in September 2009, he had the platforms across which he could push them.

It helped that he knew what to do. Breitbart was no internet ingénu. He had honed his techniques over more than a decade, with two of internet news's most talented innovators. From 1995, he worked with Matt Drudge, founder and editor of the *Drudge Report*, where he learnt to scour the net looking for nuggets of political clickbait. In 2005, he collaborated with Arianna Huffington to launch the *Huffington Post*, where he learnt how to use comment and media critique to nurture outrage and play off the news cycle. Perhaps even more than Drudge or Huffington, Breitbart believed he was a creature of the modern communications matrix, never more at home than when in multiple conversations on multiple different screens. "I am complete in this environment," he told *New Yorker* journalist Rebecca Mead in a revealing 2010 interview. "This is the environment I needed in order to become what I needed to become. With the Internet, I have communication with large amounts of people, in perpetuity. Always having a new war, a new battle."[12]

Breitbart was insightful enough to see that many of the methods that worked in old media worked much less well in the brave new world of tech platforms. Print-era newspapers would get a scoop and do everything in their power to own it: in some cases, actually secreting people in hotel rooms for days until the moment of publication. Then, all at once, they would splash the story as an 'Exclusive!' in a single outlet. Even the language print media used – *exclusive* – was symptomatic of their desire to keep a story tied to one outlet. Breitbart realized that to give a story impact in the digital era he had to do the opposite. Rather than keep it to himself he had to spread it as widely as he could. He had to find people who could blog about different angles. He had to push the videos out through social media influencers. "Ubiquity", he wrote, "is key. Ubiquity is about growing the pie for everyone, spreading the stories, the channels of distribution, the resources around so that the entire [conservative] movement can benefit, because our chunk of the public square gets bigger and bigger each time we break something huge."

Breitbart wrote up his manual on how to destroy the 'Democrat-Media Complex' as he flew coast to coast in 2010. Shortly after the book became available online, and less than a month before its official launch in April 2011, he went to speak at a conservative conference in the Ritz-Carlton in Palm Beach, Florida. There he met the billionaire who would transform his manifesto and his methods from a personal animus into a national crusade.

*

Robert Mercer's political donations had, up to that point, been sporadic and eclectic. His beneficiaries shared political beliefs, though they lacked any consistent approach to change. When he met Andrew Breitbart in Florida in 2011, he met someone who not only shared his rage at the 'Institutional Left' but had a method by which to sabotage it. Mercer had seen the noise that Breitbart made with clever use of digital platforms and very little funding (he set up his Big Government site with $25,000 borrowed from his father). The billionaire then gave him the chance to take it much further, by investing four hundred times the initial investment – $10 million. Breitbart immediately set to work preparing to relaunch his family of websites. He was, however, unable to see the fruits of his work, dying in March 2012, days before his new site was due to launch. The new Breitbart.com went ahead anyway, with the founder's friend and colleague Steve Bannon – who had been instrumental in securing Mercer's investment – at the helm. Bannon originally met Breitbart in 2005, after a screening of Bannon's biopic of Ronald Reagan. Breitbart reportedly came up to Bannon after the film, hugging him and saying, "Brother! We got to change the culture."[13] The two became friends and, in February 2010, Breitbart moved into Bannon's office in Westwood, Los Angeles.

With Mercer's $10 million investment, Bannon and a small coterie of Breitbart loyalists pedalled furiously to transform Breitbart.com from a basement blog to the "*Huffington Post* of the right".[14] By the summer of 2012 they were publishing hundreds of stories in their different sections – or 'verticals' – about Big Government, Big Hollywood, Big Journalism and Big Peace, and had grown the audience to almost three million monthly users by the end of September. Still, few saw the site achieving Andrew Breitbart's aims, or even lasting for long after his death. "I said at the time, when Andrew died," a Breitbart staffer told *Buzzfeed* in October 2012, "they gotta shut this thing down or else it's going to fall apart. I think I was right." Even a year later, and despite a slew of new hires – many from right-wing rival the *Daily Caller* – Breitbart.com was yet to distinguish itself from its competitors online, and was failing to drive the media agenda. According to Pew research from 2014, Breitbart.com did not appear amongst the top ten news sources for conservative voters.[15]

Yet it continued to grow, and even expand internationally, thanks to further investment. In early 2014 Breitbart opened branches in Texas and London, with plans to open others in California, Florida, Cairo and Jerusalem.[16] Central to its audience growth was its use of the techniques set out by its visionary founder. Creating stunts to gain attention – such as heavily edited videos captured by hidden cameras. Viewing everything as political – especially culture. Finding divisive news in one of the key verticals – like Big Journalism – and then presenting it in a deliberately emotive and highly partisan frame to prompt a reaction. Only going with news that had 'legs' – multiple threads and storylines that would last consecutive news cycles. Then using the social media outrage dissemination machine to make the news ubiquitous.

By the second half of 2014 Breitbart was getting into its provocative stride. It leapt in to defend the police after they shot Michael Brown; it supported male gamers during #Gamergate rather than the women they had attacked online; and it published a steady stream of anti-migrant stories. These presented migrants as criminals and claimed they were taking US jobs and welfare, costing a fortune to educate and bringing in diseases such as Ebola.[17] The site's approach fitted with what sociologist Stan Cohen identified in the 1970s as the media of 'folk devils and moral panics'.[18] The media outlet – in this case Breitbart – takes a particular incident, such as the Ferguson riots, and presents it as evidence of the material and moral corruption of society. Certain groups – the folk devils – are then consistently blamed for this corruption. The narrative is repeated often enough that it takes on the pattern of a folk tale, an underlying truth about society.

The focus on migrants as the root of America's problems became more pronounced on Breitbart from early 2015, from when the site sought to turn it into one of the defining issues of the US election. By July, Breitbart had so successfully cultivated this theme that, according to a study by the Southern Poverty Law Center, it overtook the *Daily Mail* as the most cited outlet from the neo-Nazi *Daily Stormer* site. The same month links to Breitbart from white-nationalist site *Stormfront* rocketed, rising to more than three hundred a month in the second half of 2015. Breitbart "really changed from being this kind of basic cuckservative type website", the owner of the *Daily Stormer* told Swedish radio, "to being this, I mean, the articles that they publish about blacks in America and about Muslims in Europe, it's basically stuff that you would read on the *Daily Stormer*."[19]

Throughout 2015 Breitbart saw its traffic climb. Its deliberate outrageousness and politically divisive approach provoked plenty of reaction online. On social media platforms like Facebook, where reaction meant engagement and engagement meant attention, its audiences soared. In July, Breitbart's Facebook audience shared, liked or commented more than that of the *New York Times*. Over the course of that year Breitbart grew from having 100,000 likes on its Facebook page to just under 1.5 million. At the end of that year, Alexis Madrigal wrote in *The Atlantic*, Breitbart's page had ten million interactions a month.[20] The site's social media presence also helped it grow as a news source. In the autumn of 2014 only about three per cent of the general news audience were getting their news from the site.[21] By July 2015 this figure had doubled to six per cent, and the site was getting almost nineteen million visitors a month.[22] By the end of November that year it had climbed to almost eight per cent. The site's chief, Steve Bannon, understood how important social media had been to its rise. "Facebook is what propelled Breitbart to a massive audience," he told *Bloomberg* in 2016. "We know its power."[23]

The rise and rise of Breitbart was not simply due to its courting of the far right. It also managed to subvert the mainstream media. It did this thanks to a story that Breitbart's chief, Steve Bannon, had been instrumental in engineering. Here again we see the remarkable success of Robert Mercer's investments in shaping the digital media ecosystem to his ends. In 2013, on Bannon's advice, the Mercer Family Foundation started supporting the Government Accountability Institute (GAI) with Peter Schweizer as its president.[24] In 2013 the Mercer family gave the GAI a million dollars, followed by another million in 2014 and then almost two million in 2015. Along with the family donation, Robert Mercer's daughter Rebekah joined the board. The ostensible goal of the GAI was to "expose cronyism and corruption" in politics. What this meant in practice was a two-year investigation and exposé of the Clintons.

When the Mercers made their investment in Schweizer's GAI, there was little doubting what his approach, and his conclusions, would be. Schweizer had written half a dozen books between 2005 and 2013, five of which were attacks on established liberal elites and the political establishment. The book's titles give a good flavour of both their tone and the author's perspective: *Extortion: How Politicians Extract Your Money, Buy Votes, and Line Their Own Pockets* (2013); *Throw Them All Out: How Politicians and Their Friends Get Rich off Insider Stock Tips, Land Deals, and Cronyism That Would Send the Rest of Us to Prison* (2011); *Architects of Ruin: How Big Government Liberals Wrecked the Global Economy – and How They Will Do It Again if No One Stops Them* (2009); *Makers and Takers: Why Conservatives Work Harder, Feel Happier, Have Closer Families, Take Fewer Drugs, Give More Generously, Value Honesty More, Are Less Materialistic and Envious, Whine Less . . . and Even Hug Their Children More than Liberals* (2008); and *Do as I Say (Not as I Do): Profiles in Liberal Hypocrisy* (2005). It was pretty clear, therefore, that Schweizer was never going to write a book that found liberal politicians to be, on the whole, honest and trustworthy. Sure enough, in 2015 HarperCollins published Schweizer's book *Clinton Cash: The Untold Story of How and Why Foreign Governments and Businesses Helped Make Bill and Hillary Rich*, based on material unearthed by a team of people working with Schweizer at the GAI, raising multiple questions about donations to, and connections of, the Clinton Foundation.

The Mercers' investment in the GAI took advantage of another key weakness of mainstream commercial media, its increasing inability to support lengthy and expensive investigations. *Clinton Cash* was the product of more than two years' research, much of it on the dark web, containing a legion of story threads and network connections that spread all round the world. This was a story that conformed perfectly to Andrew Breitbart's dictum about multiple storylines and narratives. This one had the legs to run and run. Schweizer and Bannon also made sure that the story emerged first in the liberal media. They knew that its credibility amongst those in the centre and on the left would be immeasurably enhanced if it originated in big legacy outlets. For this reason the GAI gave exclusive advance access to three pillars of the US mainstream media – the *New York Times*, the *Washington Post* and Fox News. It worked. When *Clinton Cash* was published in May 2015, all three splashed on the story.

Therefore, by the summer of 2015, Breitbart was not only legitimizing the virulent anti-immigrant rhetoric of the far right, but building on and linking to stories in the mainstream media of the centre and centre left. It was, therefore, acting as a digital bridge. A host of far-right sites were now linking to it, including the *Daily Stormer*, *Stormfront* and 4chan. At the same time it was linking out to cornerstones of the US media establishment, the *New York Times* and the *Washington Post*. When combined with its voluminous publication of stories and its deliberately provocative social media strategy, this was like rocket fuel to Breitbart online. It hit all the key measures of the tech platforms' algorithms: recent, relevant and regular stories linked to both from the open web and on social media that were generating high levels of engagement across the political spectrum.

One further Mercer investment strengthened Breitbart's position and consolidated the distortion of the digital news ecosystem prior to the election in 2016. This was in a self-styled 'media watchdog' called the Media Research Center (MRC). Now, there are two very contrasting ways in which you can run a media watchdog. The first is to give people the tools and information so they can make up their own minds about different news stories or outlets. The second is to start from the premise that all existing media is inherently biased and corrupt, and spend all your time collecting evidence to prove it. The MRC took the second approach. From its founding in 1987 the MRC presented mainstream media as a single coherent entity – the 'MSM' – an entity that was fundamentally prejudiced and untruthful. As Brian Montopoli wrote for the *Columbia Journalism Review* back in 2005, the "MRC persists in pretending that there's a vast conspiracy at hand, consistently portraying itself as a voice in the wilderness fighting against a corrupt system".[25]

Even before they discovered Breitbart, the Mercers were supporting the MRC. Rebekah Mercer joined the board of the MRC in 2010 and *Politico* reports that the family foundation gave the centre more than $10 million.[26] The support from the Mercers supplemented the centre's already sizeable budget (its revenues between 2010 and 2014 averaged over $14 million a year), which allowed it to do all it could to undermine trust in mainstream media and convince the public that all legacy media was lying to them. "Everyone now knows the news media have a liberal agenda because of the MRC," a radio presenter said to the MRC's founder and president, Brent Bozell, in 2015. "Do you feel you've succeeded?" Yes and no, Bozell replied: "Yes, a majority of Americans now understand this reality, and the Media Research Center deserves the credit, but still all Americans don't understand this."[27] Whether or not the MRC was responsible, it had worked tirelessly over almost three decades to discredit the US press and broadcasters. The consequence was that many people, especially on the right, treated with suspicion, if not disbelief, the reporting of the vast majority of media in the centre and on the left, and left them open to a site like Breitbart that more closely aligned with their partisan political beliefs.

At the beginning of 2016 Breitbart held a position in the news media ecosystem that was unthinkable just three years earlier. As a seminal research study from Harvard's Berkman Klein Center shows, Breitbart had become "the nexus of conservative media".[28] Set in a network map representing two million news stories published during the US election campaign, Breitbart was by far the largest star in the right-wing universe. In the eighteen months up to the election, Breitbart was shared more on Facebook, tweeted more on Twitter, and linked to more on the open web than any other right-wing site. It was all the more influential since, as the study shows, the right-wing news ecosystem was much more contained and inward-looking than the left. Critical stories about right-wing candidates were filtered through this lens, if reported at all.

In a remarkably short space of time the Mercer family had transformed the political media landscape through their investments in digital media. They had incubated a hyper-partisan right-wing media network, whose audience was largely sealed off from mainstream news sources. Their news site – Breitbart – had, only four years after launch, come to dominate that network and set its political agenda. On top of this, they had subverted mainstream media, and inflamed partisanship and distrust. It would be difficult to argue that the Mercers had not travelled a long way towards achieving one of their apparent goals – of capturing the political narrative and undermining mainstream media.

Yet, had the Mercer family's investments been restricted to digital media, principally Breitbart, the MRC and the GAI, then you could arguably claim that their influence was equivalent to that of an early-twentieth-century press baron like William Randolph Hearst, Lord Beaverbrook or Lord Northcliffe, each of whom had considerable influence over contemporary politics. After the First World War, for example, the British prime minister David Lloyd George sought the support of Northcliffe, who responded: "I do not propose to use my newspapers and personal influence ... unless I know definitely and in writing, and can consciously approve, the personal constitution of the government." But the Mercers' pursuit of political disruption went beyond digital media, and included another investment in 2013 that, though complementary, took them into new and uncharted territory. This was the $5 million Robert Mercer invested in what would later become a globally notorious company, Cambridge Analytica.

★

Taking to the stage in Hamburg in March 2017, Alexander Nix looked like he had modelled himself on Don Draper, the ad man played by Jon Hamm in the TV series *Mad Men*.[29] The chief executive of Cambridge Analytica (CA) was dressed in a black suit, black tie and grey shirt. Even his hair was slicked back, Draper-style. The look fitted with the subject of his talk, 'From Mad Men to Math Men', in which he lectured his audience on the revolution in political and commercial communication. We have gone, Nix said, from an era of top-down messaging to an age of bottom-up. From an era where we guessed the mind of the public to an age where – thanks to 'big data' – we know the mind of the public. Nix then helpfully laid out what he thinks of as big data. It includes all the basic factual stuff – how old we are, where we live, what we earn – plus how we behave – where we go, what we buy, what media we consume – but also our attitudes and what makes us tick – our passions, our prejudices and our politics. To create persuasive communication today, Nix said, means pulling together "as many data points as you can get your hands on". This is exactly what CA, which he led until being suspended in 2018, had done. It claimed to have more than five thousand data points on over 230 million American voters, which it could use to profile, model and target during election campaigns. "Data", the company slogan read, "drives all we do."

By 2018 only those people who avoided the news like the plague had not heard of Cambridge Analytica. A lengthy investigation, driven by Carole Cadwalladr of the *Observer*, exposed the company's methods of mass data-harvesting from Facebook, its willingness to entertain the dark arts of election-fixing, and its propensity – in common with other political consultancies – to over-hype its capabilities. Besieged by allegations of illegal and unethical behaviour, it closed in 2018. As for its effect on the US 2016 election itself, after a brief initial honeymoon period when it gained garlands for Trump's win, critics spent many months pouring cold water on both its claims and on its use – or lack of use – of its so-called 'psychographic profiling' methods. Even CA itself toned down its role, saying it did not have time to implement some of its more sophisticated approaches when working on Trump's campaign, and that it could not do its proper psychographic profiling. Some of the cold water was welcome and entirely valid. No one organization or method swung the election. And one should always take stories about technological innovation winning elections with a spoonful of salt (who now remembers Hillary Clinton's super-algorithm called Ada?).

Yet those playing down the part CA played in the 2016 US election failed to look at its most interesting, and significant, aspects. By focusing on whether or not CA won the election for Trump (it didn't), and on the application of psychographic profiling (which it may or may not have partially applied), they missed the two more important roles it played. The first was as a vehicle to collect huge amounts of personal data on the electorate, data that put the Mercers in a powerful position to offer patronage and to proffer power – challenging even the established Republican Party machine. The second was its role as a laboratory through which to conduct experiments with voter data to see what works. These experiments, and the data and knowledge gained, not only informed CA's approach, but can inform the approach of anyone trying to use data and digital platforms for political ends.

On the face of it, Cambridge Analytica was a strange company in which to invest. It was British, not American – spun off from Strategic Communication Laboratories (SCL). It had no experience in US election campaigns. It had no connections to either of the main US political parties. It did not even have a detailed understanding of the nuances of the US political system. Yet Robert Mercer reportedly screened many companies before making his investment. So why Cambridge Analytica?

In 2012–13, when Mercer was considering which political firm to invest in, CA had two main distinctions from other firms. The first was its commitment to data. It took a similar approach to politics as RenTech took to finance. It gathered as much data as it could, then relied on computer scientists, behavioural scientists and software engineers to analyse it and look for patterns. Mercer had always taken a purist approach to data. At IBM he and his colleague Peter Brown took just such an approach when creating language translation software. Rather than try to teach a computer the rules of language, as you might a child, they uploaded hefty books of equivalent text – one in French and one in English – and let the computer figure out the rules for itself. Contrary to the expectations of their peers, it worked, and the approach became the foundation for Google Translate and subsequent approaches to computer translation.

The second distinctive feature of CA was its founders' experience of strategic communications to influence behavioural change. In practical terms, this means that SCL, from which CA emerged, advised governments and militaries how to persuade their populations to do something. SCL's founder, Nigel Oakes, described this approach, sometimes called psychological operations or 'psy-ops', to a trade magazine in 1992 by saying that "we use the same techniques as Aristotle and Hitler ... We appeal to people on an emotional level to get them to agree on a functional level."[30] SCL Elections claimed, in January 2013, to have more than fifteen years of experience on thirty-five elections globally. "To date," its website said in 2013, "we have an unrivalled 100% record in election management."[31]

For someone as disenchanted with Washington politics as Mercer, CA's distance from the DC circuit would also have been an asset rather than a disadvantage. Being British it would not bring any of the American firms' political baggage or preconceptions. Lacking links to the established political parties, its data and methodologies could be kept distinct and separate.

Still, CA's emphasis on personal data was far from unique in 2013. After Barack Obama's technologically sophisticated election victory the year before, data campaigning was the new new thing. In 2012, "we measured and tested everything," Jim Messina, Obama's campaign manager, said afterwards. With over a hundred people in his digital team, Obama had experimented with tailored and targeted online messages to specific groups, leading his chief strategist, David Axelrod, to call their previous 2008 tech efforts "pre-historic".[32]

It was not so long ago that democratic campaigns functioned with virtually no voter data. The collection and use of personal voter data for political campaigning emerged in the 1970s, grew to the turn of the century, and has snowballed since then. In the 1970s, as professional political consultancies sprang up in the US, so did interest in the potential of voter data. By the late 1990s, Sasha Issenberg writes in his influential study *The Victory Lab*, political scientists were running randomized control trials of voters. And, by the time George W. Bush took on Al Gore in 2000, the Republicans had built up a 'Voter Vault', which segmented voters and helped the party decide who to target. After their 2004 election defeat the Republicans fell behind technologically, and even in 2012, despite Mitt Romney's investment, the sophistication of their data operation lagged far behind Obama's. Their supposedly state-of-the-art 2012 get-out-the-vote system, ORCA, failed dismally on election day.

In many ways, when it comes to personal data use, private companies have distinct advantages over political parties. They can do commercial as well as political work – meaning there is no downtime between elections. Equally, the knowledge and experience gained from commercial work can be used in campaigning. As Alexander Nix told his audience in Hamburg, selling a candidate can be treated in the same way as selling toothpaste. Private companies are also less constrained by party processes and party members. They also tend to attract less public scrutiny (Cambridge Analytica being a notable exception).

It had also become far easier and cheaper for campaign groups, candidates and political consultants to gather and store personal data. There is a multi-billion-dollar data broker industry in the US that collects and sells vast quantities of online and offline information about what people do, buy and think. Companies like Acxiom, Experian and Datalogix accumulate oceans of consumer data, in most cases unbeknownst to the consumers themselves.[33] A Federal Trade Commission report in 2014 found that one data broker's database "has information on 1.4 billion consumer transactions and over 700 billion aggregated data elements", and yet individuals have almost no knowledge of what is collected or how it is sold (there are few limitations on personal data use in the US, in contrast to Europe). In a digital era, once you have gathered lots of personal data for a political purpose, you can use it to do two things. You can analyse it to decide who to target and how. You can also, as long as you have people's contact details, get direct access to each voter. Previously, the only way to reach someone was at their home – knocking on their door, shoving a leaflet through their letter box, posting them a letter or, if you were lucky, giving them a call (and hoping you got the right person). With their email address, access to their social media profile, or their mobile number, campaigns suddenly had alternative – and more direct – means of reaching the electorate.

Mercer was not the first to recognize the power of personal data to someone acting outside a political party, or to invest in a company that harvested it. The Koch brothers had got there before him. They invested in a firm started by John McCain's chief technology officer, Michael Palmer, in 2011. Over the next four years, *Politico* reported, the Kochs invested over $50 million in the organization.[34] By 2015 their data was richer and had better voter profiles than that of the Republican Party. The GOP was so worried about the data accumulated by the Kochs that, according to one Republican, it went to "all-out war" with them over it. Very unusually, the Republican National Committee's chief of staff, Katie Walsh, made a public statement attacking the power grab. "I think it's very dangerous and wrong", Walsh said, "to allow a group of very strong, well-financed individuals who have no accountability to anyone to have control over who gets access to the data when, why and how."[35]

Though the Koch brothers and the Mercers made early strategic investments in voter data, their approach is not hard to copy. Any plutocrat with the finances and inclination can develop pop-up party machinery given the availability of personal data. Of course, it is one thing to have the data; it is how you use it that makes all the difference. Having collected its mountain of data, Cambridge Analytica employed teams of data scientists, physicists, behavioural scientists and software engineers to aggregate it, to dissect it and to search for patterns. This is where CA played its second critical role in US political campaigns – as an experimental laboratory in which to analyse and experiment with vast amounts of personal data in order to work out how to influence voter behaviour.

Working out how to influence voter behaviour, or 'behavioural analytics' as CA calls it, was central to the company's distinctive approach. Essentially, this means analysing lots of personal data and then figuring out, on the basis of the results, how to make someone do something – like vote or not vote. This is quite different from trying to change someone's mind. In his enlightening book *The Righteous Mind*, Jonathan Haidt describes how our non-rational and rational brains are like an elephant and its rider. We like to think that the rider makes the decisions and tells the elephant where to go, though in actuality the rider spends most of his or her time rationalizing the direction in which their elephant is already heading. When candidates try to convince us their policies are the right ones, they are appealing to the rider. When candidates make visceral or emotional appeals, they are appealing to the elephant. For centuries, political thinkers have worried away over the damaging influence of our irrational brains, and associated rationality with free will. At the same time, successful political propagandists have long known that propaganda is much more effective at provoking a response than at changing people's minds. Mao Zedong saw propaganda as a way of mobilizing large numbers of people, not converting them.

"Cambridge Analytica", the organization asserted on its homepage, "uses data to change audience behavior", not to change people's minds. It went, in other words, for the elephant not the rider. The way it tried to do this was by building up detailed profiles of each individual, combining data on everything from basic demographic information, to browsing habits, to social life, to spending habits. It meshed this with primary data it collected through surveys and polling, and used all this to group people by their personality and by the issues they cared most about. Tailoring political communication for people based on their personality was, CA argued, much more likely to trigger a behavioural response than communication based on less intimate factors. Subsequent postmortems of the election campaign obsessed over whether 'psychographics' won it for Trump, and whether or not CA were charlatans, forgetting to ask a more fundamental question: is it now theoretically and practically feasible to influence people's vote through their personality? If it is, does this undermine the democratic ideal of the rational voter?

★

Attempts to define and measure personality go back over a century. The psychoanalyst Carl Jung developed a series of psychological 'archetypes' which he believed were universal. Building on Jung's work, a mother and daughter developed a test, the Myers–Briggs test, to give people a practical way to assess personality. The test, though used for many years, was essentially a product of trial and error, not based on scientific study. It was not until the last decade of the twentieth century, after much Ivory Tower bickering, that researchers moved towards a consensus about how to define and assess personality. This consensus formed around the five-factor model – or so-called 'Big Five' – which was found to be the most consistent and accurate measure of human personality. The five factors are: openness (how open you are to ideas, people, experiences), conscientiousness (how responsible, organized and controlled you are), extroversion (how sociable and outgoing you are), agreeableness (how easygoing and trusting you are) and neuroticism (how anxious or fearful you are). How someone rates on each of these five factors will give a good indication of who that person really is. We are born with most of these personality traits, and they stay pretty much the same throughout our adult life. They are, if you like, what makes you who you are.

Once scholars had reached a consensus about personality, they had a foundation on which to build research. Studies then took off in many and varied directions. Researchers studied how personality affects people's lifespan, career prospects, educational achievement and earnings potential. Some scholars also started to look at how personality influences our political attitudes and behaviours. Of course, this idea – that your personality affects your politics – was not new. Back in 1950, Theodor Adorno and his colleagues tried to determine which individual characteristics formed the 'authoritarian personality'. In 1960, in the classic *American Voter* study, Angus Campbell and his co-authors found that personality was crucial in helping people develop political allegiances. Yet, Campbell and others lacked the theoretical framework to explore how personality affects politics. The Big Five personality test provided this framework.

Initially, there were a lot of conflicting results. Yet soon some clear findings started to emerge. The first, and most fundamental, is that there is indeed a link between our personality and our political attitudes and behaviour. Certain personality traits correlate closely with people's political beliefs, their stance on particular issues and how they engage with politics. It is possible to predict, for example, on the basis of someone's personality, whether they will explicitly identify with a political party, and how intensely partisan they will be. You can tell, in other words, not only if a person is likely to join the Democratic Party, but if they will support the Occupy movement. Or similarly, whether they will join the Republicans and if they will go further and support the Tea Party. Other aspects of personality are similarly indicative of political perspectives and persuadability. If someone rates high on openness, they are likely to be more politically persuadable. If someone is particularly conscientious, they are likely to be more conservative.[36]

Other studies looked at the connection between personality traits and specific political issues. In 2014 Aina Gallego and Sergi Pardos-Prado published research examining whether there was a link between attitudes to immigration and personality type.[37] They found there was, even when one accounts for other factors. If you rate high on agreeableness, then you are likely to have a positive attitude to migrants and towards immigration. If you rate low on agreeableness, and high on neuroticism, then you will probably have negative views about immigrants.

Now researchers had the framework – the Big Five model – and were starting to find correlations, but they still struggled to get the quantity of personal data they needed to document the links between personality and politics. Gallego and Pardos-Prado's study focused on the Netherlands, partly because immigration is a hot political topic there, but also because they could get the data. Since 2007 the MESS project in Holland has surveyed around five thousand households and made the data it collects available for research. Other studies have not been so lucky. Collecting enough personal data to be able to assess someone's personality, and correlate it to political beliefs, can be an exhausting and expensive process. One of the best-known tests – the Revised NEO Personality Inventory – has 240 questions. This has been simplified – for example into a fifty-question test – although simplifying necessarily means sacrificing some of the personal details and nuance. In practice this has meant personality research has often been done on relatively small sample sizes of people who have the time to fill in long questionnaires (hence why lots of research is based on university students). Jeffery Mondak and Karen Halperin rather creatively used data gathered from jury participants from nineteen randomly selected US counties, combined with other telephone and pen-and-paper survey results.[38] Even the best survey data is far from ideal. It relies on people's perceptions of their behaviour rather than their actual behaviour. People also have a tendency to embellish some aspects of their character, and forget or disguise others. On top of which, on the basis of a questionnaire alone it is hard – if not impossible – to put people's personality in the context of their social network, in order to understand the dynamics between the two. What researchers really needed was not just a lot more personal data, but personal data combined with personal connections and behavioural data. Luckily, a digital platform was about to oblige.

In June 2007 David Stillwell had just graduated with a first in psychology from Nottingham University. He was staying on at Nottingham to do his master's, followed by a doctorate, so had some time to kill over the summer. Facebook had just launched an app platform and Stillwell, who knew the basics of coding from an A-level in computing, figured he would build an app. He was curious to know if, by combining the answers to a personality quiz app with Facebook profile data, he could correlate people's personality with particular attitudes and behaviours. He built the app and shared it with a few of his friends. They were so taken by it that they shared it with their friends, who then shared it with theirs. Within months the test had gone viral, and hundreds of thousands of people had completed it. At first, given it was just meant as a personal project, Stillwell did not collect any data, but, after other researchers told him how valuable a resource it could be, he changed the terms and – with users' consent – began capturing the results of the tests. When he stopped, in 2012, he had personality data from more than four million people and, for over a third of them, had the data from their Facebook profiles too.[39]

Initially, Stillwell and his colleagues used the data to see which types of personality liked different consumer products. What is the personality of someone who likes Coke as opposed to someone who likes Pepsi? But then they thought they would try looking at it from the other direction. Could what you liked on Facebook tell the researchers what you were like as a person? It turned out that it could. Based on your Facebook likes, the researchers were able to tell, with a high degree of accuracy, your personality traits, your political views, your religion, your sexuality and your ethnicity. They used Facebook likes since this was what they collected, though – as they write in their much-cited 2013 paper – there are plenty of other online traces you can use. "Human migration to [the] digital environment renders it possible to base such predictions on digital records of human behavior," the authors write, going on to say, "Similar predictions are unlikely to be limited to the Facebook environment."[40] Stillwell and his colleagues had shown that, thanks to the galumphing digital footprints we all now leave, gathering personal data to predict someone's personality and political perspectives is no longer expensive or exhausting. Indeed, it has become frighteningly easy.

Stillwell and his colleagues' paper was published in April 2013. Cambridge Analytica was established at the end of that year in Delaware. From the outset the company raced to collect personal data, online and off, and analyse it using, amongst other criteria, the five-factor model. As revealed subsequently, it harvested some of this data thanks to a Facebook app developed by a colleague of David Stillwell's at Cambridge University, Aleksandr Kogan. Yet it was also gathering data and voting behaviour from each campaign it worked on. In 2014, it was involved in forty-four campaigns across the US.[41] The company said it ran its trademark psychographic messaging campaigns on behalf of Republican candidates in three Senate races, working for a John Bolton political action committee. It went on to work on Ben Carson's presidential campaign and on Ted Cruz's. As Alexander Nix said to the writer and political journalist Sasha Issenberg in 2015, "Your behaviour is driven by your personality and actually the more you can understand about people's personality as psychological drivers, the more you can actually start to really tap in to why and how they make their decisions. We call this behavioural microtargeting and this is really our secret sauce, if you like. This is what we're bringing to America."[42]

Using people's personality as a way of tailoring political messages to them was both conceptually and practically impossible before 2013. Until the 1990s there was not a consensus on how to define and assess our personalities. Only since then have researchers started to show the links between personality and political beliefs. Only in the last few years have we been able to gather enough personal data to associate specific attitudes and behaviours with personality types. And only since 2013 has it been possible to use this personal data to predict personality and target political messages based on personality types. It seems rather short-sighted, therefore, to fixate on whether or not this approach was effective in the US election, as opposed to trying to understand its effectiveness and potential use in politics in the future.

★

It was not just in the US in 2016 that a plutocrat was investing in innovative technology to capture personal data and influence voter behaviour. Across the Atlantic another wealthy businessman, Arron Banks, was funding the unofficial campaign to persuade the public to vote to leave the European Union. Banks was, for the most part, the polar opposite of Mercer: garrulous where Mercer was almost mute; laddish where Mercer was reserved; and accessible where Mercer was secretive. They did, however, share two things in common. Both recognized, and sought to leverage, the astonishing power of data and digital platforms; and both loathed the political establishment. In his triumphalist diary of the campaign, Banks writes how pleased he was to be trying something that had not been tried in Britain before and that was giving his campaign unprecedented knowledge of voters. "Using – new to the UK – social media polling technology developed in the US," he said, Leave.EU understood "exactly what was on people's minds, where they lived, and how they would vote".[43] They were able, Banks claimed, based on their use of machine intelligence, to change headlines on social media "to reflect the moods of their audience as much as 20 times a day". By the day of the vote itself, Leave.EU had managed to build up "a million online followers and a huge database". After the Leave campaign won, Banks was convinced that it was the data and the technology they employed that secured their victory. When "we deployed this technology in leave.eu we got unprecedented levels of engagement. 1 video 13m views. AI [Artificial Intelligence] won it for leave."[44]

After its establishment in 2013, Cambridge Analytica became a vital tool in the Mercers' campaign to take a wrecking ball to the political establishment. First it was used in the presidential prima-ries. The Mercer family gave $11 million to an election fund supporting Ted Cruz, the Republican candidate most hated by the Republican Party. As part of the deal the Cruz campaign engaged CA. CA then, as they had on previous campaigns, orchestrated a massive data-gathering exercise – including "a nationwide supersample of up to 50,000" people questioned each month. Combining this with openly available data, and the data they had gathered through apps, they determined which voters were most receptive and, on the basis of their personalities, crafted messages that would appeal directly to them. Someone high in neuroticism, for example, might receive a photograph of a burglar breaking into someone's house with a Cruz quote supporting gun ownership for self-protection.[45]

Out of a field of seventeen candidates, including heavily backed establishment figures like Jeb Bush and Marco Rubio, Ted Cruz won the Iowa caucus. This despite being on a radical platform that proposed returning to the gold standard and denied climate change. He went on to be the main challenger to Donald Trump. As Cruz's popularity waned and Trump's grew, so the Mercers shifted their focus to the rising anti-establishment candidate. In August 2016, Trump got rid of Paul Manafort as his campaign manager and brought in Steve Bannon and Cambridge Analytica. By election day, CA had been gathering data for consecutive presi-dential campaigns for almost eighteen months.

By 9 November 2016, the Mercers could feel justifiably pleased with the return on their investments. Through the individuals and organizations they backed, they had been able to reconfigure the digital public sphere, subvert trust in mainstream media, create a new hyper-partisan centre of gravity in right-wing news, and assemble a huge US voter database with which they could chal-lenge the power and patronage of the Republican Party and test experimental methods of altering voter behaviour. Should we care? Perhaps we should accept, or even applaud, the investments of Robert Mercer. They were, after all, astonishingly effective in helping him to achieve his aims. Other plutocrats have spent as much – and more – money and managed to exert far less influence. Yet, democracies have spent decades, and in some cases centuries, building up protections against over-powerful individuals and interests.

Data and digital platforms give individuals and organizations ways to circumvent democratic principles and electoral law and raise the prospect of elections being 'bought'. Money spent on supporting data-driven campaigning can be much more easily hidden. Personal data can be collected, bought, combined, analysed, modelled, used and sold like a commodity. Companies can, if they choose, take advantage of differential laws and regulations worldwide, offshoring data in the same way as they offshore money. Indeed, the best way to think about personal data, especially in politics, is as a virtual – and parallel – currency. Like money, data can give a candidate or political faction power. It can provide detailed knowledge of voters, the issues they care about and how to reach them. It can – thanks to social media – allow campaigns to map people's personalities, their characters and their hopes and fears, and then tailor messages that they know will resonate with them. A plutocrat with a prodigious quantity of voter data, combined with analytic intelligence, can dispense it just like money, choosing to give one candidate access, but not another. It is another source of power and patronage. Yet it is very difficult to keep track of how this patronage is dispersed, due partly to the willingness of the tech platforms to effectively collude in the opacity.

The use of personal data and digital platforms cannot help but threaten existing democratic principles and practice, particularly in the US, where the 2010 legal decision in Citizens United vs. Federal Election Commission removed most remaining restraints on election spending. There is now a massive asymmetry of information between campaigns and individual voters. Cambridge Analytica boasted over 5,000 data points on each voter; the Koch brothers' i360 claimed 1,800. Political messaging is most effective, communications theory tells us, when the recipient does not realize they are being targeted. The cognitive defences we put up when we know a political message is advertising rather than news, for example, or when we see an ad not aimed at us, are muted. Yet the asymmetry now extends far further than this. Thanks to the traces we leave in our digital past, campaigns can assess our personalities and figure out what makes us tick. With this information they can, if they are so minded, try to avoid the rational rider in our brain and go straight for the emotional elephant.

Democracies rely on a free and diverse press. This is where, the theory goes, citizens find the news and information that helps them decide who to support. Yet by all accounts, Mercer and others made a conscious and persistent effort to destroy people's trust in the mainstream media – not in one individual outlet, or one journalist, or one story, but in the entire media that did not share their perspective. To do this, these plutocrats were willing to support an approach to news that saw it not as an attempt to report the events of the day as fairly as possible within the time available, but as a tool with which to pursue political ends. Journalism as a pursuit of power rather than as a pursuit of truth.

This is where Mercer, and others who adopt similar tactics, such as the freextremists described in the last chapter and the Russians in the next, represent the greatest apparent danger to democracy. In their Nietzschean urge to break the current system, they seem willing to let democratic principles and norms be collateral damage. The best illustration of this is when, in November 2013, the author and historian Ronald Radosh asked Steve Bannon what he meant when he described himself as a 'Leninist'. "Lenin wanted to destroy the state and that's my goal too," Bannon told

Radosh. "I want to bring everything crashing down and destroy all of today's establishment."[46]

The plutocrats might counter that they, like the Silicon Valley platforms, are disrupting a system that needed disrupting; destroying a 'rigged system' to create a new and better one. Such a rationalization could be justified were they doing it all openly and accountably. Yet they are doing this from outside the system, without ever being elected or seeking democratic approval. They are doing it because they want to and because they have the money. And, they are doing it in such a way that makes accountability almost impossible. At many stages in recent history they would not have been able to use their money to support division, conflict and anarchy. Yet the revolution in our global information system has given them an opportunity, an opportunity that has been enabled by the digital platforms. "The internet is the first thing that humanity has built that humanity doesn't understand," Eric Schmidt, former executive chairman of Google, said, "the largest experiment in anarchy we've ever had."[47] Where Mercer led, others will follow.

3

STATES: THE RUSSIA MODEL

Efforts will be made in such countries to disrupt national self-confidence, to hamstring measures of national defense, to increase social and industrial unrest, to stimulate all forms of disunity.

George Kennan, telegram to State Department, 1946

Vladimir Putin smiled wryly as he listened to NBC journalist Megyn Kelly list the multiple allegations of Russian interference in foreign democracies at the St Petersburg International Economic Forum in June 2017. The experts say "it's not just one factor, it's a hundred factors that point to Russia," Kelly told the Russian president, "it's the forensics, it's the digital fingerprints, it's the IP addresses, the malware, the encryption keys, the specific pieces of code ..." Putin waited for the translation through his headphones before replying. "What fingerprints?" he said to a ripple of laughter in the audience. "What are you talking about? IP addresses, they can be invented, you know there are very many specialists that can invent or fix it up, you know a kid of yours can do it." Then, in an unnecessary and slightly sinister aside, Putin referred to Kelly's small child. "Your girl", he said, "that is three years old can perpetrate such an attack."[1]

Putin's denial seemed extraordinary given the length and detail of the charge sheet against Russia. As well as hacking almost twenty thousand Democratic Party emails in the US, in addition to the Gmail account of Hillary Clinton's campaign chairman, John Podesta, Russian intelligence had been accused of hacking political parties, politicians and government ministries across Europe. Two Russian groups, described as Advanced Persistent Threat (APT) 28 and APT 29, both of which were alleged to have hacked the Democratic National Committee, were blamed for hacks in Germany, Norway, France and Denmark. In Germany, in 2015, APT 28 was alleged to have hacked Chancellor Angela Merkel and fifteen of her Bundestag colleagues. The same year, and during 2016, APT 28 was accused of hacking emails and servers at the Danish defence and foreign ministries. In early 2017, Norwegian intelligence accused APT 29 of hacking its foreign ministry, its intelligence service (the PST) and the Norwegian Labour Party. In May 2017, just before polls opened in the French election, Emmanuel Macron's campaign team announced they were the victims of a "massive and co-ordinated" hack. APT 28 was once again blamed, this time by cyber-intelligence firm Flashpoint.[2]

On top of all this, hacking was alleged to be just the tip of the iceberg. It was seen as simply one element of a much broader information warfare campaign that Russia was waging to undermine democracies across the world. This included employing people to publish articles, blog posts and tweets aimed at promoting political division, disharmony and discord in other countries. Disinformation factories, such as the Internet Research Agency at 55 Savushkina Street in St Petersburg, were charged with deliberately seeking to undermine confidence in democratic systems, spreading malign falsehoods across platforms such as Facebook, YouTube, Instagram and Twitter, and promoting conflict between partisan groups. In addition to their extensive activities during the US election, these Russian trolls and bots were accused of interfering during the UK's EU referendum campaign, in subsequent national elections in Holland and France, and in the independence referendum in Catalonia. A study commissioned by the Democratic Party and published in January 2018 examined claims that nineteen countries – from the US to the Baltic states – had been subject to active Russian interference.[3]

These disparate campaigns of information warfare were then given oxygen and credibility by Russia's international news media outlets, RT (Russia Today) and *Sputnik*. In Italy, before a key referendum vote of late 2016, *La Stampa* reported that RT had broadcast live footage of "anti-Renzi [Matteo Renzi, then Italian prime minister] protestors massing in Rome" to 1.5 million viewers on Facebook. It turned out they were actually marching in favour of Renzi. In Germany, before the September 2017 election, RT gave full voice to the AfD. In the UK, after the poisoning of Sergei Skripal with nerve agent Novichok in March 2018, a columnist for *Sputnik* alleged that the British might be responsible. "Given their inveterate anti-Russian agenda," Finian Cunningham wrote, "the British authorities have much more vested interest in seeing Skripal poisoned than the Kremlin ever would."[4]

Yet Putin repeatedly denied any involvement or malign interference by the Russian state in other countries' affairs, often with a casual, confident insouciance. Before his denials to Megyn Kelly, he – or those speaking on his behalf – denied any Russian involvement in Brexit. Brexit was "none of our business", he said in St Petersburg in June 2016. Allegations that Russia had hacked French political parties were not based on facts, he said while standing next to Emmanuel Macron at Versailles. In response to Denmark's accusation his spokesman, Dmitri Peskov, responded, "Russia does not do hacking attacks." After US Special Counsel Robert Mueller directly indicted the Internet Research Agency, Peskov said, "There are no indications that the Russian state could be involved in this, there aren't any and there can't be any." Every time a new allegation popped up, Putin or his spokesman dismissed it, saying there was no evidence linking the interference to the

Kremlin, and asking what motive the Russian state could have for doing such things.[5]

Putin's denials seemed like brazen and flagrant refusals to acknowledge the growing mountain of evidence. Yet, in one sense at least, Putin was right: there were precious few direct links connecting the Kremlin to the many and varied efforts to hack or game Western democracies. Prior to 2018, the US intelligence agencies had made lots of assertions but presented little technical proof. When the head of French cyber-security, Guillaume Poupard, was asked by the Associated Press who had hacked the Emmanuel Macron presidential campaign in May, he echoed Putin's response to Megyn Kelly: the French pre-election hack, he said, was "so generic and simple that it could have been practically anyone".[6] The operations at 55 Savushkina Street were funded by Yevgeni Prigozhin, a caterer and restaurateur who, though known as 'Putin's Chef', did not have formal connections to the Russian government.

Why was it so hard to link the Kremlin to an aggressive, multi-faceted, global information warfare campaign? Assuming that Russia was responsible, then what was Putin's motivation for trying to disrupt democracies across the world? And why did Russia approach it in the way that it did – using hacking, disinformation and deliberately divisive propaganda to undermine confidence in other countries' political systems? Most people were convinced by the evidence that the Russian state was directing widespread interference in foreign states but were left scratching their heads at its motivation and the rationale for its modus operandi. To understand why Putin acted as he did, why he adopted the methods he did, and where Russia's information war may be leading, entails delving into Russia's Soviet past, exploring the forces that shaped Putin's experience and worldview, and charting the rise of a new Russian nationalism that has emerged since the turn of the twenty-first century.

What we eventually discover is that Putin and his intelligence services have not, like some omniscient cat-stroking Bond villain, figured out how to use modern technology to game democratic elections. Rather, he and his regime have reverted to a global perspective more characteristic of the twentieth than the twenty-first century – a dark and paranoid Soviet perspective that sees plots against Russia from every direction. In response to these 'plots', Putin and his court adopt approaches and methods familiar to them from their past. The difference is that their approaches and their methods – many of them remarkably similar to those of the Cold War era – work so much better in the world of Facebook, Instagram, YouTube and Twitter. Where operations then took months or years to prepare and develop, in the digital era they take hours or even minutes. Where propaganda and disinformation previously required detailed forethought and complex planning, they can now be programmed into social media accounts. Where the Soviet intelligence service used to go to huge efforts to cover its tracks and avoid sourcing and attribution, anonymity and non-attribution are intrinsic to modern tech platforms. It is not that the Russians have figured out how to engineer politics on the net, it is that their tried and tested methods are so much more effective now than they used to be.

Explaining Russia's motives and methods is both reassuring and disturbing. It is reassuring to know that Russia has not suddenly worked out how to play democracies. But it is disturbing to discover how effective modern technology is at disrupting politics – especially democratic politics. It is more ominous still to realize that other states have seen the political impact Russia has had using these platforms, and have concluded that information warfare will be a feature of the twenty-first-century world. For some states, such as in Scandinavia, this has meant building up their defences against hacking and disinformation. For others it has meant developing their own offensive capabilities, from national bot armies to state-sponsored hackers. We may come to see 2016 as the year in which Russia fired the starting gun on a global information arms race, in which our digital space is in a permanent state of conflict, states fight proxy battles across virtual platforms, and democratic politics becomes collateral damage.

Before fretting about the future, we need to understand how we got to where we are now. We need to explore why Russia acted as it did, and why it thought its information offensive against the West was justified. To answer these questions, we have to go back fifty years, to the height of the Cold War, back to a time when information was well and truly weaponized.

*

The Black Lake is a beautiful dark glacial lake nestled in the Bohemian Forest, close to the Czech border with Germany. In the 'Ballad of the Black Lake', the poet Jan Neruda called it the "resting place of our Czech heroes" and the "moot of ancient gods". Shortly after 2 a.m., on a clear night towards the end of May 1964, Ladislav Bittman and his small team of divers pulled on their scuba gear and dived to the bottom of the lake. There, fifteen to thirty feet down, they placed four metal boxes, covering them partially in mud to give the impression they had been there for years. Each box was full of papers – all of them blank. Six weeks later Bittman returned, this time with a Czechoslovak TV documentary team, to make a film about the legends of the Bohemian lakes. The documentary team did not know about the previous night-time dive, or about Bittman's real employer. Shortly after they started filming, Bittman and four other divers 'discovered' the boxes. From that instant, he later wrote, "the propaganda merry-go-round was off at full speed."[7]

The thirty-two-year-old Bittman was, at the time, a member of the Czech intelligence service, working in 'Department D', its department of disinformation or 'black propaganda'. The department was a satellite of the KGB's Department for Active Measures, and had been established – like others across Eastern Europe – to help the Soviet Union disrupt and divide the US and other NATO countries. The Czech "disinformation factory", as Bittman called it, organized hundreds of campaigns during the 1960s, as did its sister offices in Eastern Europe and its parent in Moscow. Each department, though it had a degree of autonomy, worked to a set of narratives drawn up by the Kremlin. Propaganda should aim to turn public opinion against the leaders and policies of the Eastern Bloc's primary enemies – the US and its allies – discredit them, enhance internal discord and distrust, and create rifts between them and the international community. Operations could use any methods that worked – forgeries, rumours, front groups, invented stories – with one proviso: they could not be traced back to source.

The boxes in the Black Lake were hauled up and – due to concerns they might contain explosives – were not opened but driven straight to Prague. The find itself provoked lots of public interest, thanks in part to the film footage of the divers emerging from the lake with mysterious sealed boxes – obligingly filmed by the independent film crew. The story then became an international sensation when the interior ministry announced that the boxes contained Nazi papers from the Second World War. This was not true; the pages were entirely blank. Without revealing any of the pages publicly, the ministry then secretly transferred real Nazi papers from Moscow and replaced the blank ones in each box. The process took months since many had Cyrillic notes scribbled in the margins. Each of these pages had to be laboriously removed or doctored before any could be made public. Then, with great fanfare in September, the ministry hosted a major press conference and gave the press access to the papers.

This was 'Operation Neptune'. It was Czechoslovak intelligence's most successful disinformation campaign of the Cold War.

It was designed to discredit the West German government, open painful wounds about Germany's recent Nazi past, and prolong the prosecution of Nazi war crimes, most of which it achieved. It was also one of the rare occasions that a disinformation operation was broadcast internationally on TV. It was a clever, well-planned and well-executed hoax worthy of a John Le Carré novel. It was also one of hundreds of operations, the vast majority of which were far less successful.

Intelligence, propaganda and disinformation were inherent to the Soviet system and had been since its inception. The Cheka, established by Lenin immediately after the October 1917 revolution, was founded to protect the new regime from counter-revolution. Surveillance and information gathering were core to its original functions. As far back as 1923 Felix Dzerzhinsky, a terrifying Belarusian-born ideologue appointed by Lenin as the first head of the service, created a dedicated office of disinformation. The Cheka's successor, the NKVD, used falsehoods, inventions and smears to help Stalin engineer and execute the Soviet purges and show trials of the 1930s. But it was the KGB, the grandchild of Dzerzhinsky's Cheka, that invested huge amounts of time, energy and effort into gathering, producing and disseminating propaganda and disinformation. As one former Soviet major general described it, disinformation was the secret service's "heart and soul", its way of continuing to fight the Cold War when mutually assured destruction prevented direct military confrontation with the US or its allies.[8] So important was disinformation – in all its forms – that when the KGB set up a Department for Active Measures in Moscow in 1958, disinformation was one of its leading responsibilities. Following the establishment of the department in Moscow, satellite units were set up across Eastern Europe in the early 1960s, of which Bittman's was one.

As a consequence of the resources and attention devoted to them, Soviet intelligence services became very skilled. To be successful, they worked out, disinformation had to have some basis in fact, or correspond to a widely accepted belief. It should fit with prevailing narratives in the target population, play to people's prejudices and nurture innate suspicions. To be credible it needed to appear to come from trusted sources – preferably some distance from where it actually originated. To have an impact it then needed to be spread as far as possible and repeated regularly. The reiteration of the same news story – even if it was entirely invented – would eventually seep into people's minds and gain a sense of veracity. The ultimate sign of success was when someone came to believe what you wanted them to believe, but thought they had come to the conclusion themselves. The Russians even have a term for this: 'reflexive control'. Distance and deniability were crucial to the success of reflexive control. As Felix Dzerzhinsky told all members of the secret service, "A Chekist has to have a passionate heart, a cool head, and clean hands."

The purpose of Soviet Cold War propaganda and disinformation was to weaken and demoralize the enemy, to limit their power to hurt the USSR and to sow division within their populations. For the Soviets anything that sapped the strength of their opponents, particularly the United States, increased the strength and sustainability of the Soviet Union, and fostered pro-Soviet sentiment abroad. To weaken the enemy meant identifying and exploiting vulnerabilities in their systems, opening and widening existing political wounds and social fissures, highlighting hypocrisies, and accentuating partisanship. This meant being opportunistic, taking advantage of political crises and set-piece events like elections and referendums, and promoting divisive characters and extremist groups. All propaganda should work towards the long-term goal of undermining the legitimacy of the adversary's government and the integrity of their political system. This was, and was intended to be, the pursuit of war through other means. It was, by the definition of Jacques Ellul in his eminent 1962 study of propaganda, psychological warfare: "Here [in psychological warfare] the propagandist is dealing with a foreign adversary whose morale he seeks to destroy by psychological means so that the opponent begins to doubt the validity of his beliefs and actions."[9]

The KGB was, for example, well aware of the racial divides in America. From the 1960s through to the mid-1980s, it used whatever means it could to provoke and inflame these divides. We know this thanks to copies of secret intelligence files spirited out of Russia by the KGB archivist Vasili Mitrokhin shortly after the end of the Cold War. After the assassination of Martin Luther King in 1968, the KGB spread rumours that he had been murdered by white racists with the support of US authorities. In September 1980, a forged National Security Council memo to the president was leaked to several African-American radio stations, and to selected US newspapers. The fake presidential memo proposed American support for apartheid South Africa, surveillance of black American leaders, plus "a special program designed to perpetuate divisions in the black movement" in America. The aim of the disinformation was twofold – to stir up anger amongst black Americans towards the government, and to discredit the hardline anti-Soviet national security adviser, Zbigniew Brzezinski. Prior to the 1984 Olympics in Los Angeles, Soviet agents in Washington posted letters, purportedly from the Ku Klux Klan, to the Olympic committees of African and Asian countries. "The Olympics – for the Whites Only", read the letters. "The highest award for a true American patriot", they continued, "would be the lynching of an African monkey." These forgeries were meant to embarrass America and foment racial hatred on the eve of the Olympics (which Russia was boycotting).[10]

Many of these campaigns had only limited, or fleeting, success. Occasionally, one took hold and proved much more long-lasting. In India in 1962, Soviet intelligence officer Ilya Dzhirkvelov was instructed by his employers – the KGB – to help set up a newspaper. The paper, *The Patriot*, was intended as a vehicle for Soviet propaganda or disinformation since it was often difficult to place such 'news' in the non-Soviet press. In the 1960s and 1970s it published occasional pieces critical of the US and in favour of non-alignment. But it was not until over two decades after its founding that it played its most effective – and destructive – role for the KGB. In July 1983, the *Patriot* published a letter – ostensibly from an American scientist and anthropologist – which falsely claimed that the AIDS virus had originated from Pentagon experiments to develop new biological weapons. The KGB planted the letter as part of a carefully conceived operation called 'Operation Infektion'. Initially it was largely ignored, but two years later a weekly Soviet journal, *Literaturnaya Gazeta*, published a longer piece on the history of AIDS that referred to the claims made in the *Patriot*.

Fast forward a further six months to April 1986, and a host of Soviet media, as well as a growing number of international outlets, began picking up the story and reporting it as news – most notably TASS (the official Soviet government news agency), *Pravda* (the official newspaper of the Communist Party) and the Novosti press agency (a second official news service). The hoax was then given new – and international – stimulus by a report released that September by Jacob Segal in Harare, Zimbabwe, titled 'AIDS – Its Nature and Origin'. Segal was a seventy-six-year-old East German biophysicist based in Berlin (though Soviet media repeatedly referred to him as a French researcher, presumably to give him greater credibility). The Segal report was enough to make the news go viral, and it was published in papers from Cairo to Buenos Aires.

As with all successful disinformation, there were some elements of the story that had foundation. Two US government organizations were, in the 1980s, doing research to find a cure for AIDS at Fort Detrick, which had been the US Army's biological warfare research and development centre from 1943 to 1969. The rest was invention. Yet that was enough for the KGB to concoct a divisive and corrosive story that persisted decades later. A 2005 study found that over a quarter of African Americans believed AIDS had been produced in a US government laboratory.[11]

Many more Soviet attempts to distort, divide and disrupt the politics of its adversaries had far less impact. This was particularly true of the various attempts to interfere in US elections. From offers of help from the Soviet ambassador to the presidential campaigns of John F. Kennedy and Adlai Stevenson in 1960 (which were rebuffed), via the failed Russian offers to subsidize Hubert Humphrey's presidential campaign in 1968, to the efforts made to derail Ronald Reagan during the primaries in 1976, Soviet attempts to influence US elections had precious little effect. Even in 1982, when outgoing KGB chairman Yuri Andropov told his agents that "it was the duty of all foreign intelligence officers, whatever their 'line' or department, to participate in active measures" to discredit the policies of the Reagan administration, their efforts achieved little.

Most difficult of all was disseminating and amplifying the propaganda widely. Access to foreign audiences was controlled by their domestic media – TV, radio and newspapers. If the Soviets were to have any influence they had to get things published abroad. This is why they set up and subsidized newspapers like the *Patriot* in India, as well as cultivating foreign journalists, editors and academics. But this was a long, laborious process, with lots of opportunities for failure. Even when Soviet intelligence was able to get something published in a foreign media outlet, spreading the message was equally fraught. Official Russian news sources like TASS and Novosti could be counted on to republish the stories, but these were regarded with suspicion by those outside the Soviet bloc. KGB agents were pressed into extensive letter-writing campaigns to newspapers, pretending to be angry workers, though again this was labour intensive and had only sporadic success. Seeding a story that made the leap from print to broadcast media was vanishingly rare. The pre-internet Soviets therefore recognized that disinformation, if it was to work, had to be part of a long-term strategy. As Ladislav Bittman wrote, a "single covert action ... cannot tip the balance of power ... [but] mass production of active measures will have a significant cumulative effect over a period of several decades".

★

By the time of the 1984 US election, Vladimir Putin had already been in the KGB for almost a decade, having been recruited during his fourth year at Leningrad University. He was to stay until 1990 when he left to work with the mayor of Leningrad (later renamed St Petersburg). He returned to head the Russian intelligence service (later called the FSB) in 1998, before becoming Boris Yeltsin's successor as president in 2000. Prior to becoming leader, therefore, Putin spent much of his career either within, or closely connected to, the intelligence services. Few contemporary heads of state have anything close to as much experience or knowledge of covert operations as the Russian president.

As a teenager, Putin was in no doubt what he wanted to do with his life. So taken was he by the Soviet secret service that he first tried to get a job there at the age of sixteen in 1968. This was a period, Masha Gessen writes in her fascinating biography of the Russian president, in which television programmes and popular books presented the KGB as thrilling and glamorous. The recruiting officer who met the teenaged Putin told him to go to university or join the army and, were he to be needed, the service would contact him. Putin took the advice and was accepted into Leningrad State University where he read law, and where the secret service did, in his fourth year, come and recruit him.

During Putin's formative years – from when he first tried to apply to the KGB through to his early thirties – Soviet intelligence was at its most internationally active. Under the chairmanship of Yuri Andropov the service significantly increased its planning and execution of active measures overseas. Andropov had a particular bent for conspiracy theories, seeing the US behind almost every anti-Soviet activity. Soviet defectors, Andropov believed, did not defect but were kidnapped by the CIA. The Prague Spring of 1968 was, he thought, orchestrated by Washington. Human rights groups were simply US front organizations trying to undermine the USSR. In response to these perceived threats, the KGB chairman prepared a whole series of ambitious, even reckless, foreign interventions. These included a coup d'état in Greece, the disruption of Prince Charles's investiture in Wales, and the sabotage of a major oil pipeline in Austria. Each of these was eventually abandoned for fear they could be traced to Russia, but many other measures were put into effect, such as shipping arms to the IRA, the Basque separatist group ETA and the German Red Army Faction, and attempts to smear US politicians. For Andropov, anything that caused political discord and unrest outside Russia was to its benefit, as long as it could not be traced directly. Andropov was essentially adopting the tactics of the guerrilla fighter, acknowledging the growing asymmetry of power between the Soviet Union and the West, but using it to his advantage.

Putin was a product of the Andropov KGB. By the time he joined, in the mid-1970s, Andropov's perspective and his methods of response were firmly established. In Putin's youth and early career, he too came to see everything as a plot against Russia, and was trained to believe that interfering in other people's political systems was a natural and justified response, provided one did not get caught. After he left the service, in 1990, this conspiratorial perspective on international relations was encouraged further by actual US political interference in Russia. In the 1990s the US and others interfered freely in Russia's domestic politics. After Boris Yeltsin's re-election as president in 1996, *Time* magazine even published a cover story – 'Yanks to the Rescue' – subtitled 'The secret story of how American advisers helped Yeltsin win'. The advisers' role was doubtless over-played, but the story reaffirmed Putin's impression that, in international politics, every nation did as much as it could get away with – including interfering in elections. It was this background, and this paranoid view of international relations, that framed Putin's thinking in 2011 when his leadership, and the Russian regime he had established, came under mortal threat.

*

Sakharov Avenue, named after the Soviet dissident and Nobel Peace Prize winner Andrei Sakharov, runs from north-east Moscow down towards Red Square. On 24 December 2011, in temperatures of -5°C, it was host to the largest protest in Russia since the end of the Cold War. A hundred thousand people gathered there to protest against the recent parliamentary elections and the imminent return of Vladimir Putin to the presidency. Placards called for a 'Russia without Putin' and compared him to Muammar Gaddafi, the Libyan dictator killed two months previously. The protest on Sakharov Avenue that day was not the first, but it was the biggest, and had a profound effect.

For Putin, the protest showed how close he and his government were to suffering the same fate as Mubarak's Egypt, Ben Ali's Tunisia, and Gaddafi's Libya. As with the so-called 'Arab Spring', this incipient 'Slavic Spring' was focused on Putin as leader: it condemned his 'managed democracy' and called for his overthrow. Similarly, as in Egypt and elsewhere, it was being organized and coordinated through US social media platforms. Over fifty thousand people signed up to go to Sakharov Avenue via Facebook, and throughout the day Cyrillic hashtags trended on Twitter – including the protestors' nickname for Putin, #ботокс (#botox). Social media was fundamental to the escalation and coordination of the revolutions across North Africa and the Middle East. These protests started out small but quickly snowballed until their momentum carried away the leader and his government.

Putin could have taken the December protests at face value. He could have seen them as spontaneous public anger at what looked like a rigged electoral system. This was not how he, or his government, interpreted them. Putin said he was convinced that they had been orchestrated by America. Specifically, he said he believed they were initiated by the US secretary of state, Hillary Clinton. Clinton "gave them [the protestors] a signal," Putin told Russian state TV within days of the first demonstrations. "They heard this signal and started active work." The signal, Putin asserted, was coordinated via US-funded NGOs in Russia. "It is unacceptable", he said, "when foreign money is pumped into election processes."[12] Putin read the protests, and indeed the wave of global disruption in 2011, as part of an orchestrated American plan to extend US hegemony. And the major US tech platforms, he believed, were an integral part of this plan. This was made evident by protestors' use of US social media to organize in preference to Russia's home-grown social media platform, VKontakte.

Prior to 2011, Putin had not focused on the internet. Though extremely conscious of the political power of media, he had concentrated on harnessing traditional media within Russia in his first two terms. For Russians this meant television, and Putin gained control of independent television channels such as NTV, and established a new state-run international news broadcaster, Russia Today (later renamed RT to obscure its origins). Tactically, ignoring the internet made sense; it had only two per cent penetration in Russia in 2000 when Putin came to power and only sixteen per cent when he shifted his role to prime minister in 2008. But in the absence of state control the Russian internet flourished. A domestic search engine, Yandex, grew faster than its US equivalent, Google. VKontakte, founded by twenty-two-year-old Pavel Durov in 2006, soon became Russia's most popular website.[13]

It was Putin's successor as president, Dmitri Medvedev, who first really engaged with the internet, though he saw it simply as an engine for economic growth and as a way of appealing to Russia's web generation. In June 2010, President Medvedev, in an open-necked blue shirt, blue blazer and jeans, stared wide-eyed as Steve Jobs demonstrated the latest iPhone. It was just days before the launch of the iPhone 4, and Medvedev was in Silicon Valley for a three-day whirlwind visit. From Apple, the Russian president went to meet Eric Schmidt at Google, and then on to Twitter to meet Evan Williams and Biz Stone, where he posted his first tweet from @KremlinRussia. The interim Russian leader had already tried to embrace the tools of the tech platforms, starting a video blog in 2009 – earning himself the nickname 'Blogger-in-Chief' – and subsequently set up his own Facebook page in 2011. It was on this page, on 11 December 2011, that Medvedev condemned the Moscow protests of the previous day. Within two hours, over three thousand people had posted comments to the page, most of them negative or abusive. "Dim, are you taking the mick?" one comment read. "Go now, shame of the country," said another, and "Your time has gone."[14]

December 2011 proved to Putin that Medvedev's approach had been a spectacular failure, and that the internet, especially the US tech platforms, now posed a grave danger to the Russian state. Medvedev had embraced these platforms and tried to use them in a conventional way. His attempts backfired and he found the tools used against him, and against the political system he led. This was just the sort of threat Putin had been afraid of when he first came to power, over a decade previously. In September 2000, Putin approved a new 'information security doctrine' that explicitly warned against "a deformation of the system of mass information [in Russia] owing to media monopolization as well as to uncontrolled expansion of the foreign media sector in the national information space". If this 'information space' evolved in such a way, the doctrine warned, there was a danger that "foreign special services" would use the media system within Russia "to inflict damage to the nation's security and defence capability and to spread disinformation". This, Putin believed, was exactly what the US was now doing, trying to topple the Russian regime in partnership with the major American tech platforms by spreading false information and provoking dissent.[15]

As with most conspiracy theories, there was a kernel of truth around which Putin could construct his thesis. In May 2009, for example, Hillary Clinton launched a '21st-century diplomacy' initiative, in which the US State Department said it would help civil society groups around the world transform politics using the internet and social media. "We need to build new partnerships from the bottom up," Clinton told an audience in New York, "and use every tool at our disposal" to kickstart "Civil Society 2.0".[16] The following month, the US State Department asked Twitter to delay maintenance work on its network, in order to keep the service open for anti-government protestors in Iran, during the country's election campaign. Speaking in Morocco later that year, Clinton then put money behind the State Department's plan for 'Civil Society 2.0', including grants for the Middle East and North Africa.[17]

Nineteen months later, some members of the State Department seemed to be relishing the first wave of revolutions in the Middle East. Alec Ross, Clinton's senior adviser for innovation at the State Department, told a *Guardian* conference in London in June that the internet had become the "Che Guevara of the twenty-first century". Facebook and Twitter were giving people the power to challenge autocratic regimes. "I think this is fun," Ross said, "it's going to be wildly disruptive in the next few years and net-net I think this is a good thing."[18] Ross's attitude may not have been typical of US government personnel, and his relish obscured the trepidation with which the US administration responded to the initial wave of anti-government protests, but it fitted with Putin's interpretation. Moreover, there is no doubt that the threat to Putin and his regime at the end of 2011 was genuine. In addition to the mass protests, there was increasing rivalry amongst Russia's political elites. This "is precisely the most dangerous time for an old regime," Richard Sakwa, an acute observer of Russia's politics, wrote, "and the moment when a democratic breakthrough becomes possible".[19]

Putin desperately needed a strong narrative with which to stabilize and maintain power. He found it in his claim that foreign forces were actively destabilizing Russia and using tech platforms to interfere in its politics with the aim of toppling the government and installing a compliant leader. Whether Putin believed this or not, it is the story he told the Russian people. The US and its allies, he said, represented a hostile, existential threat to the Russian state. They were interfering in its elections, supporting civil society groups in order to create unrest, encouraging anti-government protests, and coaching people to use tech platforms to coordinate action. Putin was, in other words, ascribing to the US exactly the sort of tactics that Soviet intelligence engaged in during his time as an agent.

This narrative was then made explicit in a speech by the chief of the general staff of the Russian armed forces, General Gerasimov, published in February 2013. The Arab Spring represented a new type of warfare, the general said, one characterized by a blurring of the lines between war and peace, where non-military action is as important as military action, and where asymmetrical tactics, such as the use of digital information networks, come to the fore. In response to this new approach to warfare, an approach Russia believed to be led by the US, "it is necessary", Gerasimov said, for Russian forces "to perfect activities in the information space". That was where Putin, the Russian intelligence services and the Russian military then focused their attention.[20]

The digitally enabled protests of late 2011 and early 2012 therefore led to a major shift in Putin's approach. Not only did they change his politics, they turned his focus to the internet, and to the platforms that – as he saw it – had almost enabled another Russian revolution. From then on, he sought to tame the internet domestically, and to use it internationally to his advantage – "to perfect [Russian] activities in the information space".

Within Russia, Putin could replicate the approach he had taken with television in his first term. He could force out the current heads of the internet companies and install more accommodating ones in their stead. The founder and chief executive of VKontakte held out against government pressure until 2014 when, after refusing to disclose personal data about his users, he was forced to resign and left Russia. The search engine Yandex was already majority owned by Sberbank, a state bank, so it was easier to influence. Its founder and CEO, Arkadi Volozh, also resigned in 2014.[21]

Outside Russia, Putin had to take a different approach. He could not pressure the US tech platforms like Facebook and Google in the same way as he could VKontakte and Yandex. If he wanted to respond to what he saw as concerted attempts by foreign actors to destabilize Russia's politics, he would need to find another way. It was only natural that he and his ex-FSB colleagues should look to their past experience, at the way they had previously dealt with such external threats, and the methods they used in response. Central amongst these was the effective use of information to protect your own system and to weaken others, to exploit their communications systems against them.

Still, if the Kremlin wanted to adopt an aggressive new approach internationally, and produce effective propaganda and disinformation, it needed people who were adept at using social media, at producing and commissioning digital content, and at making sure that content spread. At the same time these people had to be patriotic, nationalist even, and unfailingly loyal to the Kremlin. Fortunately for Moscow in 2012, these people were close at hand.

★

Reading through Kristina Potupchik's emails from 2011, you could be forgiven for thinking that she ran a hip, ambitious social media marketing agency. In her mid-twenties, and in constant communication with her colleagues, Potupchik shares advice on how to be an effective influencer on Facebook, how to promote blog posts and where to find good internet memes. She talks about online branding, commissions YouTube videos and discusses how to optimize posts in Google's search rankings. Like any successful social media marketer, she is obsessed by how popular her content is. "The material", she writes, "must contain 'viral' elements, that is, use the motivation of people to distribute it."[22]

Yet in 2011 Kristina Potupchik was not running a social media marketing agency. She was press secretary for Nashi ('Ours'), a pro-Putin nationalist youth brigade. Nashi was one of a number of groups set up or supported by Putin's mercurial political technologist, Vladislav Surkov, in response to the Rose and Orange revolutions of 2003 and 2004 in Georgia and the Ukraine. Surkov believed that in order to counter those protesting against Moscow, the Kremlin needed its own protestors and demonstrators. Directly and indirectly, he encouraged the formation of various nationalist groups – of which Nashi was the biggest – that would loyally support the Kremlin. The groups themselves had to be distant enough from the state to seem organic; that way their support would be more credible and effective.

Every summer Nashi would organize a summer camp up in the Seliger lakes, north of Moscow. There, up to twenty thousand young Russians would play games and do bonding activities – mass weddings included, overseen by Nashi 'commissars' and surrounded by posters of Putin and Medvedev. Russian leaders would often visit the camp, to the great excitement of participants. Financial support for Nashi and other pro-Kremlin groups was funnelled through various channels, from obliging oligarchs to institutions like the Orthodox Church. Neither Nashi nor other similar groups like the Eurasian Youth Group were given orders directly from the Kremlin. As Charles Clover writes in his illuminating study of Russia's new nationalism:

> They represented something more complex [than official organizations] – a milieu of deniable, autonomous groupings of money, executive power and ideology, the wishes of which were carried out by operatives who most often functioned without central direction and clear leadership, responding instead to ideological 'signals'.

These groups functioned as networks, linked and empowered through modern technology, working to an agenda loosely drawn up in Moscow. The key, as Clover writes, was deniability. No actions could ever be traced directly back to the Kremlin.[23]

Potupchik joined Nashi the year it was established, in 2005, and within two years she was its spokeswoman. By 2011 she was in charge of its media output, commissioning scores of young people to post comments online, to write blog posts, to produce YouTube videos and to attack opposition politicians. All this was done to promote Putin and the Kremlin's agenda, making it appear as though it emerged spontaneously from civil society. It was as if Potupchik and her colleagues were an in-house public relations agency for the Russian leadership, yet without any formal ties.

"Putin must become a brand again," Potupchik wrote in April 2011. To promote the brand, Nashi had to adopt whatever online tactics worked. As the head of Nashi, Vasili Yakemenko, explained, when commissioning people to write comments online they had to find "people with balanced language, who write well, not idiots, [who are] capable of maintaining a debate, of developing it. They will comment on our posts, on forums – basically slandering the opposition and praising Putin . . . [creating] the impression that the majority supports us."[24]

However, useful as Nashi was, it was unable to counter the rising anti-Putin sentiment of 2011. Surkov's whole postmodernist approach to state communication, which was reliant on taking advantage of fragmentation, ambiguity and the general confusion of the web, fell out of favour. As Surkov's star waned, so too did Nashi's. Kristina Potupchik herself left in mid-2012, posting on her blog that "it's time to say what was long overdue. I'm leaving".[25]

Yet, though the Kremlin's approach to the internet took a more authoritarian turn in 2012 – especially at home – the methods used by Nashi and other groups were not discarded; rather they were formalized and made more systematic. In September 2013, the independent Russian newspaper *Novaya Gazeta* discovered that a company had been established in a suburb of St Petersburg two months earlier, employing people to comment, post and blog online in favour of the Russian government, and to discredit opposition politicians and enemies of Russia (particularly the US). These 'trolls' were given criteria and guidelines, and publication targets (such as a hundred comments per day). They were doing work similar to that done by Nashi and other pro-Putin youth groups, except in a more structured and targeted way, and at scale. By the summer of 2014, Max Seddon reported, the Internet Research Agency, as the company was called, was employing six hundred people and had a budget of $10 million that year.[26]

The St Petersburg 'troll factory' had many similarities to the Soviet disinformation factories set up fifty years earlier. Hundreds of people were employed to churn out propaganda and false news to promote Russia and to undermine the US and its allies. As in the Czechoslovak department in which Ladislav Bittman worked, they each had specific roles and hierarchies. Similarly, they focused on fostering political divisions, eroding trust in authorities, encouraging partisanship and nurturing anger towards US and European political systems. In the US in 2016, this meant posting on issues about race, immigration, guns, gender and gay rights. Like the Soviet satellite disinformation departments, the St Petersburg office was distant enough from Moscow and the Russian government to claim plausible deniability.

Yet there were also important differences from fifty years previously. There was no need for the directors of the St Petersburg operation to study Western opinion polls in meticulous detail – if they wanted intelligence about public attitudes, they could just scroll through Twitter feeds, look at public pages on Facebook or explore Google Trends. Responding quickly was no longer such a problem either. They could comment beneath news articles as soon as they were published, retweet pro-Russian tweets and like anti-liberal Facebook posts. They could even buy Facebook ads that deliberately stoked racial tension and target them at areas in the US where they knew such tension was high (as, in September 2017, Facebook revealed they had).[27]

Still, useful though it was for pushing the Russian perspective abroad, the Internet Research Agency, and other services like it, was less able to take on some of the other tasks performed by the Soviet departments for active measures. It was less equipped, for example, to do 'black hat' online tasks like hacking into personal emails, putting together compromising personal dossiers (*kompromat*), or installing malware. This is not what the Internet Research Agency was set up for. Moreover, there was a higher risk associated with these types of operations, and therefore an even greater need for 'clean hands'. Fortunately for the Kremlin, there were readily available alternatives.

★

As the snow fell in Kiev in late January 2014, and temperatures dropped to -15°C, thirty-four-year-old Mykhailo Gavrylyuk stood naked in the street, posing for photographs. Stripped and beaten by the Ukrainian government's paramilitary group, the Berkut, he was then handed an axe and made to stand waiting to be photographed for a trophy shot by the dozen or so militiamen surrounding him.[28] Gavrylyuk was being summarily punished for joining a protest against the pro-Kremlin Yanukovych government. The Berkut, or 'Golden Eagle', militia was renowned for its intimidation and violence against protestors. Originally established to fight organized crime, after 2004 the group shifted to disrupting anti-government protests and fixing elections. After Yanukovych had been deposed, the new Ukrainian government disbanded the Berkut. Yet less than two months later, in March 2014, this brutal militia was revived by the Russian government and incorporated into the Russian interior ministry. In the same month an anonymous hacking group calling itself 'CyberBerkut' announced its formation online. "As an inflexible 'Berkut' stood to the end," the website posted, "so 'CyberBerkut' will hunt the fascist evil spirits." The site's emblem was a play on the Berkut badge, with a golden eagle landing and the name 'Berkut' replaced with 'CyberBerkut'.[29]

From the start, CyberBerkut said it would use whatever means necessary to disrupt and depose the Ukrainian government. It began by launching DDoS attacks against government sites, crowdsourcing incriminating information about public officials on its Facebook page, and blocking mainstream media online. By the end of its first month it had hacked and leaked its first emails, claiming they proved that the US had organized the revolution in the Ukraine.

In 2016 CyberBerkut had turned its attention to hacking emails much further afield, including in the US. On Friday, 7 October 2016, the journalist and writer David Satter received an email telling him that someone had just used his password to sign into his Google account, and that he therefore needed to confirm his password. The sixty-nine-year-old Satter had been writing about Russia and the Soviet Union for four decades and had recently published a book detailing the origins of the current Putin regime. By 2013 he had so successfully got under the skin of the Russian government that he gained the accolade of becoming the first US correspondent to be expelled from the country since the end of the Cold War. Assuming the Google email was genuine, Satter clicked on the link.

Satter was not the only one to receive the email that day. Two hundred others, including senior politicians, high-ranking military officers, academics and activists, received the same Google warning. Except that it was a 'spear phishing' email from a hacking group – meaning it looked like it came from a trustworthy sender requesting confidential information, but in fact had malign intent. As soon as Satter clicked on it he gave the hackers access to all his emails. A fortnight later, less than three weeks before the US election, CyberBerkut published a carefully selected tranche of them, claiming they showed that "the United States is preparing a 'color revolution' in Russia on the Ukrainian model". Only that was not what they showed at all.

A meticulous and illuminating investigation by the interdisciplinary Citizen Lab at Toronto University discovered that, as well as selecting which emails to publish, CyberBerkut carefully edited a small number of them, changing their original meaning so that they fitted with the story the hackers wanted to tell. This story, the Citizen Lab writes, was "to make Satter appear to be paying

Russian journalists and anti-corruption activists to write stories critical of the Russian government". Shortly after the doctored emails were published on CyberBerkut's site they were picked up by the Russian government's news agency RIA Novosti and *Sputnik* radio. From there the story was tweeted, liked and shared on Twitter and Facebook.[30]

The Satter affair has lots of similarities to the hacking and release of the John Podesta emails during the US election campaign, hacked six months earlier. Like Satter, the chairman of Hillary Clinton's campaign clicked on a fake Google email warning and changed his password. Like Satter, the emails were then leaked – via WikiLeaks. And, like Satter, it was impossible to link the hack and leaks directly back to the Kremlin. In the Podesta case, the Clinton campaign chose not to validate the emails or confirm whether they were selectively edited to change their meaning. In the case of the Macron hack, the campaign said, many false documents were added to genuine ones, in order to do more political damage.[31]

Trolling and hacking both proved highly effective methods of propaganda and disinformation. Moreover, both were carried out far enough from the Russian state to ensure a veneer of deniability and, though their exact cost is unknown, the approaches were certainly much less expensive than those employed during the Cold War. At the same time, they were not – in Silicon Valley jargon – very scalable. If Moscow wanted to challenge Western dominance of the global information system, it would need greater speed, scale and reach. It would need automation.

*

In Soviet times, it would have been hard, if not impossible, to push alternative news narratives widely in the US or beyond. Yet by 2017, Russia could use not only trolls and hackers but bots and cyborgs. Bots are fake accounts – made to look like real people – which are programmed to react to particular cues. Cyborgs are a combination of a bot and a real person – harder to spot and trickier to respond to. You can see the activities of these micro-propaganda machines play out after almost any newsworthy event, across each of the dominant tech platforms, whether it be a far-right rally or a school shooting.

Ben Nimmo, who analyses global disinformation campaigns at the Atlantic Council's Digital Forensic Research Lab, tracks bot activity after major news breaks. In the days following the 'Unite the Right' rally at Charlottesville, Virginia, on Friday, 11 and Saturday, 12 August 2017, where far-right nationalists clashed with counter-protestors, Nimmo noticed that many of the Russia-linked and pro-Russian bots and cyborgs started to push three narratives. These were: that the far-right protestors and counter-protestors were as bad as one another; that US politicians who criticized the far right were hypocrites (since, it was claimed, they had previously supported the Ukrainian right); and that the counter-protests had been organized by George Soros (no evidence emerged of this). These narratives downplayed and legitimized the actions of the far right, challenged the authority of those criticizing the far right, and presented the counter-protests not as a popular response but as one orchestrated by a liberal billionaire. The aim was to diminish the voices of those condemning the US far right, dilute consensus on the social unacceptability of the march, and increase sympathy for the far right amongst the wider population.[32]

Compare this to Soviet methods. When the KGB sent fake KKK letters before the 1984 Los Angeles Olympics to foster racial tension they were quickly denounced as forgeries by the US attorney general. In the era of Twitter, Facebook and YouTube it had become easy to throw out multiple alternative narratives and push them far and wide. As Nimmo documented in this case, as soon as the Russian news outlets presented their perspectives, other pro-Russian sites repeated and amplified them. From there they were spread further on Twitter, both by real people and by Twitter bots. Hundreds, if not thousands, of bots can be connected together so that they respond simultaneously to the same cues. A Twitter account called 'Kyra', for example, set up a few weeks before the Charlottesville march, retweeted posts about the hypocrisy of US politician John McCain thirty-one times in less than five minutes. 'She' then continued retweeting after Charlottesville – over 140 times a day on average – on everything from Bernie Sanders (pro) to Hillary Clinton (anti) to Donald Trump (anti) to Julian Assange (pro). Kyra-bot's political aim, if one can be gleaned from her thousands of tweets, was to promote partisan extremes and attack the political centre.

The pro-Russia bots, like the trolls in St Petersburg, were engaged in what Russia expert Mark Galeotti calls 'guerrilla geopolitics'. Like Soviet intelligence services in the 1960s, 1970s and 1980s, they were identifying vulnerabilities in other countries' political systems, and then targeting these in order to encourage tension and division, to widen partisanship and existing social fissures and to undermine trust in authority. As with guerrilla fighters, the trolls and bots can inflict thousands of tiny wounds and then disappear into the ether. Plus, unlike the Soviet attempts to encourage racial tension in the early 1980s, they can push alternative narratives while the news cycle is still live.

False amplification using bots is all the more appealing on modern tech platforms since it is so hard to attribute. It can be virtually impossible, for Ben Nimmo or anyone else, to trace the bots back to their controller. This is partly because many bot networks (or botnets) are run as businesses and can be bought or rented at will. Cyber-security journalist Joseph Cox found a thousand plain new Twitter accounts going for $45.[33] If you have the money and would rather buy 'real' popularity, then Russian companies like Vto.pe offer access to over two million users across all the major tech platforms including YouTube, Twitter, Facebook and Instagram. As an alarming report by the IT security firm Trend Micro discovered, for example, you can buy forty thousand 'high-quality likes' for your cause for about $6,000. For $5,000 you can buy twenty thousand comments beneath news articles, "which in the underground come in templates that a customer can choose from". Services like these are certainly not restricted to Russia. You can find social media popularity companies everywhere from China to India to the Middle East. The burgeoning market illustrates how easy it is to do. It can also have a hugely distorting effect on democratic politics. During the 2016 US election campaign, it was estimated that almost one in every seven political tweets was from a bot.[34]

*

Sitting on stage in St Petersburg in June 2017 beside Indian prime minister Narendra Modi, Putin could afford to smile. At this stage, he could still claim that the US had yet to find Moscow's 'fingerprints' on pre-election hacking. Though evidence was piling up about Russian influence on operations in the US, it remained very hard to draw a direct line from these to the Kremlin. Putin's one concession, made earlier that day at the St Petersburg forum, was that "patriotic" Russians may well have launched attacks on Western democracies. Presumably, he was referring to organizations like the Internet Research Agency, hacker collectives like CyberBerkut, and pro-Russian bots. It was not until a year later, in July 2018, that Robert Mueller would finally present detailed evidence of a coordinated hacking operation against the Democrat campaign by twelve members of Russian military intelligence.

The real problem for Putin was that Russia's propaganda and disinformation offensive had been too successful (or had been perceived to be too successful – the two having become synonymous). After 2012 he and his intelligence services adopted the same playbook they had used in the Cold War, creating hundreds of fake news stories, cultivating social tensions, and fomenting division and distrust in the US system. In the Soviet era, this had occasional, sporadic success. In the second decade of the twenty-first century, thanks to radical changes to the information ecosystem, its success surpassed all expectations. So influential was it that many came to believe Russia actually tipped the balance in the US election. As with any retrospective reading of an election, the true impact of Russia's interference will ultimately be impossible to prove. We can never know what swung the minds of individual voters, though it is always very unlikely that any one factor changed the outcome. That said, in the end it does not matter whether Russia did or did not influence the outcome of a US election, if enough people think it did. And many Americans believe it did.

This has led, in some quarters, to mounting Russophobia, an anti-Russian hysteria reminiscent of the early stages of the Cold War. At that time, the shrewd and reflective diplomat George Kennan – himself no Russophile – cautioned against over-simplified Red scares and called for greater knowledge and understanding to counter the Soviet threat. "I am convinced", Kennan wrote in his legendary Long Telegram to Washington, "that there would be far less hysterical anti-Sovietism in our country today if realities of this situation were better understood by our people. There is nothing as dangerous or as terrifying as the unknown." Greater understanding of Russian attitudes and methods would not diminish their significance, but would make other countries better able to counter them. This is all the more necessary given that Russia shows no signs of reducing its information warfare efforts. As well as serving a valuable domestic purpose to Putin in his fourth term as president, they help obscure Russia's material weaknesses.

Yet to fixate on Russia distracts from the extent to which other states have learnt from the Russia model. The 'Gerasimov doctrine'

– like the Cold War arms race before it – is self-fulfilling.[35] Once one state believes another has an advantage that threatens its security and stability, it will take measures to counter it. Other countries saw Russia's actions and, like General Gerasimov, took this as a signal of how twenty-first-century conflicts between states would play out. They therefore had to adapt or risk being left behind. A 2017 study by the Computational Propaganda project at Oxford University found that the governments of twenty-eight countries had already engaged in some form of social media manipulation. In Vietnam, in 2017, it was revealed that the government had recruited ten thousand people to a cyber-warfare unit. Across many countries – from France to Singapore to Malaysia – governments sought to bring in laws to police disinformation. Other countries were even accused of adopting Russia-like offensive information tactics. In May 2017, the Qatari government claimed its neighbours came close to instigating a military conflict after the Qatar News Agency was hacked and explosive false news published.[36]

The dominant US tech platforms are fundamental to this new form of inter-state conflict. They are the virtual battlegrounds on which these information wars are being played out. It is on these platforms – on our Facebook pages, in our Twitter feeds, in our email and on YouTube – that states are deploying their bot armies, launching their spear phishing attacks and battling for supremacy over the news agenda. It is a continuous fight where the measures of success are public support and ownership of the narrative – a global propaganda arms race to sow confusion, division and disinformation.

Part 2
SYSTEMS FAILURE

4

THE FACEBOOK ELECTIONS

It is they who pull the wires which control the public mind, who harness old social forces and contrive new ways to bind and guide the world.

Edward Bernays, *Propaganda*

His election victory in 2016 came as a tremendous shock. He was not supposed to win. He was an outsider from way beyond the political mainstream who entered the campaign late and without the political legacy or campaign infrastructure of the other candidates. He presented himself as a man of the people, who was standing up to a crooked establishment. He had little actual policy programme of his own, choosing instead to rail against the corruption and failure of the political elites, and promising, should he be elected, to provide the leadership to tackle crime, root out government corruption, and rebuild the country's infrastructure. At theatrically staged campaign rallies he would play up his patriotism by kissing the national flag and calling for his audience's help to mend a broken nation. "Together," he said, "let's fix this country." Throughout the election campaign he outraged people with his vulgar boasts, crude language, rape jokes and bellicose rhetoric. Lacking the funds of other more established campaigns, he focused his attention on social media, organizing and mobilizing his supporters on Facebook and Twitter. Using a combination of brash statements and a strongman leadership style he captured public attention and energized his base.

The candidate was not Donald Trump but Rodrigo Duterte, who stunned the world with his landslide win in the Philippine election of May 2016. He was not the only candidate to make populist appeals, nor the only one to claim he would tackle corruption. But he flaunted a provocative macho style and was "the first to make full use of the power of social media".[1]

At the previous election, six years earlier, this would have made little difference to the result. But, in the intervening years, Filipinos had adopted social media – and particularly Facebook – with astonishing gusto. By 2016 about half the Filipino population were online (about three quarters of those eligible to vote) and almost as many were on Facebook as were online. They had also gained the dubious accolade of being world leaders in the amount of time they spent on social media – using it for, on average, four hours and seventeen minutes per day, or as long as it would take to fly from Manila to Tokyo.[2]

Duterte's campaign was the only one to take full advantage of this. Its digital activities were closely integrated with, and considered equally important to, the rest of its election activities. The campaign team scoured social media looking not just for Duterte supporters but for social media influencers. It then wooed them to its cause. Once on board it encouraged them to mobilize their networks, to create viral content, to evangelize online and to swamp the opposition. Thanks to the interconnectedness of social media, the multiplier effect of this was remarkable. The independent Filipino news outlet *Rappler* reported that the campaign enlisted four to five hundred influencers, each with networks of between three hundred and six thousand members (though one had 800,000 members). This gave it a direct social media reach of well over a million people. It became the campaign's unofficial networked army, even being referred to in military terms (with Facebook page names like 'Duterte Warrior'). These digital brigades could be mobilized to flood Facebook or Twitter with the 'message of the week' or to amplify specific campaign videos, messages or hashtags. Equally, they could be geed up to support and defend Duterte – as when they rallied round #DuterteTilTheEnd when the candidate was accused of corruption.[3]

Yet, as politicized vigilantes, Duterte's online battalions could also become vicious and aggressive. One young Filipino woman, Renee Juliene Karunungan, published a Facebook post saying that choosing "Duterte is a lazy choice". She received so many rape and death threats that she filed criminal charges against over a dozen of her abusers. So nasty did some of the online attacks get that Duterte himself even stepped in, his campaign putting out a statement asking for people to "exercise civility, intelligence, decency, and compassion". As with Trump and his 4chan and Reddit footsoldiers, Duterte had no formal connections with these motley crews so could distance himself from them when necessary. And also like Trump, the aggressive, brutal, no-holds-barred approach to campaigning – especially across the dominant tech platforms – worked, and the seventy-one-year-old Duterte became president of the Philippines in June 2016. He did not tone down his belligerent style after the election. "Just because you're a journalist", he said at a press conference shortly before he was sworn in as president, "you are not exempted from assassination, if you're a son of a bitch."[4]

Donald Trump's election victory in November 2016 astonished many people. Yet his success needs to be seen in the context of a whole series of election and referendum upsets in democracies around the globe after 2012. In February 2013, Beppe Grillo's Five Star Movement – a movement that the Italian comedian only properly started in September 2009 – won more than a quarter of the national vote. Less than a year before it had been polling at only five per cent. In January 2013, in the Czech Republic, Karel

Schwarzenberg rocketed to second place in the presidential election, having been considered a joke candidate when he launched his campaign the previous October. In April 2014 in Hungary, the far-right Jobbik party won twenty-one per cent of the vote, far exceeding public expectation. The following month in India, the world's largest democracy, BJP leader Narendra Modi upset all predictions by securing the first absolute majority for a governing party since 1984. In Indonesia in July, Joko Widodo, 'Indonesia's Obama', completed a miraculous ascent from the riverside slum in Surakarta where he grew up to win the presidency. The following year in Argentina, Mauricio Macri, leader of Republican Proposal (PRO), surged from behind to overturn the Front for Victory (FPV), the party of the Kirchners that had governed Argentina from 2003 to 2015. "Even by the operatic standards of Argentine politics," the *New York Times* reported, "the upset victory of Mauricio Macri, the mayor of Buenos Aires, on Sunday was a stunner." From Indonesia to Italy, from Argentina to the Czech Republic, outsider candidates and parties were surging to new heights.[5]

Established parties, incumbent candidates and defenders of the status quo also found themselves battered by unexpected waves of frustration and ire. In Malaysia in May 2013, the ruling Barisan Nasional coalition, which had won every election comfortably since 1974, won less than half the popular vote (though it retained enough seats to stay in power, at least until 2018). In Scotland in 2014, just under forty-five per cent voted for independence, a figure that had risen from twenty-eight per cent just three years before. In October in Brazil, after what *The Economist* called "a wild and nasty campaign", Dilma Rousseff just managed to hold onto office. In June 2016, in a result that flabbergasted much of the world, Britain spurned its stable image and voted to leave the European Union. The following May Emmanuel Macron, having created a party from scratch and run a 'people-powered' campaign, beat all the established parties to win the French presidency.[6]

Each of these elections and referendums was nationally and culturally distinctive and each had its own complex confluence of causes. But many shared common characteristics. Pollsters' predictions regularly turned out to be wrong. Polls fluctuated wildly, often contradicting one another, often showing unprecedented swings. Compelling, charismatic candidates outshone their parties. Rank outsiders, dark horses and newly created parties did much better than expected. Special-interest groups, single-issue voters and previously inactive voters turned out in far greater numbers than envisaged. The campaigns themselves were generally characterized by intense partisanship, divisiveness and high emotion. In all of them, social media played a starring role. And the daddy of all social media was Facebook, along with its various progeny – Instagram, WhatsApp and Messenger. In these years, Facebook became the context for digital campaigns, the leading space in which election campaigns were fought. For some candidates, the platform was simply the quickest and most effective way to build a following, engage that following, and speak to them directly – bypassing mainstream media channels like TV and print. For others, it became a way of reaching key voters with exactly the right message at exactly the right moment. It was not that all these candidates or campaigns necessarily mastered Facebook (though some certainly did), but rather that they recognized the power of the platform and embraced it. It helped, of course, that the rules and boundaries that existed in other media were for the most part absent from Facebook. In the absence of boundaries, political activists, like twenty-something testosterone-fuelled males let loose on a stag weekend, went wild. And democratic processes and protections were trashed in the process.

That Facebook had become so central to, and disruptive of, democratic politics is ironic, given that for much of its short life Facebook did not think especially deeply about politics. It spent far more time thinking about growing its user base, about UX (user experience), about user engagement and time on site, and about building services – walls, groups, the News Feed – that kept users on Facebook (and it was 'users' rather than individual people). When it did consider politics, it tended to assume the platform was by its nature democratizing, that political identity was just another thing to add to your profile, and that if the organization had a political role, it ought simply to encourage participation. A role that was – perhaps unsurprisingly – consistent with Facebook's overarching aim of driving growth, maximizing activity and pursuing dominance at all costs (which in turn grew its advertising revenue). Essentially, Facebook thought political engagement was great, as long as political engagement happened for the most part on Facebook. The seismic consequences of becoming the main platform for global political debate do not seem to have occurred to those running the company. Nor did they consider that not all those using its platform for political ends would have the best interests of democracy at heart, or that the platform might enable people to sidestep protections designed to make the democratic process free, fair and open. Indeed, Mark Zuckerberg and his colleagues appear to have blithely assumed that Facebook's ambition to make the world more open and connected – and its pursuit of its commercial goals (more engagement, more clicks, more shares, more comments) – were both synonymous with, and complementary to, the enhancement of liberal democracy. This naïve and self-interested assumption was to have irremediable global repercussions.

It's not as if Zuckerberg was entirely unaware of the political power of his creation. Less than three years after he launched the site from his Harvard dorm room, and just as he opened it up to non-student users, the twenty-two-year-old consciously inserted Facebook into a US election campaign. It was the autumn of 2006 and, with the US midterms fast approaching, Facebook created profiles for each candidate. The candidates could, if they wanted, take over their page and use it to start a discussion, post comments, tell people about events and build up a base of Facebook support- ers. Tellingly, the pages were active whether candidates wanted them to be or not. And, if you registered your support for the candidate you could post freely on their page, even if they had not claimed it. As it turned out, despite thousands of public posts on candidates' pages, the candidates themselves almost never responded. Facebook also gave its users the chance to express their politics to friends in their network, and in 2008 it added an 'I voted' button to some US users' profiles which alerted their connections that they had voted. In this way politics, for Facebook, was like so much else on the platform, an expression of personal identity – just like being a cat lover or a Manchester United supporter.[7]

It was in 2008 that Facebook's political potential really started to become evident, and this was more a consequence of one of its co-founders than the site itself. Twenty-five-year-old Chris Hughes, a roommate of Zuckerberg's at Harvard and one of the original Facebook crew, left the company in 2006 to work with the Obama campaign. There he created My.BarackObama.com, or MyBO, which gave Obama supporters the digital tools to become active campaign organizers. Hughes took his learning from Facebook and gave the Obama campaign the networking capabilities it otherwise would not have had. Over the course of the campaign two million volunteers organized 200,000 events via the site, formed 35,000 groups and raised $30 million.[8] Barack Obama's team used Facebook too, though as one of many social media tools it was experimenting with to reach voters directly. This reflected the limited reach that social media – Facebook included – had in mid-2008, when only one in ten Americans was using it for politics.[9] Obama saw, far earlier than almost any other democratic politician, the capabilities of digital social networks in mobilizing supporters around a candidate – especially when that candidate was advocating change. In this sense, this was not the

'Facebook election', as it was prematurely called, but it was the first election in which the political power of social networks started to become apparent.[10]

Two years later, at the US midterm elections in 2010, almost every American candidate had a Facebook page.[11] Almost three quarters of US internet users were getting political news online, and almost two thirds of Amserican voters who were online used social media.[12] This did not mean all candidates benefited equally. On the contrary, political popularity on Facebook looked a lot like many 'winner-takes-all' graphs of internet industries. Politicians such as Barack Obama and Sarah Palin gained millions of followers, while less engaging and less emotionally stimulating candidates earned just hundreds.[13] It helped if the candidate was polarizing. Keeping to the middle ground, searching for consensus, and seeking to mollify rather than excite, were not winning strategies on Facebook. Still, in 2010, though an increasing number of users were discussing politics on social media, the discussions bubbled up organically, and politics was certainly not the main reason most people were logging on. Catching up with friends, sharing holiday snaps and posting baby photos had far greater appeal than politics. Only one in twenty American social media users said that they used it to read comments by politicians, celebrities or athletes.[14]

For Facebook too in 2010, US politics was still a long way down the list of priorities. It was scrambling to become the leading social network, and racing to avoid being superseded by upstart rivals. Measured by its rocketing growth, its strategy was succeeding. Between the autumn of 2008 and the end of 2010, the number of people using the platform had exploded, leaping from 100 million regular users to over 600 million. Much of this growth was outside the US, such that by late 2010 seventy per cent of users were non-American. Facebook was pedalling furiously to build on this momentum and take the platform to its first billion users. It pushed the service in Brazil and India, looking to overtake

Google's own social media offering, Orkut, in both countries (it soon did). It ruthlessly cannibalized its competitors' successful features, adapting its News Feed into a stream and encouraging users to share, in order to undercut the fast-growing Twitter. In the UK, it flew past social networking site Bebo, and in Germany past the leading domestic service, StudiVZ. The media, meanwhile, was too mesmerized by Facebook's growth to assess its political significance. Indeed, it is striking, reading news reports about Facebook in 2010, how few articles mention politics. The press was too busy commenting on Aaron Sorkin's new Facebook movie, *The Social Network*, or reviewing David Kirkpatrick's glowing biography of Facebook's first five years, *The Facebook Effect*.[15]

It was Twitter's capacity to upend international politics, not Facebook's, that first drew public attention. The protests in Iran after the 2009 election were, misleadingly, dubbed 'the Twitter Revolution'. Misleadingly since most of those participating in the protests were not using Twitter, and it did not result in a revolution. Still, the message many people took away was that social media tools had intrinsic political potential, and that this potential was inherently democratizing. This impression was compounded by the credit given to social media – and specifically to Facebook – for the wave of revolutionary protest across North Africa and the Middle East in 2011. This credit was not entirely undeserved. As techno-sociologist Zeynep Tufekci's research shows, "people with a presence on social media, especially Facebook and Twitter, were much more likely to have shown up for the crucial first day that kicked off the avalanche of protest that was to come."[16]

This astonishing illustration of the political potency of Facebook did not lead Mark Zuckerberg into a period of self-reflection. It did not lead Facebook to pause and consider the implications of such political power, or to become more self-conscious about what its role ought to be or what responsibilities the platform should acknowledge. From Zuckerberg's perspective, whatever disruptive impact technology was having on politics was not a consequence of Facebook, but of the internet. It "would be extremely arrogant for any technology company to claim credit" for the Arab Spring, he told the eG8 summit in 2011. "People are having the opportunity to communicate. That's not a Facebook thing. That's an internet thing." And anyway, the company did not have time to worry about politics; it had more pressing matters to take care of. It was working overtime to kill off Google's new social network, Google+; it was launching a separate Facebook Messenger service; it was preparing to buy photo-sharing site Instagram for $1 billion; and it was heading towards an initial public offering (IPO) in May 2012. Politics was less important than accelerating global growth and engagement, and figuring out how to turn Facebook's growing international dominance into dollars.

And boy, was Facebook growing. As American voters woke up on the morning of 4 October 2012 to news reports about the first presidential debate between Barack Obama and Mitt Romney, Facebook announced that it had hit its milestone of one billion users. In just over two years it had added half a billion people, equivalent to more than the entire population of South America. Outside the US, the fastest-growing Facebook nations were also the world's biggest democracies. In India, the number of Facebook users grew from less than 45 million in 2011 to 112 million in 2014. In Brazil over the same period it grew from 28 million to 72 million, with Brazilians spending between three and four hours a day on social media (mainly – but not only – on Facebook). In Indonesia, of the 71 million people online in 2014, 65 million – a whopping ninety-two per cent – were active Facebook users. Plus, not only was Facebook fast becoming the dominant social network across the world, it was also becoming a space where people talked about politics. In 2012, the US election was the most discussed topic on Facebook, and more than four in ten Americans said they had taken part in at least one political act on social media in the last year. In 2013, 'election' was the most discussed topic on the site. In 2014 the Brazilian election was the third most discussed topic on Facebook across the world.[17]

When it came to politics, whether your government was authoritarian or democratic, Facebook was increasingly the main public space – the digital market square. The candidates that realized this, and were able to take advantage of it, benefited disproportionately. When Beppe Grillo captured Italians' frustration with their political system in September 2009, he had announced that he was starting a new movement that "will be born on the Internet". By November 2012 Grillo had a million supporters on Facebook, almost five times the number of his closest opponent. He used the platform to organize political rallies and demonstrations, rail against the *casta* – the Italian privileged establishment – and convert his followers into votes.

Narendra Modi saw this too. Modi, the leader of India's BJP and their candidate in the 2014 election, built a huge number of followers on Facebook, and engaged with those followers throughout the campaign. From the date the election was announced to when voting closed, *Quartz* reported, "13 million people engaged in 75 million interactions regarding Modi" on Facebook. Like Grillo, Modi encouraged his supporters to become activists in what he called Mission 272+ (272 being the number of seats the BJP needed for a majority), through one of the campaign's Facebook or Android apps. Volunteers signed up in every one of the country's 543 constituencies.

The contrast between political communication in this Indian election and the previous one in 2009 was like the difference between the telephone and the loudhailer. In 2009, social media was virtually irrelevant. There was one Indian politician on Twitter – Shashi Tharoor – and he had only six thousand followers. During the 2014 campaign there were 227 million Facebook interactions (posts, comments, shares and likes), and Modi had sixteen million Facebook followers by the time he was sworn in. As Facebook's policy manager told the *Times of India*, "Facebook is really the key place of the conversation that is happening." Modi's embrace of social media – his rival Rahul Gandhi, who led the Indian National Congress, did not have a Facebook or Twitter account – galvanized the campaign, animated his supporters, boosted his volunteer network and drove people out to vote. When the results of the election came in, to almost everyone's surprise, Modi's BJP exceeded its target of 272, winning 282 seats and more than doubling its votes from 2009.

From Facebook's perspective all this political activity on the platform was great and should be encouraged. It added an 'I'm A Voter' button to Indian voters' Facebook pages in 2014, which they could press to let their network know that they had voted. After the company first tried this in the US in 2008, it rolled it out across the world, and by 2016 it was active in forty-seven countries.[18] This was in addition to Facebook apps tracking candidates' popularity and a global outreach programme to increase political interactions. Politicizing voters was, Facebook thought, entirely consistent with its global mission to make the world more open and connected. "Part of that [mission]", Facebook's Katie Harbath told *Buzzfeed* in 2014, "is helping to connect citizens with the people who represent them in government." Like the host of a children's party filling toddlers up with sweet fizzy drinks, Facebook just wanted to energize citizens, without considering where they might direct this energy.

In 2014 there was still no sign that those running the platform were anxious about the unintended repercussions Facebook might be having on democratic politics. The way in which, for example, those candidates pushing strong anti-establishment messages – like Narendra Modi, Karel Schwarzenberg or Beppe Grillo – seemed to gain bigger and more active followings than those with a more centrist or conservative message. Or the way in which far-right parties with anti-migrant and anti-Semitic messages, like Jobbik in Hungary, were growing large support bases. Indeed, Jobbik was the most popular Hungarian party on Facebook prior to the 2014 elections. Nor did they seem concerned about the way in which political engagement on the site was often coupled with vehement partisanship. In the lead-up to Brazil's election in October 2014, for example, "a war raged on social media," the *Washington Post* reported, "with friends and even family members falling out over political affiliations and unfriending one another on Facebook." In Thailand, research on the 2014 election found that Facebook may be "exacerbating existing divisions" in an already deeply divided society, and that partisan Facebook groups were ignoring "discrepant information" that conflicted with their political views.[19] Also in Thailand the same year, Facebook-based political vigilante groups emerged, including the 'SS' and the 'Rubbish Collector Organization', targeting users they saw as anti-monarchist.[20] Still, despite its distorting effect on democratic politics, had Facebook restricted its role to enabling civic action and coordination, and providing a space in which candidates and parties could post messages and coordinate supporters, then the company might justifiably have claimed that its actions were not dissimilar to those of other digital platforms (and much more responsible than those of, say, 4chan). But Facebook did not stop there. Facebook went further, much further, in enabling motivated actors to game democratic politics.

In 2012 Facebook shifted from being a relatively passive enabler of democratic disruption to an active agent. This was the year in which it chose to turn its phenomenal reach, its remarkable depth of personal data and its increasing grip on the world's attention into dollars. It did this by transforming the platform into the most powerful behavioural advertising system the world has ever known.

Up to 2012, advertising on Facebook was not exactly smart. It relied not on intelligence about the behaviour of users or details of their profile, but on sheer numbers. In his fabulously gonzo memoir, *Chaos Monkeys*, Antonio García Martínez, who worked as product manager at Facebook from 2011 until 2013, describes his astonishment at how bad Facebook's monetization of its users was when he arrived. Facebook monetization was "bottom of the barrel stuff", Martínez writes. "Before 2013, if you wanted to know how Facebook made money, the answer was very simple: a billion times any number is still a fucking big number."[21]

In 2012, as its IPO approached and Facebook realized it had to prove its market value to investors, the company went all out to create an intelligent, scalable, global, targeted advertising machine. In pursuit of its commercial goals, it introduced a raft of new ways in which businesses could target users more accurately, reach them more effectively and learn – through people's response – how to make their advertising more powerful. In one sense this was simply doing what everyone else on the internet was trying to do: monetize users' attention. Yet Facebook was in a unique position to do this. By 2012, no other company had a billion regular users around the world; no other company knew as much about its users; and no other company had such intimate access to them via their friends and family. From Facebook's perspective, it was just building better commercial tools to help business advertise to customers. It is not even clear that Facebook considered how powerful these commercial tools could be to political campaigns, or what implications they might have for democracy. Yet it was not long after these tools had been introduced that candidates, campaigners and parties began to recognize, and take advantage of, their political potential. And even though it might not have been the original intention, it was not long before Facebook itself started to encourage people to use them for campaigning – no matter what their political purpose.

There were three elements to Facebook's drive to enable much more sophisticated targeting of its users. The first was about giving advertisers a much richer range of criteria by which to identify who they wanted to target: letting advertisers reach people who played golf or loved gardening, for example, rather than restricting them to standard measures like age, gender or relationship status. The second was about giving advertisers the power to reach people in a comfortable and familiar context, and in a way that made the ad more trustworthy. They did this by slipping advertisements into people's News Feed from January 2012, something they had tried briefly in 2007 but pulled after users protested.[22] This time, since Facebook had taken much greater control of what posts you were shown in your News Feed in 2011, it could introduce ads more strategically. These were not ads like you would see elsewhere on the web. They were called 'featured' posts, and included what looked like an endorsement from someone in your network at the top (such as 'Sarah Smith likes Amazon.com'). The third element of Facebook's transformation was about enabling advertisers to link together what they already knew about people with what Facebook knew about those same people. Facebook did this through something called 'Custom Audiences', launched in autumn 2012, which let companies link their customers with the same person's Facebook profile, creating a bridge between Facebook and the real world.[23] Over the following months and years, the company would develop these features and add new ones, giving advertisers ever more options for targeting users and for evaluating and developing their messaging. In February 2013, for example, Facebook announced it was linking up with big-data companies like Axciom and Epsilon so that businesses could merge real-world personal data with their audiences on Facebook.[24] And, the following month it launched 'Lookalike Audiences', letting businesses use Facebook's behavioural data to find new customers who were similar to their existing ones.[25] If Facebook was a poker player, and its chips were its users' personal information, then from 2012 onwards, the company was going all in.

Up to this point, all these new product launches sounded pretty corporate, and unrelated to politics. But what may – to a car maker – be a much more efficient way of selling a car is – to a political candidate – a fantastically potent instrument of propaganda. Facebook's targeting tools are, for political campaigns, like firing a high-powered scope-sighted rifle after having made do with a smooth-bore cannon. On top of which, unlike previous campaign tools (and cannon), Facebook could tell you if you hit your target and whether you needed to alter your method of attack to get better results. Best of all for propagandists, it gave them the chance to reach prospective voters directly (via their mobile phone), in a trusted environment (their personalized News Feed), with a specially tailored message that had already been ratified – or 'liked' – by someone in their personal network. On this last achievement alone, Facebook had managed to resolve a problem that had dogged political propagandists for almost a century. How do you reach voters directly without having your political message filtered by friends, family, work and all our other social influencers? To understand the extent of Facebook's achievement you have to go back to the early twentieth century, to the period just after the Great War, when we were just getting to grips with the idea of mass propaganda.

*

In 1926, twenty-four-year-old Harold Lasswell completed his doctoral thesis at the University of Chicago. In the thesis, the young political scientist described British, French and German government propaganda efforts during the First World War. Lasswell believed each government had manipulated the mass media in order to justify its actions to domestic populations and those abroad, especially in the US. The British were particularly clever propagandists, Lasswell wrote, and the American public was particularly vulnerable to manipulation. "American public opinion", Lasswell wrote, "has often been a cockle-shell, floating helplessly and unconsciously in the wake of the British man-of-war." Lasswell's thesis fed into contemporary fears about the public's susceptibility to propaganda, fears already fanned by the journalist and writer Walter Lippmann, and subsequently by the 'father of public relations', Edward Bernays. These anxieties then seemed to be borne out by fascist demagogues who used radio and film to inflame populations across Europe in the 1930s.[26]

While Lasswell was turning his thesis into a bestselling book, another young academic was teaching maths in Vienna. Paul Lazarsfeld, who was later to become the 'the founder of modern empirical sociology', did not start out studying the effects of mass propaganda.[27] In the 1920s he researched and wrote about youth camps, statistics, the working class and the social effects of unemployment. This last research project caught the eye of the Rockefeller Foundation, which gave Lazarsfeld a grant to travel to the US to conduct research in the early 1930s, before permanently emigrating in 1935. Then, in 1940, he started a research project that would overshadow our understanding of the effects of mass communication for the rest of the century, and cast doubt on Lasswell's claims about public susceptibility. Lazarsfeld, working with his colleagues Bernard Berelson and Hazel Gaudet, set out to discover whether the mainstream media really did influence people's political views as much as was thought. In the first ever large-scale panel survey, he and his fellow researchers interviewed three thousand people in Erie County, Ohio, during the 1940 US presidential campaign. They broke these down into five groups of six hundred each, one of which they interviewed multiple times to see how their attitudes changed over the course of the campaign, while the others acted as control groups.[28]

Lazarsfeld, Berelson and Gaudet discovered that people's political views were not, as contemporaries thought, much changed by what they read or heard in the media. Voters were far more influenced by their friends, their family and their colleagues – in other words, by their social network. "Personal influence is more pervasive and less self-selective than the formal media," the researchers wrote. "In short, politics gets through, especially to the indifferent, much more easily through personal contacts than in any other way, simply because it comes up unexpectedly as a sideline or marginal topic in a casual conversation."

They also made another unexpected discovery: not everyone's political views counted equally. Certain people in each social network had an outsized impact on the views of others. These 'opinion leaders', as they called them, tended to take more notice of politics, to consume more media and to be more vocal about what they thought. They acted, in other words, like powerful political filters. The researchers termed this a 'two-step flow' of influence since they found most people's political views came not directly from the media or politics, but via an opinion former in their social sphere of influence. Since this finding emerged so unexpectedly from the interviews, Lazarsfeld returned to it the following decade to check it was right. This later research, with sociologist Elihu Katz, consolidated the findings of the first project and reaffirmed the central role that social networks and opinion formers have in shaping our political opinions.

Arguments about the influence of mass media on political perspectives waxed and waned over the following decades, particularly as television took a strong hold on the public's attention. But, at the turn of the century, political propagandists still had to accept that the effects of any mass media communication were liable to be limited and filtered by those in our social network, which no-one had the omnipotence to oversee, nor the power to control. Until Facebook came along.

Using Facebook's new tools, campaigners could not only reach voters directly, they could have their message effectively endorsed by people in a voter's social network. How? Facebook knows, since it records everything we do on its platform (and lots of things we do off it), which members of each social network are Lazarsfeld's opinion leaders. This is not rocket science. It can see, from activity on the platform, the people who have large personal networks, who post frequently, and whose posts and links are shared, liked and commented on regularly. If campaigns target these opinion formers, they do so in the knowledge that these people are likely to share their messages. When they do share them, other people in their network see a political message endorsed by someone whose opinion they know and respect. For political campaigners, being able to access friendship networks with a direct message that has social endorsement is like a linguist discovering the Rosetta Stone.

Facebook gave campaigners the Stone, the translation and a how-to guide on Egyptian hieroglyphs. Barack Obama's 2012 campaign was the first to capitalize on direct access to Facebook's social networks. Using a tool called Facebook Connect (subsequently discontinued), the campaign asked supporters to log into its website via Facebook. This gave Obama's team access to supporters' friendship networks. Combining its own knowledge about voters with Facebook's, the campaign then used these networks to distribute tailored messages to the specific types of voters it needed to reach. One million supporters signed up for the app, and 600,000 shared pro-Obama messages.[29] "This is the Moneyball moment for politics," Obama's 2008 blog director told the *Guardian* in 2012. "If you can figure out how to leverage the power of friendship, that opens up incredible possibilities."[30] Facebook gave campaigns a way to reach voters directly, and at the same time the ability to hack Lazarsfeld and Katz's two-step flow.

As well as leveraging the power of friendship, Facebook made it so much easier – and cheaper – to target specific voters in specific places. Since most democratic representatives represent a particular geographical area, this could – and did – give campaigns a huge leg up. In Britain until 2014, for example, if a political party wanted to post something to every voter in a specific constituency, they had to ask the Royal Mail for their addresses. The Royal Mail could provide addresses at a constituency level, but it was a hassle, and since the only people who were really interested were political candidates, it was – from the Royal Mail's perspective – hardly worth the bother. As a consequence, campaigns would spend huge amounts of time and effort collecting and checking address lists so they could post campaign literature. Then, in 2014, Facebook 'onboarded' Axciom's data in the UK. Onboarding is a term digital marketers use when they meld real-world data with online data to create richer online user profiles for advertisers. In this instance, the Axciom data contained lots of different ways to split users geographically – including by constituency. All of a sudden, for the first time, a political party could reach every voter in a specific constituency with a specific campaign message. And they did not even have to pay for postage! This was transformative, says Craig Elder, the joint digital director of the Conservative Party's 2015 campaign.[31] Along with the ability to target individual constituencies, the party could upload its own voter data to Facebook, and fire pre-tested messages at particular sets of swing voters.

The benefits to the Conservative Party of mastering Facebook's new targeting tools became strikingly apparent during the 2015 election campaign. The Conservatives had identified twenty-three seats which, if won, would give them a majority in Parliament. Most of these seats were in the south-west of England, many of them held by the Conservatives' coalition partners in government, the Liberal Democrats. Unbeknownst to the Liberal Democrats, the Conservatives embarked on what they called the 'Black Widow' strategy to take over their seats – since a black widow spider eats its partner after mating. The strategy relied heavily on Facebook, backed up with copious direct mail shots. "We were able to work with Facebook using constituency targeting to focus just on the constituencies that were going to decide the election," Elder told journalist Tim Ross, "and then based on what we already know about the demographics of the people who are going to decide this election, we could do demographic targeting, and interest targeting."[32] It had the added benefit that it was almost invisible to the Lib Dem incumbents. "We didn't see any canvassers out on the streets," the Lib Dem leader Nick Clegg said after the election. "We would send out teams of canvassers, in the old 'shoe-leather' way. And you just wouldn't see [the Tories], which is why in some significant parts it did completely blindside us." The Conservatives took every Lib Dem seat in the south-west at the election.[33]

Facebook also proved to be the best way for campaigns to reach and motivate the young, the unconfident and the downright apolitical. The platform gave campaigns access to a friendly space where people, including many young people and those with no interest in politics, would spend large chunks of their day – the News Feed. Here campaigns could reach them via their peers, with messages which they already knew would provoke a reaction, at the moment when they were making their decision on how to vote. This was the strategy – driven by data analysed by data scientists – that Dominic Cummings, the director of the official Leave campaign, used during the EU referendum campaign in Britain in 2016.[34]

In what Cummings called 'Project Waterloo', Vote Leave deluged nine million people they had identified as 'persuadables' with videos and messages in the last ten days before the vote. Almost all of these were versions of three powerful but questionable Leave campaign claims: that Turkish migrants would flood Britain if it stayed in the EU (of which there was an extraordinarily small chance), that the EU cost the UK £350 million a week (later called "a clear misuse of official statistics" by the UK Statistics Authority), and that this money would flow to the NHS if Britain left (a commitment abandoned after the vote). Facebook was the primary delivery mechanism for these messages. Between eight and twelve million people saw Vote Leave content on Facebook in each of the last few days of the referendum campaign, with the number of impressions exceeding forty million by the end.[35]

Britain was hardly the only place where campaigners saw the potential of the platform to energize the young. Savvy campaigners across the globe were using it. In Indonesia, where over a third of the population were under twenty-four, Joko Widodo's election campaign team could see Facebook would be crucial. "We knew that first-time voters . . . have the tendency to be very highly influenced by their friends," the head of digital strategy for Widodo's campaign said, "especially on political affiliations or likes and dislikes. So that was very much determined by their social network and . . . social media."[36]

Facebook gave campaigns the power to reach precise sets of people individually, to infiltrate their social news at a moment of the campaign's choosing, and to apply peer pressure. No wonder it made for a fantastically powerful motivator to political action – both in the digital and in the real world. We know that Facebook's political power extended to the real world thanks to experiments on the company's own data. Back in 2010, it allowed researchers to measure whether adding the 'I voted' button to people's profile page – and letting them know when someone in their network clicked it – increased the likelihood of them voting. Being Facebook data, the researchers did not need to rely on a small sample size – 61 million people unknowingly took part. "The results show", the researchers concluded, "that the messages directly influenced political self-expression, information seeking and real-world voting behaviour of millions of people." Particularly striking, they found, was "the effect of social transmission on real-world voting", in other words, the importance of peer pressure.[37]

Following Paul Lazarsfeld's discoveries in the 1940s and 1950s,

Donald Green and Alan Gerber, world leaders in the science of voter turnout, have conducted repeated experiments that show social pressure, especially when it is visible to your social network, makes it more likely people will vote.[38] When Katherine Haenschen conducted similar experiments on Facebook itself in 2014, she too found that "it is the heightened visibility of individuals' voting behavior made possible on Facebook that appears to be driving turnout."[39] This may also help explain unexpectedly high registrations and turnouts in recent elections. In California, in September 2016, for example, the number of voter registrations per day leapt from just over 9,000 to more than 120,000 after Facebook posted registration reminders. At the UK Brexit vote in June 2016, three million more people voted than in the general election the year before, and increased turnout was highest in areas that voted to leave.[40]

Had Facebook not become so dominant, its political tools – powerful as they are – would not have had nearly such an impact. But with over two billion active monthly users, Facebook was the world's largest online social network, larger and more active than most world religions. "Always be where your audience is," the Conservatives' Craig Elder said in a speech to campaign professionals shortly after the 2015 election, and in democracies all around the world, the audience was on Facebook. Not only were they on the platform, many were getting their news there too. By 2016, in twenty-six countries more than half the population were using social media as a source of news. For more than a quarter of young people in those countries it was their main source of news. As *Bloomberg* reported in November 2016, America had just "endured its first presidential election in which the majority of the electorate got its news from social media". The chief source of news on social media was Facebook's News Feed. "If it's an exaggeration to say that News Feed has become the most influential source of information in the history of civilization," the *New York*

Times' Farhad Manjoo wrote in April 2017, "it is only slightly so."[41]

So why is this a problem? Isn't political engagement a good thing for democracy, especially after many years of declining civic participation? If Facebook, and its various vast subsidiaries – WhatsApp, Instagram and Messenger – is enabling and driving this engagement, should we not applaud it? At the very least, shouldn't those who lamented the decline of political engagement pause before heaping opprobrium on the company? At the turn of the century, political scientist Robert Putnam pulled together a mountain of evidence to show what many had long suspected about civic engagement in the US – that people had become less involved in their communities. More and more Americans were, as his book title said, 'bowling alone'. If Facebook helped buck part of this trend, by increasing voter registration, voter turnout and political discussion, then it is hard to argue that this is not a good thing for democracy.

Yet Facebook pushed political engagement on its platform without considering whether it supported or undermined democratic processes. Whether, for example, Facebook algorithms would expose people to diverse and conflicting news and information, or to perspectives that confirmed or even polarized what they already thought. Whether Facebook Groups would recreate democratic communities or simply encourage echo chambers. Whether the Facebook News Feed and Groups would give people a chance to deliberate on political issues or just to promote partisanship.

When Facebook thought about its civic roles, it assumed these roles were consistent with, and complementary to, its business goals. It was helping, for example, to give people their own voice online. What "we're trying to do", Mark Zuckerberg told the audience at one of his global town halls in December 2014, "is to make it so everyone has a voice". He was right; Facebook was giving more and more people the chance to communicate. It just so happened that by doing so, Facebook was gaining more and more users, and making its platform more and more powerful for advertisers. Then, prior to and following its IPO, Facebook went further. On top of being an acquiescent enabler of divisive and sectarian politics, it turned its platform into an active propaganda weapon that could be used for political campaigning by anyone, including those who wanted to circumvent democratic protections.

In 2013 Facebook introduced 'dark posts', also called unpublished posts, in the News Feed. The company was responding to businesses who wanted to be able to test a few different versions of an ad with different audiences, without all the different versions appearing on someone's Facebook page and making the advertisers look foolish. Dark posts let these companies do their own 'A/B testing' – testing, in other words, whether version A of an ad worked better with audiences than version B. When Facebook introduced the service, it was aimed squarely at the commercial sector, not political campaigns. It did not know that three years later the Trump campaign team would take advantage of dark posts to create a remarkably sophisticated behavioural response propaganda system. Every day of the campaign, the campaign team would test not just two or three versions of ads, or even a few dozen versions, but around fifty thousand different versions of campaign ads. Each ad would be slightly distinct, with a particular font, an alternative background colour, a different format or different text. Artificial intelligence software would capture feedback from Facebook about user engagement, and then keep the features that performed better and discard the rest.

Dark posts were, by their nature, only visible to those at whom they were targeted. It was therefore almost impossible to compare claims made in dark posts, or challenge them publicly. If, for example, a campaign wanted to use dark posts to run a voter suppression campaign, it could do this with little fear of being exposed. And the Trump campaign did try to suppress votes for Hillary Clinton, particularly amongst supporters of Bernie Sanders, black voters and young women. We discovered this not through Facebook, but because a senior member of the campaign team told journalists Joshua Green and Sasha Issenberg. "We have three major voter suppression operations under way," he said.[42] The first pushed a message that Clinton had been corrupted by big money; the second presented her 1996 remarks about 'super-predators' as indicative of her attitude to black men; and the third alleged that Bill Clinton was guilty of sexual assault. The approach may well have worked, with Democrat turnout lower than expected in key battleground states.[43]

When Facebook helpfully layered Axciom geographic data onto UK Facebook profiles in 2014, it gave politicians the opportunity to focus lots of attention – and resources – on specific voters in marginal constituencies. Some "Labour insiders who worked for former party leader Ed Miliband" even insist, journalist David Bond wrote in the *Financial Times*, that "the 2015 UK general election was won and lost on Facebook". There is nothing in UK electoral law that prevents the Conservatives – or any other party – from doing this, though it does make existing local spending limits seem faintly ludicrous. Candidates for Parliament are allowed to spend a maximum of around £15,000 campaigning in their constituency (the exact amount varies by size of seat). This restricts the role that money can play, makes the contest accessible, and provides a level playing field for candidates. Yet if, in addition to this £15,000, a party can spend another £100,000 or so communicating with specific voters in the same constituency via Facebook, but none of this counts towards the local limit, then it hardly makes for a fair and level playing field – as the spending constraints intend.

When Facebook gave businesses the opportunity to coordinate their own data and ads with the platform, the company could not have known the UK Leave campaign would employ physicists and specialists in 'quantum information' to work out how to identify persuadable voters, and how and when to mobilize them. Yet this is what the campaign did, flooding these voters with exactly these messages in the days leading up to the 2016 Brexit vote.

When the social media giant introduced Instant Articles in 2015, as a way of letting news organizations publish their stories directly to the platform, it did not know that it would be used to publish hyper-partisan and distorted political information during the US election campaign the following year. The intention – Facebook said at the time – was to improve their users' news experience and make news articles load faster on the site. Initially, the social network only opened the service to a few big name news organizations – the *New York Times*, the BBC, the *Guardian* and a handful of others. Over the next year it started to let others in until, in April 2016, Facebook opened Instant Articles "to all publishers – of any type, any size, anywhere in the world".[44] For Facebook, this was part of its "journey of informing people and connecting them to the news that matters to them". For anyone who wanted to publish invented, clickbait, divisive or grossly distorted news, this was an invitation. It was far from Facebook's intention that some of the most widely read and shared stories on the site shortly before the US election would be false or hyper-partisan, but this is what happened.

Nor could Facebook have known that political campaigns would use every opportunity to infiltrate friendship networks, to promote smear stories about opposition candidates, to stir up vehement partisanship, or to identify vulnerable voters and target them with singularly one-sided information. When Facebook provided an open, automated system for advertisers, where anyone could run their own campaign as long as their ads kept within Facebook's community standards, they did not know that the Russian Internet Research Agency would take advantage of this to target over three thousand divisive, inflammatory and polarizing advertisements at around ten million US citizens before the 2016 election. This included an ad showing Satan ("If I win, Clinton wins!") arm-wrestling Jesus ("Not if I can help it!"), with the instruction "Press 'Like' to help Jesus win!". The ad, *Wired* magazine reported, was targeted specifically at people interested in "Laura Ingraham, God, Ron Paul, Christianity, Bill O'Reilly, Andrew Breitbart, the Bible, Jesus, Conservatism in the United States".[45] The advertisements would have given those at the Internet Research Agency useful data, provided by Facebook, about which ones provoked the greatest reaction. Once people liked this or other Russian-bought advertisements, then the Internet Research Agency could channel further politically polarizing messages to them, and via them to their networks. According to evidence given to the US Congress, the agency created 120 Facebook pages between 2015 and 2017, where it published eighty thousand posts. These reached, Facebook reckoned, about 126 million people.[46]

Facebook did not know this at the time, but that is at least partly because prior to 2016 it gave it very little thought. It was too busy outperforming its earnings schedules, competing with other Silicon Valley tech giants, growing manically and figuring out ways to heighten its users' engagement with the site. If Facebook had put obstacles in the way of those wanting to use its platform for political campaigning, it would have impeded its own growth. So it didn't. Instead it did the opposite, leaving its door wide open to political campaigns that wanted its help, no matter what their political inclination, using whatever currency they wished, and even advising them on how to get the most out of the platform's powerful propaganda tools. In the process, Facebook enabled the distortion, division and destabilization of the democratic process.

Still, Facebook might legitimately counter, it did not invent the advertising model that fuelled the economy of the web, Google did. The social media giant may have taken the Google ad model and supercharged it, but it was still the Google model. And, it was this model that created perverse incentives. So perverse that a cheap, low-rent site full of misinformation could be more competitive than a well-respected, reputable, high-end one. If you want to apportion blame for the systems' failure, then you have to look at Google's role in it, too.

On Saturday, 20 May 2017, Mark Zuckerberg and his wife, Priscilla Chan, went hiking on the Appalachian Trail. This was not, however, an ordinary hike. As Zuckerberg remembers, he and Priscilla met "local residents – former mill workers, teachers, small business owners, a librarian, and a trucker".[47] These were pre-arranged conversations with everyday folk, not accidental chats with other walkers. The conversations were filmed, photographed and documented on the Facebook founder's profile page. Zuckerberg was talking to them as part of a listening tour of the US, his New Year's resolution for 2017. This was not, he repeatedly stressed, the start of a political campaign. He had – he said – no ambition to be elected (despite hiring Obama's 2008 campaign manager). Whether this is true or not, should Zuckerberg or anyone close to him ever choose to run for election, they would have personal access to the most powerful platform for influencing elections in the history of modern democracy.

5

ANARCHY IN THE GOOGLESPHERE

"Have you guessed the riddle yet?" the Hatter said, turning to
Alice again.

"No, I give it up," Alice replied. "What's the answer?"

"I haven't the faintest idea," said the Hatter.

"Nor I," said the March Hare.

Lewis Carroll, *Alice's Adventures in Wonderland*

It was a made-for-TV scene. US senator Al Franken, author,
actor, comedian, radio show host and politician, who resigned
from the Senate over allegations of sexual harassment in late
2017, leant forward in his seat at the Senate hearing and eyeballed
Colin Stretch, Facebook's general counsel, sitting ten feet away
from him. "You put billions of data points together all the time,"
Franken said, "that's what I hear that these platforms do." Stretch,
who was sitting beside Richard Salgado from Google and Sean
Edgett from Twitter, was answering questions put by Franken
and other members of a Senate judiciary committee about
alleged Russian interference in the US 2016 election. Senator
Franken could not understand why Facebook, Google and
Twitter, companies that collected vast quantities of data for a
living and which employed some of the smartest people in the
world, had not noticed that a Russian agency was buying partisan ads aimed at US voters. Even when it was paying for them in

rubles! The more questions he asked, the more exasperated Franken became. These platforms are, Franken said, starting to gesticulate widely with his hands, "the most sophisticated things invented by man. Ever . . ." He then paused before levelling his accusation. "You can't put together rubles with a political ad and go like, 'Hmmm . . . those two data points spell out something bad.'" Stretch, who had been at Facebook for seven years and the firm's general counsel for four, stared down at the desk in front of him, looking deeply uncomfortable. "Senator," he replied, "it's a signal we should have been alert to and, in hindsight, it's one we missed." Head in hands and visibly frustrated, Franken then pressed Stretch to commit at least to not accepting political ads paid for with foreign currency in future. Stretch would not make this commitment. He would only go as far as saying that Facebook would require all political advertisers to provide information showing they were allowed to advertise in the US. Despite Franken's interruption that "you can't say no" to the currency commitment, Stretch did just that.[1]

This exchange between Franken and Stretch during Senate hearings in October 2017 provides a perfect illustration of how broken political communication on the web had become, and a glimpse of how hard it would be to fix. What, to Franken, seemed like a pretty straightforward problem – a foreign power trying to distort another country's election by pumping propaganda at its citizens – could require, Stretch recognized, an incredibly complicated solution. Facebook's chief lawyer had to equivocate, because allowing people to buy ads in different currencies had become an integral part of Facebook's global, open, self-service, automated, carefully tailored, and extremely lucrative, business model. More than just being a part of its business model, it was part of the philosophy and principles that underlay Facebook's growth and dominance. In fact, you could go even further, and argue that such a globally open ad system was fundamental to the way in which news and information were fuelled and sustained across the entire web.

Since the web took off in the late 1990s, online news and information have been funded chiefly by advertising. Yet digital advertising does not work the same way as advertising did in the old world. Indeed, if you think you can understand digital advertising based on the way advertising worked in the twentieth century, think again. Scotch any impressions you have of Mad Men labouring over storyboards on New York's Madison Avenue. Digital advertising – or 'ad tech' as it is known in the industry – is something quite different. You could go as far as to say that ad tech is a different species to its pre-internet ancestor. Where old-world advertising was slow, digital advertising moves at lightning speed. Where it was broad and mass, digital advertising is forensically narrow. Where old-world ad firms were populated by creatives, account directors and copywriters, digital firms have software engineers, system administrators and data scientists. A specialist at the IT research company Gartner called ad tech 'more complicated than Wall Street'.[2] Commercial firms like Adobe and Quantcast employ trainers dedicated to educating people on how ad tech works.[3] Google even has an Academy for Ads. Bob Hoffman, who worked in advertising for many years and has written what he calls "a small, hysterical book" about ad tech, describes how the digital journey from advertiser to publisher now "weaves its way through trading desks, DSPs (Demand Side Platforms), data providers, targeting programs, verification software, ad exchanges, and an insane and murky gauntlet of other toll takers who each extract a little money from the advertiser's media budget".[4]

Given its baffling impenetrability, it is tempting to turn away from the strange new world of digital advertising and leave it to run itself. This would suit those profiting from it very well but would be a terrible mistake for politics and society. Without lifting the lid on this horribly Byzantine virtual world, it is impossible to explain not just Russian interference, but much of the political turbulence and upsets of the last decade. Or indeed to understand why and how it has been possible to hack democracies using digital tools. Understanding how ad tech works does not, by itself, explain the shocks and surprises. But these cannot be explained without understanding how ad tech works. Colin Stretch could not explain to Al Franken how Russian agencies could buy and distribute ads so easily on Facebook without describing how Facebook's advertising model functions. Equally, you cannot explain why, in the lead-up to the US presidential vote in November 2016, scores of Macedonian teenagers in the town of Veles were publishing hundreds of invented news stories about Donald Trump and Hillary Clinton, without looking at how digital advertising funds news. The reason why companies like Cambridge Analytica were able to target behavioural ads at people based on intimate attitudinal profiles only becomes clear once you figure out the dynamics of digital advertising. Similarly, to understand the way the Trump campaign A/B-tested thousands of political messages each day in order to create the most persuasive content, why Vote Leave set so much store in physicists, mathematicians and data scientists when planning its Brexit campaign, and why bots have become such a feature of modern digital election campaigns, you need to understand ad tech.

Ad tech is both the sustenance and the poison at the heart of our digital democracy. The sustenance because it supports a huge proportion of the political and non-political content on the web. The poison because it cannot function without behavioural tracking, it does not work unless done at a gargantuan scale, and it is chronically and inherently opaque. Constant and intrusive behavioural tracking is intrinsic to ad tech. Advertisers have been sold on the idea that in the digital world they can reach exactly who they want, when they want. The only way to give them this sort of access is to follow you everywhere you go online (and beyond). To capture everything you do, where you go, what you're like, who you're connected to and what you're likely to do next. This gives enormous – and asymmetric – knowledge to those who want to influence your behaviour, whether for a commercial or a political purpose. It also means ad tech providers have to collect phenomenal amounts of information all the time, about as many people as they possibly can. As you can imagine, this mounts up pretty quickly. The only way ad tech can work at this scale is if it is as open and frictionless as possible. Being open and frictionless means almost anyone can use it, at any time. It is equally open, therefore, to those with good or honest intentions and to those with malign ones. Ad tech is also inherently dark – in the sense of being very hard to assess or monitor externally. This darkness is, in some cases, conscious (for example within platforms like Facebook); but in other cases, simply because ad tech is so big and so complex, trying to follow any single ad to any single destination is virtually impossible. So vast is the digital ad system, so multi-layered and so labyrinthine, that no-one knows exactly what anyone is doing at any one time. It is, to all intents and purposes, anarchic. Should states want to interfere in other states, plutocrats play politics, or radicals subvert the status quo, they can, safe in the belief that they can hide most of their tracks.

Given how fiendishly complicated ad tech has become, it is hard to explain how we got here without quickly disappearing into a maze of acronyms, technical jargon and corporate-speak. Fortunately, much of the convoluted history of ad tech can be told through the story of two companies, Google and Facebook. This is partly because, by 2018, these two companies squatted like virtual hippopotamuses across this brave new world of ad tech. Together, they accounted for half of the money made in digital advertising across the world, and for more than $6 in every $10 in the US. So dominant had they become that the media had started referring to them as 'the duopoly'. Advertising is also each of these companies' main source of revenue. About ninety per cent of Google's income, and over ninety-five per cent of Facebook's, comes from digital advertising. And it is because these two companies either invented or appropriated the methods that now define ad tech that they jointly became dominant and utterly integral to our digital universe.[5]

★

When they started Google, Larry Page and Sergey Brin would have been appalled by the idea that they would eventually find themselves running the world's largest advertising company. In their seminal 1998 academic paper introducing Google, they made clear they saw advertising as a corrupting influence on search. They even went so far as to include an appendix deploring the reliance of search engines on ads. "We expect", they wrote, "that advertising funded search engines will be inherently biased towards the advertisers and away from the needs of the consumers." Yet, in a crucial subsequent sentence, the pair wrote that although they had a purist attitude to search results, they had no theological objection to advertising per se. It was just that in general, "the better the search engine is, the fewer advertisements will be needed for the consumer to find what they want."[6] This conflicted attitude to advertising – an inherent distaste coupled with a recognition that it served a practical purpose, as long as it was done well – characterized the approach the founders took to it over the next two decades. They would resist introducing or developing Google's advertising until they could see others taking a lead, then they would leap in – taking a more 'Googley' approach (more data, more engineering, cleverer) – and, having made the leap, do their utmost to dominate. Once they became dominant, their approach would then become industry standard. Of course, they did not have to make advertising their primary source of revenue, and they certainly did not have to take the distinctive approach to advertising that they did. But, through their early decisions – often made belatedly for the sake of expediency – they set off in a direction that would define not only their own future, but the future of communication on the web.

In the film version of David Mamet's play *Glengarry Glen Ross*, there is an iconic scene in which Blake, the representative from head office (played by Alec Baldwin), reads the riot act to three salesmen in the down-at-heel Premiere Properties (the fourth – Ricky Roma – is busy pitching to a gullible drinker in the Chinese restaurant opposite). Having just told them they are all fired, and have to earn back their jobs by the end of the week, Blake then gives them a harsh lesson in how to sell. "Because only one thing counts in this life!" he yells at the three of them, "Get them to sign on the line which is dotted! You hear me, you fucking faggots?" He then walks to a blackboard and flips it over. "A-B-C. A-always, B-be, C-closing. Always be closing! Always be closing!!" This is sales at its most brutal and raw. It is a long, long way from promoting a brand, or raising a buyer's awareness. This is simply about contacting people who have already shown an interest in investing in property and converting them to a sale. No conversion, no commission, no job. Or, as Alec Baldwin says in the movie, "The money's out there, you pick it up, it's yours. You don't – I have no sympathy for you."

When Page and Brin made their momentous commitment to fund Google through advertising, this is the type of selling they went for. That is not to say that the Google method had anything to do with hard-bitten salesmen in down-at-heel offices pulling every trick to get people to sign on the dotted line. Their approach was, however, ferociously focused on conversion. Before October 2000, Google sold advertising in a pretty traditional way. It employed advertising salespeople who sold banner advertising on its site, based on the number of visits people made. This was less a conscious choice than an indication of just how little the founders thought about advertising. They were so focused on building the most effective search engine that they, for the most part, ignored ads. This changed in the autumn of 2000, when Google adapted its approach to the one taken by various other search engines, selling search terms. This meant letting advertisers pay for specific words which, if typed into Google, would prompt the advertiser's text ad to appear beside the search results. From the outset this was self-service, promoted with the straightforward line "Have a credit card and 5 minutes? Get your ad on Google today". Yet, though self-service and linked directly to what someone was already searching for, advertising on Google was still not fully 'Google-ish' – in the sense of being distinctive and unconventional. Advertisers were still charged based on the number of people who saw their ad.

It was two years later, in 2002, that Google went the full *Glengarry Glen Ross*. At the time, the company had to do something radical. The first internet bubble had burst, Google's funding was running low, and investors were unhappy at its rate of return. Or, in Steven Levy's words from his 2011 biography of Google, "The VCs were screaming bloody murder." In response Google upended the way it charged advertisers. Rather than making them pay for the number of people who saw their ad, it would only charge them for the number of people who actually clicked on their ad. Success would not be measured by exposure, but by behaviour. The approach was not entirely new – a version of it had been developed by Bill Gross at the end of 1997 and integrated into his search service GoTo.com – though Google adapted it. Google's ads would not be integrated into organic search results as they were on GoTo.com. Ads would be ranked according to quality (on criteria decided by Google), and people would bid via so-called 'Vickrey auctions' or second-price auctions. This meant that the winner of the auction – the advertiser who bid the highest price – would not pay the price they bid but the price of the second bid, plus a penny.

There are lots of reasons why Google felt pleased with itself when it adopted its behavioural approach. For a start, it bucked against convention and ran counter to the way most advertising worked. Second, it was measurable, based on actual behaviour backed up with data. Advertisers could be shown the exact number of people who were taking action in response to their ad. Third, it was highly efficient. Advertisers could choose words, create ads and make bids themselves. The market would then decide the value of the words, not Google. For this reason, it could also be run at scale by algorithms, as long as you had access to enough processing power. The Vickrey auction also made it seem fairer. And finally, it appeared to work for all parties. People had already indicated what they wanted by typing in the search terms ('cheap flights to Paris'). The search results coupled with the ads made for a happy marriage. As Google frequently liked to say, everybody wins! Google certainly did: its $7 million profit in 2001 jumped to $100 million in 2002.[7]

Yet this approach, which quickly led to these ads becoming Google's main source of revenue, would also have significant side-effects. It committed Google to the hard sell – to Always Be Closing. It also obliged the company to track consumption and behaviour. Advertisers and content creators were motivated always to be thinking about what would make people click, while Google had to measure not only the total number of clicks, but who clicked what and when, and what happened as a result. A whole online culture developed from this obsession with clicks – a culture not limited to commercial websites, but to news and to political communication. Google's decision to take this approach set it on a path that would lead far beyond where it originally intended. It would eventually lead, for example, to Google trying to figure out not just if you bought something online after seeing an ad, but even if you went to the store and bought it.

Still, at this stage Google's ambition was simply to fund search. With its new text ads it did this with a healthy income left over. At this point Page and Brin could have decided that since they had successfully made search self-funding they could go back to safely ignoring digital advertising. But they didn't. Having tasted the fruits of AdWords (as its text ads were called), Google spread, and in so doing played its next critical role in determining the economy of the web.

By early 2003, a four-year-old Santa Monica start-up called Applied Semantics had tried seven different product ideas, changed its name (from the far less cerebral 'Oingo'), and seen six potential buyers come and go.[8] When Google got interested in acquiring it there was every reason to think they would lose interest like the rest. But this time, the seventh, the sale went through. It would later be cited as one of the most important acquisitions in internet history.[9] Working with Applied Semantics, Google was able to take its phenomenal expertise in text-mining and combine it with ad-serving technology in order to deliver contextual ads at scale. In plain English, Google could now automatically deliver an ad to a web page – any web page – that was directly related to the text on that page. If you were reading an article about skiing, Google could show you an ad for ski equipment. If you were reading a story about the financial markets, it could post an ad for bitcoin trading. The aim of this new technology was not to provide more ads on Google Search, but to give any online publisher the opportunity to show ads, simply by adding a few lines of code and letting Google do the rest. Once the ads arrived, so would the cheques – for the publisher and for Google. In the same way that Google Search had organized the new flood of information online, Google AdSense – as it was called – would help to fund the flood. As far as Google was concerned, once again everyone was a winner.

Advertisers could put their ads on lots more websites, and publishers could fill some empty space on their pages and get paid. What could go wrong?

★

In 1802 the scientist, naturalist, adventurer and polymath Alexander von Humboldt sent home from Peru a series of specimens of a substance he was sure would have agricultural value. "The name Huano (the Europeans always confuse hua with gua, and u with o) means," he wrote, "in the language of the Incas, fertilizer with which one fertilizes." Europeans knew it as guano, or more commonly as bird poo. Tests made in Paris confirmed that the substance was high in nitrogen, phosphates and potassium. Two decades later, when it was tried by farmers in America, one found it "the most powerful manure he had ever seen applied to Indian corn".[10] By the 1840s there was a guano gold rush, led by the British, with the Americans in close pursuit. For about twenty years in the mid-nineteenth century guano was the principal fertilizer used by British farmers. Initially, it seemed like everyone benefited. The Peruvian government paid off longstanding debts and guano soon became the main source of state revenue. New businesses like the chemicals company W. R. Grace took off. Some merchants and their families − like the Gibbses − made lots of money (leading to the Victorian music-hall line "William Gibbs made his dibs / Selling the turds of foreign birds"). Farmers, particularly in the UK and US, were able to increase their yields. All from a seemingly endless resource that was otherwise, quite literally, waste.[11]

In fact, not everyone benefited from the guano gold rush. Excavating bird poo was a miserable job that few people wanted to do. This led guano miners to seize labourers from Pacific islands, and to virtually enslave Chinese workers, many of whom died or suffered terrible health problems as a result. The Peruvian government, which initially made lots of money from the trade, built up major debts that it was unable to repay when the price of guano later collapsed. The United States, bristling from being beaten to the market by the British, passed a law – the American Guano Islands Act 1856 – that legalized the requisitioning of Pacific islands for the purposes of mining guano. This was subsequently called the first act of US imperialism. A colonial war broke out when Spain tried to requisition guano-rich islands off the coast of Peru, and when Peru and Chile disputed control of resources in the Atacama Desert. The guano itself soon became depleted through over-extraction, and was then replaced by synthetic alternatives. Exploitation, slavery, indebtedness, imperialism and war – such were some of the unintended repercussions, or 'externalities' as economists call them, of the nineteenth-century guano trade.

What on earth has Google's twenty-first-century approach to ad tech got to do with the nineteenth-century trade in guano? Well, in 2003 Google saw seemingly endless white space on the net, white space that was growing every day, most of which – from a commercial perspective – seemed to be going to waste. If, by mining the text on each web page, Google could fill these spaces with relevant ads, then everyone might fill their pockets. The sites themselves could earn money from ads, users could see ads that were relevant to the page, and Google could take its cut. Like the British imperialists in the nineteenth century, having seen the opportunity Google moved quickly to colonize as much of the market as it could, before others stepped in. Sure enough, Google ads spread like wildfire across the web. On top of which, Google was seen as a generous patron that had created a sort of magic money tree. As the journalist Ken Auletta writes in his book *Googled*, "Not only was Google not evil, it was beneficent." Where Google led, others followed. Outbrain, a service that similarly filled white space on publishers' sites with links to other relevant articles, ads and sponsored content, launched in 2006, and another similar called Taboola in 2007. Next time you are on a news website take a look at the ads and links dotted round the page – there is a good chance at least one of these will be provided by one of these three companies.

Yet, as with the guano trade, Google's colonization of white space on the web had many unforeseen ramifications. It gave Google authority over a massive inventory of waste space. So massive that it could only be managed through smart software and reams of data, and by publishers and advertisers doing much of the work themselves. Google might have authority, but it only exercised limited control. No single person at Google would decide which ad was shown on which page on which site. This would be done by algorithms. Publishers necessarily had to forgo control of many of the ads that appeared across their own websites, leaving that up to Google and automation. Similarly, advertisers had to cede control of where their ads went. It was a system designed to be governed by eyeballs and clicks. A system built for scale, not for control.

Such a massive change to the way news and information was funded was bound to have ripple effects. A whole fledgling market emerged of players – some more kosher than others – producing stuff purely to satisfy fleeting public demand. Clickbait took off. The poster child of this shift was even called Demand Media, a company which literally kept track of what people were searching for online, then produced super-cheap articles or videos to redirect some of this search traffic and the ad dollars associated with it. It was a fantastically ruthless free-market approach to information – and one that emerged directly from the model Google adopted. Eventually Demand Media stalled and then sank, holed under the waterline by the very company to which it owed its success. Google adjusted its search algorithm in 2011 to push the Demand Media-type content down its search results. No attention, no income. Yet the approach – producing whatever news and information attracted attention in order to earn ad income – did not die, it just evolved. Five years after Demand Media's star began to fade, a cottage industry of young people living on the banks of the river Vardar in Macedonia was inventing news about US election candidates. And – thanks in large part to AdSense – they were earning more than ten times the average monthly salary.[12]

Another unintended side-effect of Google's imperial model was that advertisers could – unintentionally – find themselves funding political extremism. A company like Walmart would pay Google to deliver ads wherever they would earn clicks. After 2012 this could be one of over two million publishers in the AdSense network. Neither Google, nor companies like Walmart, were paying a lot of attention to what their ads were appearing alongside. As long as it was not pornographic or violent, then they figured it was not their concern. Until they discovered, thanks partly to a 2017 investigation by *The Times*, that through their ads they were helping to fund sites that promoted political extremism, conspiracy theories and wholly concocted news stories.

Still, having adopted this shiny new advertising model back in 2005, Google was sitting pretty. It had solved its financial worries. It had, in 2004, successfully gone public. And it had figured out its primary source of income – web advertising. Since this included not just its own sites but the long tail of publishers across the web – a tail that was growing every day – its future income looked rosy too. Eric Schmidt, who became chief executive of Google in 2001, told Ken Auletta that 2002 was the year he realized "we are in the advertising business." The bargain had not – so far – turned out so well for online content publishers. After Google swelled the inventory of advertising space, the income they received from each web ad was a fraction of what they received from ads in print or on TV. Yet, those leading the advertising business were still sanguine. The money, they thought, would shift online. "I would hope", Sir

Martin Sorrell said in 2008, "that within five years, so let's say 2013, or something like that, we would be at least one third in digital."[13] Sorrell, then head of one of the world's largest advertising conglomerates, was right that money would flow online, but it would not go to the old advertising firms and publishers.

*

Now that it was in the digital advertising business Google could not help but notice that it was not the leader but just one of a number of competing players. There are few things Google chiefs dislike more than not leading. Especially when they think the company can do a much better job than its competitors. In 2007 it could still see a huge expanse of advertising space online that was entirely outside its ambit – all the banner ads that sit on top and along the side of the big publishers' sites. Although these ads had nothing to do with Google's core business, the company could see how inefficient the service was. Lots of these ads were sold by people. They were often the same across multiple web pages, and they could sit there for hours, days even. Unfortunately for Google, this whole sector was already occupied by entrenched players with established relationships. The most dominant amongst them was called DoubleClick, a company that boasted a roster of blue-chip advertisers and – in Madison Avenue style – hosted frequent lavish parties for its clients. One of these, according to early employee David Sidor, turned New York's Roxy nightclub into Willy Wonka's chocolate factory, complete with Oompa Loompa waiters.[14] Impatient to expand into new territory, Google bought DoubleClick for \$3.1 billion in 2007 (completed in 2008) – almost double what it spent on YouTube in 2005 and by far its biggest acquisition up to that time.

Like Alexander the Great after finally defeating the Persians at the Battle of Gaugamela, Larry Page and Sergey Brin could now gaze out across the web at their vast advertising empire. Having taken over DoubleClick, Google oversaw the ad content of many millions of pages, from high-end news publishers to tiny blogs. The breadth of the empire was especially wide since DoubleClick had, like Google with AdSense, taken over responsibility for selling the acres of waste space that publishers struggled to sell themselves – the old and rarely visited pages buried beneath the new content. Google was fast becoming the patron of the information economy. Yet, there is also no question that by buying DoubleClick, Google's founders were taking yet another step away from their early disapproval of advertising, and their initial justification of using it just to pay the bills. The search company was also moving inexorably further down the road of tracking its users, and then using this information to help target ads at them – something the founders had previously always fought against (though not enough to stop collecting this information). Indeed, in 2008, the *Wall Street Journal* reported that they had stand-up arguments about how they ought to use all the data they were now collecting.[15]

There was another reason for buying DoubleClick, and one that fitted more closely with Google's theology of engineering and with the direction in which they were driving news and information on the web. DoubleClick had been building an advertising exchange, modelled on the premise of stock exchanges. The idea, one that naturally appealed to Google's sensibilities, was that an exchange would remove lots of the friction that currently characterized the process of buying and selling digital ads. Online publishers, who had spare ad space to sell, could dump it onto an exchange, while advertisers, who wanted ad space at the best price, could find it there. Removing friction (friction for the most part meaning people) had always been a central justification for what Google did online. It did not organize the world's information using people, it did it using code. Similarly in advertising, sales people and middlemen could be replaced by code and by the market. As Susan Wojcicki, who led the development of AdSense at Google, had said about that service, "It changed the way content providers think about their business. They know they can generate revenues without having their own sales teams."[16] An advertising exchange was yet another extension of this principle.

Two enterprising students sitting in a dorm room in Philadelphia in 2007 could see the direction in which things were headed. Nat Turner and Zach Weinberg were undergraduates, neither of whom had ever worked in advertising or even had much knowledge of how the industry worked (given how different ad tech is from traditional advertising, this was probably an advantage). But the pair knew how to code. Turner and Weinberg decided "to make a bet that the exchanges would go real time". "We felt that if Google does it, everyone else will do it, and all of a sudden there was a need for a broker."[17] What Turner meant by 'real time' was that advertisers would bid for each ad space at the moment someone opened a web page. When you first go to a website, you will notice that although there is space for lots of ads, they do not necessarily appear immediately. This is not because you have a slow connection. It is because the moment you opened that page, your details were thrown onto an ad exchange where advertisers started bidding for your attention. The more you are worth to them – based on who you are, where you live, what you do and countless other gobbets of personal information – the more they bid. The winner of the auction gets to show you their ad, the loser doesn't. All this in the split second that it takes for your page to load.[18]

Turner and Weinberg were right. In September 2009, Google launched a real-time ad exchange. With immaculate timing, the pair had launched their service the same year, to help advertisers buy ads through ad exchanges in real time – all using smart software. Always alert to services that complement their own, the following year Google bought their company, Invite Media, for $81 million in cash.[19] According to Neal Mohan, Google's vice president of product management, ad exchanges would "democratize the world of display advertising and make it as accessible and as open as possible to large and small publishers, large and small advertisers – just as search advertising is today".★[20] What Mohan meant was that Google's systems would – in theory – make it cheaper for small businesses to advertise, and would give them a chance to get their ad on lots of new spaces. But even in the economic sense, it would quickly become apparent that the world of real-time ad exchanges was so complex that it would only be democratizing for those who were fluent in coding or happened to have a PhD in physics.

The move towards buying and selling through ad exchanges propelled the world of ad tech still further towards automation and personalization. Advertisers would no longer be buying space on media outlets: they would be buying you. They would not choose you by name, but by your susceptibility to their message. Therefore, the more they knew about you the better. Not just that you might have shown an interest in something, but how serious that interest was, whether you were likely to follow through on it, when the right moment was to reach you. Thanks to ad exchanges they could also figure out how to reach you most efficiently – at the lowest possible cost for the highest possible return. If this meant tracking you online, and showing you an ad on a fringe political site that you happened to be on, rather than the news site you were on five minutes ago, then so be it, that would simply be the most efficient and cost-effective way of reaching you. What this meant in the real world is that advertisers could now reach the same person more cheaply on a small, less established site – via an ad exchange. Money that previously would have flowed to long-running prominent media like the *New York Times* was being

---

★ This use of the term 'democratize', which is peppered across many of Google's announcements, is not about democracy in the political sense. It is an economic use of the term (though it conveniently blurs the distinction).

siphoned off to fringe sites. Google was effectively incentivizing low-cost, casual content by directing ad dollars away from more costly, more authoritative sites. The funding model for responsible media, already tanking, took yet another dive.

By 2012 Google had spread itself across the new ad tech ecosystem. It was selling ads on its own sites, selling ads across millions of other sites, helping publishers organize and sell their ads, running the leading ad exchange, and helping advertisers buy ads. It was, if you were to compare it to the world of finance, the company people were investing in, the company's investment adviser (its Morgan Stanley), the stock exchange on which the company was traded (like the NASDAQ), and the broker advising people where to invest. The difference being that in financial markets there are rules and regulations governing the activities of different firms. It would be a conflict of interest, for example, for someone to be both a broker and an investment adviser. There were (and are) no comparable rules in the world of ad tech. It was, essentially, a pretty rule-free world over which Google presided like an absentee landlord. In order to minimize cost while maximizing scale and efficiency, the system was built on self-service, auctions and automation. Control, for example in terms of which ads went to which sites, would mean friction, and friction would add cost.

Google had driven the creation of a whole digital ecosystem that on the one hand was open, accessible and relatively rule-free, but on the other was monumentally intricate, complex and precarious. Indeed, by the time Barack Obama was elected for a second term as US president in November 2012, the whole structure of ad tech looked like a fantastically ingenious and monstrously complicated Heath Robinson or Rube Goldberg contraption (the 'new multi-movement machine for gathering Easter eggs' comes to mind). Each cog turned another cog which rotated a lever which pulled a rope which lifted a ramp which caused a hammer to fall ... and so on and so on. To work, the whole system relied on each element operating smoothly in tandem with the next. Only if everything gelled perfectly together could millions of advertisers place billions of different advertisements on millions of different websites every second of every day. To function, the system needed to be fed constantly with mountains of personal information, updated continuously, all of which had to be carefully – and automatically – aligned with advertisers' willingness to pay and publishers' openness to sell. So big and complex had it become that only those capable of collecting and processing massive amounts of data could compete. Only companies, in other words, like Google. Add a little grit and the whole thing could fall down – and much of the web with it. On Wednesday, 12 November 2014, this is exactly what happened. A glitch in Google's ad server meant that, for an hour, ads failed to appear on publishers' sites across the web. Since the ad tech was integrated into the pages themselves, it also meant many pages could not appear, meaning that for lots of people a good chunk of the web just stopped.[21]

This Heath Robinson-esque ad tech system relied on open access. Since October 2000, Google had done all it could to let people create, buy and target their ads themselves. As long as the ads did not flag up an obvious breach of Google's ad policies, they would be delivered, friction-free, to websites. Open access for Google was both economically efficient (fewer people needed, lower cost), philosophically appealing (democratization!), and consistent with their business model (of commercializing the open web). It was also deliberately non-discriminatory – anyone could buy ads, anywhere in the world and pay for them in dollars, euros, pounds, yen or rubles. Russia's Internet Research Agency could as easily pay for hyper-partisan propaganda as Whole Foods could pay to promote meatless sausages.

Yet openness is not transparency. Indeed, as a consequence of its complexity, speed and automation, the system was unfathomably opaque. Any system this complicated, and this inaccessible to external scrutiny and internal oversight, was bound to be gamed. And it certainly was. Between 2008 and 2012 Google reported that the number of ads it disapproved rose from 25 million to 134 million. For Google this was evidence of success. "Even in this ever-escalating arms race [of ad fraud]," its director of advertising engineering wrote, "our efforts are working." This confidence was belied by the rise and rise of scams, bots, 'trick to click', self-clicking ads, deceptive ads and 'tabloid cloakers' (ads made to look like tabloid news headlines to make people click). In 2015 Google reported it had "disabled more than 780 million ads for violating our policies" and in 2016, 1.7 billion. Google pitched this phenomenal increase in gaming and manipulation as evidence that it had the problem under control. This is one reading. Another is that it had created a system that was inherently vulnerable and that more and more people were taking advantage of its vulnerabilities. As quickly as Google could stamp out one method of fraud, another popped up.[22]

Not only was the digital ad system – the Googlesphere – open to gaming, it incentivized its participants to gather as much personal information as they could about their visitors, so they could sell it on for higher prices on an ad exchange. Ad exchanges operated by matching as many buyers and sellers as quickly as possible at a price defined by the market. It was not their job to police what happened to the ads once they were placed. Perhaps not surprisingly then, it was estimated in 2011 that between fifty and ninety-five per cent of *display* ads sold on exchanges (as opposed to click-throughs) were never seen by anyone. "Literally, the exchanges are a cesspool," one ad exchange buyer told industry journal *Digiday*.[23] Agencies were motivated to reach the most valuable consumers at the lowest possible price on behalf of their clients. And their clients, the advertisers, were driven to measure their success by the behavioural responses they triggered. Just get the user to click! Everything was geared towards buying and selling the user – the user, of course, being you and me. It is like in the 1973 film *The Sting*, where

Robert Redford and Paul Newman bring together a whole crew of blaggers, hoaxers, grifters and con artists to orchestrate an elaborate sting on the 'mark', Doyle Lonnegan. Everyone is in on the hoax except Lonnegan himself, who loses half a million dollars, while never realizing he is the victim of a complex ruse.

Google never set out to build a system that would work like this. And, conscious that the system was in danger of falling into disrepute, the tech giant looked for ways to address it. At this stage, there were two routes Google could have taken. It could have tried to unravel the system, adding friction back in and reducing its role, though this would have been a huge task and would inevitably have meant reducing its dominance and its income. Or, it could have gone the other way, gathered yet more personal data and become still more dominant. Google chose the second. Up to 2012 it had held back from using all the data it gathered, keeping personal information from its different services separate. But in that year it chose to pool them together. Seventy different privacy policies merged into one.[24] This meant it could combine everything it knew about you – from what you watched on YouTube, to your Google searches to your Gmail – into one big pot. From there it went further, connecting people to their own unique identifier, and following them across their digital lives. And from there further still, tracking people's real-life movements via their mobile phone. While all this personal information no doubt helped the company tailor and develop its many and varied products, it also led it deeper in the direction of what academic Shoshana Zuboff has called 'surveillance capitalism'. In order to prove to advertisers that their money was well spent and that ad fraud was under control, Google became fixated on measuring people's every move online, to keep closer and closer tabs on them, and to record every time they 'converted'. In 2013, it even started following people into shops, to see if it could connect what people bought in the real world with what they searched for online.[25] The source of funding and the approach that Page and Brin had adopted, reluctantly, to keep the lights on was coming to lead the company by the nose. Not only that, but it now faced a major competitor for its revenue.

★

Facebook had a major competitive advantage in the digital economy that Google had played such a major part in creating. It had bucketloads of personal data. Where Google knew what you looked for online, what you did and where you went, Facebook knew your personality, your attitudes and your friends. Prior to 2012, Facebook had not taken full advantage of what it knew about its users to drive its advertising but, in order to justify its value and keep growing, it transformed itself into a people-centric propaganda engine.

A lot of what it did, initially at least, built on Google's lead. It focused heavily on collecting data to prove to advertisers that its engine worked. It spread itself across the web – using Facebook 'like' buttons, hidden 'conversion pixels' (later Facebook pixels) and Facebook logins – to capture what people were doing online even when not on Facebook.[26][27] The ads were self-service and could be paid for with any currency. Facebook also made advertisers bid for space in second-price, or Vickrey, auctions. Similarly, like Google, it tried to incentivize advertisers to make their ads compelling and relevant, by taking these criteria into account when choosing the auction winner. It even started to create an open ad exchange (though it shuttered this in 2016).[28]

Yet Facebook was able to delve deeper into people's private lives than Google, and had less reticence than its rival when using personal information. This, after all, was Facebook's greatest asset. From 2012, it melded, aggregated and filleted its users' personal information such that advertisers could target – or rather micro-target – people based on a plethora of attitudinal, behavioural, social or demographic data. It also took this personal information and connected it back to the real world, allowing companies, and political campaigns, to upload their own custom audiences to Facebook's systems. By 2015 Google found itself playing catch-up, introducing, for example, a Custom Audiences clone called Customer Match, and then Similar Audiences to compete with Facebook's Lookalike Audiences. All this meant, of course, more tracking of their users and merging together of what they knew to create a complete and intimate profile of you. A study of web tracking technology published in 2016, the largest one to that point, found that Google owned the top five most common tracking tools, and that – by combining Google Analytics and DoubleClick technology – it was following people's movements to more than seventy per cent of sites on the net.[29] The same year Google even changed its privacy policy so it could mash together data from its display ad network with whatever else it knew about you – something it had carefully refrained from doing since 2007.[30]

By the time of the Brexit vote in the UK and the Trump–Clinton campaign in the US, Google and Facebook were vying to outdo one another in data collection, surveillance tracking, onboarding, micro-targeting, multivariate testing and attribution.* The two behemoths, who by now oversaw the majority of advertising on the net, battled it out to provide advertisers with the most powerful, the most sophisticated and the most comprehensive digital targeting tools. Given their dominance, these two tech titans defined the terms on which ad tech functioned. The rest of the industry's left-behinds found themselves scrambling just to stay

---

* Multivariate testing is when someone trials multiple versions of a message on different audiences and measures the response to see which is most effective. Attribution is being able to attribute credit to whatever led someone to take an action (for example, the advertisement that led someone to buy the shoes).

in the game – accumulating whatever personal data they could, providing access to any corners of the web the big two had not colonized, and mimicking the tools of the duopoly. As the tech bible *Wired* wrote in 2017, "Wherever Facebook and Google lead, the rest of the digital advertising world will follow." Yet, as with the guano trade 150 years earlier, this system – which Google and Facebook had been instrumental in creating, and which they now dominated – had numerous damaging, if inadvertent, knock-on effects for democratic politics.

Google, like Facebook, treated political advertising like any other commercial advertising. They were happy to sell their wares to anyone who could afford them, no matter who they were, what their message was, or who they were trying to reach. They were even willing to advise their political clients as to how to get the most out of their services. Scholars Daniel Kreiss and Shannon McGregor went to the US Democratic Party convention in 2016 and found both tech giants lavishly promoting their services. The Facebook Election Space, for example, "featured a formal broad-cast studio, a Facebook Live studio, virtual reality displays, and a miniature Oval Office that the company invited Instagram influencers to visit and post pictures from during the first night of the convention".[31] During the 2016 US election campaign, Google and Facebook went as far as embedding their employees in the Trump team (they offered to do the same for the Clinton campaign). Sitting with the Trump digital team in San Antonio, Texas, these tech advisers helped the campaign "optimize, create more engagement around, and tailor and expand audiences for their ads". One of the staff on the Trump campaign even called its Facebook adviser, James Barnes, the campaign's 'MVP' (most valu-able player).[32] The platforms also advised advocacy groups. In October 2017, *Bloomberg* reported that, in the final weeks of the US election, both Google and Facebook helped a US advocacy group, Secure America Now, to target anti-Islamic messages to those who might be most receptive to them. Some of the ads showed "France and Germany overrun by Sharia law. French schoolchildren were being trained to fight for the caliphate, jihadi fighters were celebrated at the Arc de Triomphe, and the 'Mona Lisa' was covered in a burka."[33] Facebook and Google did not see it as their responsibility to police political messaging, even if these messages were contradictory or intended to provoke conflict. Clients could create whatever political ads they wanted, load them into the system themselves, and – as long as they did not breach the broad T&Cs – deliver them to whoever they liked. Heart of Texas, a Facebook group created by the Russian Internet Research Agency, was able to buy ads calling on Texans to join a rally to 'Stop Islamification of Texas' while another Russian group was able to advertise a rally to 'Save Islamic Knowledge' – both rallies were at the same place at the same time, and presumably meant to start fighting one another.[34]

Many of those taking advantage of the darkness in the system were doing it not for the politics but for the money. Security firm White Ops revealed in late 2016, for example, that a Russian group was operating a bot farm which had been earning hundreds of thousands, if not millions, of dollars every day through a sophisticated click fraud scam.[35] But techniques used for commercial gain could have political consequences or be easily spun for political ends. Botnets developed for the purposes of ad fraud could be repurposed to promote a candidate or political cause. Advertisements using provocative claims to attract attention and prompt a behavioural response could as easily be about politicians as celebrities. In 2017, *ProPublica* discovered a series of false political ads on Facebook, with headlines such as "Regardless of what you think of Donald Trump and his policies, it's fair to say that his appointment as President of the United States is one of the most …". If you made the mistake of clicking the 'ad', this ransomware froze your computer and told you your machine was now "infected with viruses, spywares and pornwares", with a phone number if you wanted 'help' to have it removed.[36] Ad tech was also helping generate income for fringe and radical political websites, as well as for sites that were inventing 'news' purely to generate advertising income. Less than a fortnight after the US 2016 election a dozen alt-right sites were showing ads from companies including American Express, Sprint and Walgreens, served up by Google.[37] Ironically, thanks to the way the ad tech model prioritized ads that were engaging, incendiary political advertisements were cheaper to post than more measured ones.

The methods and techniques of ad tech proved incredibly useful to political actors – of whatever stripe or persuasion. Campaigns and consultancies were able to use Custom Audiences to bridge their intimate voter profiles with actual Facebook users. Sophisticated conversion tracking software allowed motivated groups to follow voters, watching their movements carefully in order to choose the right moment to mobilize or convert them. Jonathan Albright, director of research at the Tow Center at Columbia University, was astonished to discover through his research that behind many hyper-partisan, conspiracy-obsessed, fringe websites, there was sophisticated ad tracking technology which enabled "a highly coordinated campaign to drive traffic" to these sites.[38] Basically this meant that if you – or someone you were connected with – went to one of these sites once, then you were on their target list and would be followed around the inter-net with hyper-partisan ads and news.

By 2016 the tech giants had become much more conscious of how politically powerful their tools could be. Indeed, they were marketing them directly to candidates, campaigners and political activists on this basis. "Voter decisions used to be made in living rooms, in front of televisions," YouTube's director of ad marketing, Kate Stanford, wrote in March 2016. "Today, they're increasingly made in micro-moments, on mobile devices," when citizens turn to Google or Facebook to figure out who to vote for. She therefore urged candidates to use Google to find out what people cared about, and to "be there" at that "micro-moment" with a tailored message.[39] The search giant and Facebook did the same, each touting its services as the best way for political propagandists to reach just the right people with just the right messages at just the right time. You could call it each voter's 'Goldilocks micro-moment'. All these tools and techniques were freely available to whoever had the money, the time and the know-how. Sign up, get an account, create some material, and start bidding in whatever currency you have to hand.

This is the answer to Al Franken's question. To stop taking different currencies would undermine the ad tech model so painstakingly constructed over the past decade and a half. It would mean unravelling the system that had enabled Google and Facebook to grow as large as they were. It would mean adding resistance to a design built to be frictionless. No wonder Colin Stretch found it difficult to commit to this. So, despite everything that emerged about the fraudulent, malign, disturbing use of ad tech after 2016, neither Google, nor Facebook, nor any of the host of players in the whole digital advertising ecosystem, committed to deconstructing the edifice. Instead, they would commit to adding a limited degree of friction, and to making the whole system more 'hygienic'. They would exercise more control, be more interventionist and, presumably, collect more data.

Anyway, by this time the problems extended far beyond just Google and Facebook. Much of the web was driven by this model. Like the multiple murderers in Agatha Christie's *Murder on the Orient Express*, almost all commercial companies producing content online were complicit in tracking users, building profiles and selling access. Add the Ghostery extension to your browser, which clocks up the number of invisible trackers on each website you visit, and you will see how rare it is not to be followed. Many news sites, which rail against the Google and Facebook duopoly, have trackers in double figures. The *New York Times* site has more than two dozen, as do the *Los Angeles Times* and *The Times* of London.[40] As a 2018 study of the 'technologies behind precision propaganda' from the New America Foundation wrote, "It cannot be understated how important personal data is to the long-term sustainability and success of the digital advertising ecosystem. Data drives commerce on the internet; every consumer-facing internet company that has a major presence in online advertising collects and shares information about individuals to help their advertising clients succeed." And these clients could be selling shoes or propaganda.[41]

Of course, even if greater duopoly dominance did lead to a more hygienic ad system, it would only resolve half the political equation. The ability of political groups to micro-target, A/B test, track conversion and accumulate intimate information would remain and almost certainly be enhanced. Already, for example, a growing number of companies have experimented with a new approach to advertising called 'emotions analytics'. Beyond Verbal offered to analyse emotions using vocal intonations. Another company called Affectiva claimed to have "emotion recognition technology" which could sense and analyse "facial and vocal expressions of emotion". Or there was Sticky, "the world's only self-serve, cloud-based biometric eye tracking and emotion measurement platform". All of these companies, and many others, were competing to find cleverer ways to get inside our heads, figure out what makes us tick, and use this to catalyse a behavioural or emotional response. Delivered, no doubt, by Google or Facebook.

No matter how anarchic and intrusive the ad tech model, as long as people focused enough of their attention on news and information, ad money could still – in theory – support the reporting and journalism on which democracy relies. Unfortunately, most people (journalists included) were not focusing as much attention. Indeed many of them found themselves perpetually diverted and distracted, ever conscious of the latest post in their feed, or the next stream of tweets.

6

THE UNBEARABLE LIGHTNESS OF TWITTER

The absolute absence of a burden causes man to be lighter than air, to soar into the heights, take leave of the earth and his earthly being, and become only half real, his movements as free as they are insignificant.

Milan Kundera, *The Unbearable Lightness of Being*

On the night of 13 June 2017, as flames engulfed Grenfell Tower in west London, Rania Ibrahim filmed the scene outside her flat on the twenty-third floor of the tower.* The corridor was dark and filled with smoke. "The building is burning from down beneath," she said in Arabic. As she filmed, the footage was being broadcast on Facebook Live. Pointing the camera out of her window, she saw many residents who had already left the tower. "You can see all the people who were lucky to leave", Ibrahim says, "are all running over there." Before she stops filming her final recorded words are, "Your prayers, peace be upon you all."[1] Rania Ibrahim and her two daughters, aged three and four, were killed by the fire along with sixty-nine others.[2]

During the night, news of the fire travelled quickly across social media. As it spread, offers of help came flooding in: volunteers,

* The fire at Grenfell Tower was first reported shortly before 1 a.m. on Wednesday, 14 June 2017.

donations in kind – clothes, blankets and food – money and shelter. By 9:30 the following morning the Kensington and Chelsea
Foundation, which was coordinating support for the victims of
the fire, was overwhelmed. "Our community partners, charities,
local churches and mosque are unable to accept any more items
for the moment," it tweeted. "Please hold on. Thank you."[3] Much
of this was documented and coordinated, *The Week* magazine later
reported, on Twitter.[4]

For days and weeks after 14 June, the terrible fire at Grenfell
Tower dominated UK national media and almost toppled the
recently elected prime minister, Theresa May. Survivors of the
tragedy and the wider public were outraged that warnings by residents about the tower had been ignored, and that cladding on the
outside of the building had fuelled the fire rather than stifled it. Yet
their anger was directed almost as much at the media as at the
government. "You didn't come here when people were telling you
that the building was unsafe," one man said to veteran Channel 4
presenter Jon Snow when he visited the burnt-out building. "That
is not newsworthy. You come here when people die. Why?"
Another held up a sign reading "This is not a photo opportunity"
and shouted, "This is real life!"[5]

The survivors were right. Before the fire, the failings of Grenfell
Tower – and others like it – had been absent from national and
local media. Only a weekly specialist housing magazine, *Inside
Housing*, had investigated safety concerns about tower blocks after
a fire in another building near to Grenfell the previous August.
There was no coverage because there were no longer any journalists dedicated to reporting on Kensington and Chelsea, the
borough where Grenfell Tower was located. As a subsequent BBC
investigation documented, the only journalist covering the area
between late 2014 and 2017 lived over 150 miles away in Lyme
Regis, Dorset.[6] Geoff Baker was news editor for the *Kensington
and Chelsea News* until April 2017, when the paper closed. He was

also its chief reporter, features editor, showbiz reporter and royal correspondent (there was only one other reporter, who covered sport). This was on top of doing the same for two other newspapers, the *Westminster and City News* and the *London Weekly News* – all on a salary of £500 a week. Given how much he had to do, and how little money he had to do it with, Baker had to do almost all his research on the internet and by phone. In the two and a half years he worked on the *Kensington and Chelsea News*, he said he was only able to actually go to Kensington and Chelsea twice.[7]

The residents themselves had raised the alarm, repeatedly, online. The previous November the Grenfell Action Group had posted that the KCTMO (the management organization running the tower) was "playing with fire" and that it had got to the stage when "only a catastrophic event will expose the ineptitude and incompetence of our landlord".[8] It was not picked up by any mainstream media outlets. "The completely man-made Grenfell disaster", Jon Snow said to the UK's media elites at Edinburgh that August, "has proved beyond all other things how little we [the media] know, and how dangerous the disconnect is."[9]

Even after the tragic fire, the mainstream media were often playing a secondary role. Twitter, along with other social media, acted as alert system, mobilizer, coordinator and newswire. News, conversations and concerns on Twitter were then amplified in mainstream news outlets, which sparked further discussion on social media. The importance of social media – and particularly of Twitter – as a source of news, a way to express concern and offer help, a means of coordination, was not new to Grenfell. Ever since Twitter had become popular, people had seen its news value, in the aftermath of – and even during – crises. "Mumbai terrorists are asking hotel reception for rooms of American citizens and holding them hostage on one floor," @Dupree tweeted during the terrorist attack on Mumbai back in November 2008. Two months later, in January 2009, a Florida-based businessman, Janis Krums, tweeted the first picture of US Airways flight 1549 floating on the Hudson River in New York. In Iran later the same year, the presidential election and the protests surrounding it were to become the most engaging topic on Twitter that year. In 2010 and 2011, following earthquakes in Haiti and Japan, Twitter was used to track down missing people, to spread official and unofficial information, and to fundraise.[10]

When Noah Glass, Ev Williams, Jack Dorsey and Biz Stone founded Twitter in 2006, they had no idea it would become such an essential news service. Reading *Hatching Twitter*, Nick Bilton's chronicle of the company's birth, it is hard to believe the service took off at all. The four of them developed Twitter only when their podcasting service, Odeo, was gazumped by Apple's iTunes. Right from the beginning, when they were not arguing over who should run the company, they were disagreeing about what the service was for. As Bilton describes it, Dorsey saw Twitter as a way to let your friends know what you were up to – "just out to grab lunch". Williams disagreed, seeing it "more like a mini-blogging project" to tell people what was going on around you. Glass, who was kicked out of the company not long after conceiving the idea with Dorsey, had found the name that he thought captured the essence of the service while flicking through a dictionary. Twitter, "the light chirping sound made by certain birds," the dictionary read, "agitation or excitement; flutter".[11]

Had Glass been using the *Oxford English Dictionary* he would have found another definition: "talk rapidly in an idle or trivial way". This is what a lot of people first thought of Twitter – that it was frivolous and superficial. "This is like the Seinfeld of the internet," Gawker's Valleywag reported in 2006, "a website about nothing."[12] "Pointless email on steroids," American productivity author Tim Ferriss called it in 2007 (before joining the service in January 2008).[13] "Inane twaddle," *Mashable* journalist Steven Hodson wrote in 2008.[14] Inane it may have been, but it was also fabulously popular. It took eight months for Twitter to gain its first twenty thousand users, but then thousands started to join each day. By the spring of 2008 there were over one and a half million people posting about 300,000 tweets a day.[15] A year later there were more than thirty million, tweeting well over two million times a day. Already, by that time, journalists were writing that it was "OK to be sick and tired of Twitter. Heaven knows, it may be the world's most overhyped technology."[16]

Yet, however overhyped and shallow people thought it was, and whatever the intention of its founders, there was no doubting the increasing importance of Twitter for news. Natural disasters, terrorist attacks, wildfires, plane crashes and public protests were appearing first on Twitter and then playing out from the platform. For many journalists, the value of the service was immediately obvious and it quickly became integral to their job. A survey of almost four hundred US journalists in late 2009 found that over half of them were using Twitter for research, and that those writing online used the service "all the time".[17] Alfred Hermida, one of the most astute academic observers of social media, wrote that sites such as Twitter were becoming like "awareness systems" for journalists, providing them with an ambient background noise of public statements and news updates.[18] Senior figures in the news industry were telling their journalists to take the platform seriously. The editor-in-chief of the *Guardian*, Alan Rusbridger, gave a public lecture in 2010 espousing the usefulness of Twitter and listing fifteen ways it could help news. "Inanity – yes, sure, plenty of it," Rusbridger said. "But saying that Twitter has got nothing to do with the news business is about as misguided as you could be."[19] The director of the BBC's global news, Peter Horrocks, went further and reportedly told his journalists in 2011 – half in jest – to "tweet or be sacked".[20] He need not have worried, as most of them already were. A survey conducted amongst British journalists that summer found that seventy per cent were using Twitter for reporting.[21]

Those running Twitter had noticed its value to news too. A "birds-eye view of Twitter reveals that it's not exclusively about these personal musings," Biz Stone wrote in November 2009. "Between those cups of coffee, people are witnessing accidents, organizing events, sharing links, breaking news, reporting stuff their dad says, and so much more."[22] As a sign of its evolving news role, Stone announced Twitter would change the text in its status bar from 'What are you doing?' to 'What's happening?'.

★

As Twitter was taking flight, and becoming a central part of the news ecosystem, so many traditional news organizations were losing momentum. Traditional news outlets had, even from the early days of the web, struggled to adapt to digital media. Print papers that relied heavily on advertising were particularly hard hit when first classified ads, and then display ads, started disappearing onto sites like Craigslist. With less ad revenue coming in, many chose to reduce their production and editorial staff. From 2000 to 2005 about three thousand staff were cut from US newsrooms. This was just the prelude.

The year Twitter launched, 2006, turned out to be the tipping point – the last year of the news as we knew it. As the authors of the landmark 'State of the News Media' report wrote in that year, "We see a seismic transformation in what and how people learn about the world around them. Power is moving away from journalists as gatekeepers over what the public knows."[23] From 2006, US newspaper advertising revenue began its inexorable decline.[24] Print circulations, many of which had already started to fall (in the UK they had been declining for decades), began to drop precipitously. Then came the financial crash. America's communications regulator, the FCC, estimated that in the four years between 2007 and 2011 there had been "roughly 13,400 newspaper newsroom positions" lost (from 55,000 to around 41,600).[25]

From a citizen's perspective, the most material change was in the number of journalists employed to report on local news. In Philadelphia in 2006, for example, there were less than half the number there had been in 1980. By 2009 the *Los Angeles Times* had fewer than 600 journalists, from a high of 1,100 just a few years previously.[26] The *Baltimore Sun* dropped from 400 journalists to around 150 in 2009. In other places the decline was less steep, but the trend was the same, meaning there were fewer people whose jobs were dedicated to keeping track of what the government was doing. At US state capitals, for example, there were 158 fewer full-time journalists in 2009 compared to 1998 – down from 513 to 355.[27] The implications for democratic accountability were not good.

The haemorrhaging of editorial staff from news organizations was best documented in the US, but it was happening in democracies across the world. Countries that shared America's liberal model of journalism – where commercial news outlets relied heavily on advertising – were most vulnerable. In Australia, between 2008 and 2013, more than three thousand journalists were let go.[28] In Britain, in the decade after the financial crash, the number of local journalists halved.[29] Continental European countries that relied less on advertising were initially shielded, though not for long. In the decade to 2007, more than half the newspaper publishing jobs in Norway were lost. In the Netherlands four in ten jobs were cut, and in Germany one in four.[30] Only in Africa and parts of Asia did news organizations see print circulations rising and newsrooms growing.

By 2011, it was already clear that – in lots of democracies – the number of people dedicated to reporting what was happening was sliding ever downwards. The response, from governments and publics, was a dismissive shrug. Why? Partly because, on the surface, it did not look as though the situation had changed that much. The corporations that ran many local newspapers (and by 2011 it increasingly was large corporations that ran many local newspapers) had figured out it was more profitable to reduce the headcount than close the title. Better to hollow a paper out from the inside and let the readership decline gradually, even if this meant far less reporting, than lose all the income overnight. This is why some of the dire predictions made about the future of the local press after the financial crash looked excessively pessimistic. In Britain, the highly respected media analyst Claire Enders forecast in 2009 that half of the country's 1,300 local newspapers would close in the next five years. Five years later, between a hundred and two hundred had closed. And yet, if you were to dig deeper, the situation – from a democratic perspective at least – was worse.

Take a paper like the *Leicester Mercury*. In 1996 it was a decent-sized city newspaper employing almost six hundred people, and serving a city of around 300,000. By 2011 it was selling fewer than 30,000 copies a day (down from over 150,000 in the mid-1980s) and was down to 107 staff (despite the city's population rising significantly).[31] Or you could look at Wales, where Media Wales owned a stable of papers including the *Western Mail* and the *South Wales Echo*. In 1999 there were just under seven hundred editorial and production staff. By 2011 there were 136.[32]

Another reason the collapse in the number of local journalists was not immediately obvious, both in Britain and elsewhere, was because it did not happen overnight and was not the same everywhere. One month there would be nineteen jobs cut from the *Yorkshire Post* and its sister titles. The next there would be seven newspapers closed with fifty jobs lost in and around Reading. The reductions were piecemeal but relentless, often going undocumented since no-one is ever keen to report their own decline. Equally, public sympathy with news organizations was not high, especially following revelations like the one that journalists at Rupert Murdoch's News Corporation had been systematically hacking people's phones to find personal information.

But the main reason why most people failed to notice the growing democratic deficit was because it seemed churlish to worry about the decline in local reporting when new media platforms like Twitter and Facebook seemed to be democratizing the world. "Information has never been so free," Hillary Clinton said while in charge of the US State Department in 2010. "There are more ways to spread more ideas to more people than at any moment in history." Or, as New York University academic Clay Shirky titled his book about the opportunities opened up by social media in 2008, 'Here Comes Everybody'. Across the world, people were starting to use social media to coordinate collective action. In Iran in 2009, Twitter was credited with enabling and enhancing election protests. After the Deepwater Horizon oil spill in 2010, thousands used Twitter to spread news and coordinate responses to the crisis.[33] And in 2011, across North Africa, people used Twitter and other social media to share their anger at authoritarian regimes and, in countries such as Tunisia and Egypt, to help overthrow them. "The communication of the future", the communications scholar Manuel Castells wrote hopefully, "has already been used by the revolutions of the present."[34]

As much as social media was transforming social protest, so it was transforming journalism. Some of the most influential early coverage of the Arab Spring in the US did not come directly from journalists on the ground, or even from someone who spoke Arabic or Farsi, but from a balding thirty-nine-year-old social media strategist working at National Public Radio (NPR) in Washington, DC. Andy Carvin started tweeting about what was happening in Tunisia in December 2010.[35] From his previous experience he knew people who lived in the country, and others in North Africa, and quickly saw the importance of what was happening. By tweeting, retweeting and verifying information he found on Twitter and other social media, Carvin covered revolutionary developments not as an eye-witness but from his office cubicle (and roof terrace, and bathroom ...). Hundreds of times a day he tweeted, for up to sixteen hours, seven days a week. Other journalists were fascinated by what Carvin was doing, saying he was "breaking ground in curation and crowdsourced verification".[36] "I see it as another flavor of journalism," Carvin told the *Washington Post's* Paul Farhi, "So I guess I'm another flavor of journalist."

A few months later in London, two reporters were also using Twitter to help reinvent how journalism could be done. At just before 9:30 on the evening of Saturday, 6 August 2011, Paul Lewis tweeted, "I'm heading to Tottenham riot. Advice anyone?" Lewis, who was working for the *Guardian* in London, then got on his bike and headed to the north of the city. Ravi Somaiya, a *New York Times* reporter based in London, learnt about the riots – like Lewis – on Twitter, and set off for Tottenham just before midnight. Over the next four days, with short breaks to sleep, both journalists embedded themselves in the riots and tweeted what they saw. Anyone following them on Twitter found themselves plunged into a visceral real-time stream of on-the-scene action. "Building in north Tottenham ablaze. Young men in masks won't let me get closer," Lewis tweeted on the Saturday night. "Police have now massed," Somaiya wrote, "dozens in riot gear. But not sure how they will break through firewall to rioters (and me!) behind."[37]

Carvin, Lewis and Somaiya were not unique, but they were exceptional, as illustrated by the number of articles and academic case studies written about them.[38] Twitter became equally central to the daily routines of other journalists, though for different reasons.[39] To put it crudely, for many journalists Twitter was great for learning about breaking news, for keeping track of trending news, and for gauging how people were reacting to news. Any self-respecting journalist had to make sure they did not miss breaking news, which, given its speed, invariably broke first on Twitter. It was useful to keep an eye on what was trending and, when news broke, to get a sense of the direction in which the herd was galloping. Not to mention, of course, that all your colleagues were on Twitter, and there are few things journalists want more than the recognition and approval of their peers. It was easy to spot how integral social media was becoming to reporting simply by looking at how often quotes from tweets were included in news articles. In a 2013 analysis of Dutch and British newspapers, journalism academics Marcel Broersma and Todd Graham found "a steep rise in the number of tweets that were included in newspaper content" after 2010, especially in the tabloid press. It indicated, they concluded, the shift in journalism from "place to space". "Reporters do not have to 'go out there' anymore to find information."[40]

★

We, the public, were slightly behind journalists when it came to changing our news routines, but they soon shifted just as radically. Up until 2011, social media had chiefly been a way of keeping up with friends or tracking down old contacts.[41] But from that year, as the mainstream media endlessly talked up the roles of Facebook and Twitter in disrupting authoritarian regimes, it increasingly became a source of news too. In America, the number of people who saw news on a social networking site the previous day more than doubled between 2010 and 2012, from nine per cent to nineteen per cent. The following year, three in ten Americans were getting their news on Facebook, and just under one in ten on Twitter. Across the globe, as people rushed to buy smartphones and tablets, so the number using social media for news climbed and climbed. In Egypt, in 2012, just under eighty per cent of people with a smartphone used it to access social media.[42] In Brazil, a 2013 survey found that social media had already become one of the five most important ways of finding news.[43]

Not only was the way we discovered news changing, so was how we decided what news was important. Instead of relying on the judgement of news editors and subeditors, we were looking to our friends, to our wider networks and to public figures – whether they be actors, singers, sports personalities or politicians. "Twitter is where I get most of my news from," replied one user when the Pew Research Center asked why people found social media useful for keeping up with the news. He went on: "I follow all kinds of politics and media personalities."[44] There was certainly a growing number of these to choose from. Where Lady Gaga and Britney Spears led the way, Ashton Kutcher and Justin Bieber soon followed, as did a growing number of campaigners, politicians and government leaders. In autumn 2011, Twitter reported that there were thirty-five global heads of state using the platform "as a primary way to communicate with their constituencies" (the heads themselves may have bristled at Twitter's use of the word 'primary').[45] It was even channelling the word of God: in June 2011 the Pope sent his first tweet.

Nowhere was the shift in news habits more obvious than amongst younger people. While the total number of people in the US getting news from social media may have jumped to one in five by mid-2012, amongst the under-30s this was one in three, and rising fast – not just in the US, but globally.[46] By 2015, in a twelve-country study that included Australia, Denmark, Brazil and the US, six out of ten eighteen- to twenty-four-year-olds said that their main source of news was online, and over one in five said their main source was social media. By 2016 this was up to almost thirty per cent.

Still, Twitter was not to everyone's taste. While for journalists the immediacy and constancy of the raw feed was addictive, for a lot of the public it was overwhelming.[47] It turned out that while we liked our social updates and we liked our news in a constantly updated stream, we preferred the stream to be more babbling brook than Niagara Falls. Facebook saw the opportunity and stepped in, adapting its News Feed to include more public news, but making sure it kept the number of updates we saw at a digestible level (ending up screening out about eight out of ten of the updates we would see if the feed were raw). Twitter appealed to a certain type of person, particularly those more interested in hard news and politics, and often strongly partisan.[48] 'Power users', who posted frequently and expressed strong opinions, started to dominate the platform. Those who wanted a less gladiatorial space in which to follow news and chat to friends chose Facebook, Instagram or Snapchat instead. Twitter's growth slowed in 2012 and by 2015 it had pretty much topped out at just over 300 million users. A huge number in absolute terms, but increasingly dwarfed by Facebook.

As people across the world turned towards their mobiles and social media for their news, so they turned further away from newspapers, especially local ones. For the younger generation particularly, walking to a shop to pay for a printed paper to find out what was going on around you seemed bizarre when you could simply look at your phone. In 2011, researchers discovered a sharp divide between those over and under forty. Those under forty already relied on the internet for local news and information, while those over forty still relied more on traditional media.[49] While "newspapers currently remain a key destination for local news and information," the report found, "most Americans would not miss [them] if [they] were to disappear." And sure enough, they were disappearing, though not as fast as the journalists within them.

The decline in the number of professional journalists, which in America had accelerated from 2007, was spreading like a virus across many other democracies. In Australia in the six years after 2011, over a quarter of journalists lost their jobs.[50] One company alone, Fairfax, which had been a giant in the Australian news land-scape, cut almost five hundred positions. In Canada, around a third of journalists disappeared over the same period.[51] In Britain, the National Union of Journalists started keeping a tally of cuts in

2014, which by the end of 2017 had well over a hundred separate updates, and reads like a slow-motion obituary of local reporting. In Spain, in the decade up to 2015, the number of newspapers sold had halved, and by 2017 not a single Spanish paper had a circulation of over 200,000.[52] In France, daily newspapers cut almost a thousand jobs between 2007 and 2016.[53] "The situation of the media in Switzerland . . . is alarming," the European Federation of Journalists reported in 2017. "Restructuring, closures or mergers of media have never been so high."[54]

With notable exceptions (like journalists' unions) it is hard to find many people or democratic governments that were especially exercised about the decline and fall of local journalism. Despite occasional displays of sympathy or earnest official inquiries, most governments viewed it simply as the waning of another industry sector. In the US, devotion to the free market and immense scepticism about the value of government intervention forestalled any concerted action. In Britain, the four corporations that monopolized local newspaper ownership were wary of any intervention that might jeopardize their monopolies or their perpetual efficiency drives.[55] Other governments struggled with similar constraints, as well as with figuring out what – if anything – they should do. Absent political will, the collapse continued. Nor did the public in most of these countries become animated about the loss. They were paying too much attention to the streams of news flowing from their phones and from social media, distracted by the vast flow of updates about celebrities, international incidents and disasters, and viral content. The ten most read news stories on the *Guardian*'s website in 2014 illustrate where many people were focusing their attention: the top story was on the hacking of celebrity nude photos; the fifth and seventh on the deaths of Robin Williams and Philip Seymour Hoffman; and, at number nine with more than 1.4 million views, 'US student is rescued from giant vagina sculpture in Germany'.[56]

We, the public, were making a trade. We were trading one way of finding out what was going on outside our immediate network of friends, family and colleagues for another. The immediate benefits of this trade are clear. It is cheaper (often free), continuous and convenient – from a consumer perspective it seems almost perverse to object. We can find out both what people are talking about, and what our friends think. We can filter out the dull stuff and be fed with just what we want. We can as easily find out what is happening in the heart of Delhi as in London or New York. We become, with the advent of mobile news and social media, 'news snackers', dipping into news quickly and often.[57] As three academics from Mainz, Germany, who researched changing news habits found, news is now more of an appetizer than a main dish. By being exposed to lots of news posts in social media (notably Facebook) we gain "the feeling of being well-informed, regardless of actual knowledge acquisition".[58]

The costs of this trade are less obvious, and less immediate. One of these is the loss of a layer of our news ecosystem, the on-the-ground reporters who witness and report what is going on in our town, or city, or near where we live. Since this loss has been haphazard and sporadic, and has happened in the context of the digital revolution, the democratic implications are only now becoming apparent. And the implications are profound and alarming. There is a good environmental parallel – bees. Bees are the main pollinators of about a third of the food we eat. As they collect nectar, they inadvertently pick up and transfer pollen from the anther of one plant to the stigma of another, fertilizing the plants and enabling them to produce seeds. Around the turn of the twenty-first century, scientists became aware that honey bee populations were dropping. A few years later beekeepers were seeing whole colonies of bees collapsing.[59] Were they to disappear entirely it would have cataclysmic consequences for our food supply. Reducing the use of pesticides has helped slow the decline, though it has not stopped it. Reporters play a similar role in the news ecosystem. As they spend their days buzzing from courts to councils to crime scenes and local football grounds, they witness and record the information that forms the basis on which the rest of the ecosystem relies. Like bees, their benefit to society is both direct and inadvertent.

Even if people do not read what they produce, local reporters – especially political reporters – perform an invaluable democratic function. Rasmus Kleis Nielsen, professor of political communication at Oxford University, tested this by analysing the ecology of the news in Næstved, a town and municipality of about 82,000 inhabitants in Denmark. For three weeks in 2013 Nielsen captured all the local and regional news published in the local paper, *Sjællandske*, online, on television, on radio and on Facebook (by politicians and public authorities) – a total of 5,298 editorial 'units' as he called them. He then separated out the news that dealt with politics (about a tenth of the total) and calculated how much each outlet had produced. He discovered that sixty-four per cent of all the political stories were produced by *Sjællandske*. The local paper was the only outlet that regularly sent a journalist to cover the city council meeting. Not only that, but the political stories the local paper covered were often then covered by the TV station. One of the broadcast journalists, when asked where broadcast journalists sourced local political stories, replied, "I read *Sjællandske*." Nielsen also saw the role of the local newspaper and its journalists in environmental terms, likening it to a 'keystone species' which, though a relatively small part of the wider system, is integral to its functioning.[60]

Still, five years after Nielsen did his research, *Sjællandske* was alive and well, in print and online. To really understand what happens to a community and its politics when you lose dedicated reporters, you would need to see what happened after a place which once had them lost them. Somewhere that once had a vibrant news ecosystem, which then collapsed and was replaced by

Facebook, Twitter and blogs. And you would need to record what happened to the community and to people's attitudes, not over weeks or months, but years. This is what Rachel Howells did in Port Talbot, Wales.

★

Port Talbot is not what most people would call conventionally pretty. Drive past it down the M4 through south Wales at night and you could be forgiven for mistaking it for a scene from a dystopian science-fiction novel. Its skyline is peppered with chimneys billowing smoke, steel roller conveyors and heavy machinery. Yet its brutal industrial architecture is also the source of its community. Port Talbot, historically blessed with access to lots of coal, grew along with its industry. It gained a dedicated local paper, the *Port Talbot Guardian*, in 1925, the year after its local MP, Ramsay MacDonald, became Labour's first prime minister. By the 1960s there were up to eleven full-time journalists working out of Port Talbot, and a thriving rivalry between competing news titles. The *Port Talbot Guardian* led the pack. If you wanted to know what was happening in the town, you knew it would be in the paper. From council meetings to court reports, from school sports matches to car accidents. As one ex-reporter from the 1970s told Howells, "It was like this huge vacuum cleaner sucking material in, stories about anything, little Johnnie winning an award for collecting £5 in his street for the Wings appeal or something." Yet, by the 1990s, the number of journalists based in the town had dropped to around half a dozen, and fell further when the *Port Talbot Guardian* journalists were moved to nearby Neath. Just before the paper closed, in 2009, there were two editorial staff, and sometimes just one, dedicated to covering the town.[61]

Howells worked for fourteen years as a journalist in south Wales, and saw the decline in local coverage first hand. After the *Port*

Talbot Guardian closed she decided to study what effect it had on the community and how people got their news. Initially, after it shut in 2009, it did not seem like much had changed. The local authorities functioned just as they had. The steelworks kept running. There was still lots of media to choose from, just not a dedicated local paper. Yet, as Howells discovered, although most of the town was functioning in the same way most of the time, there was a growing sense of confusion, of powerlessness, and of distrust.

A seemingly innocuous road closure in 2014 provided a glimpse of the damage the lack of local reporting was having on the community. On the morning of 4 August, the authorities closed Junction 41 of the M4. Junction 41 is the main junction off the motorway to Port Talbot. If you want to travel into or out of Port Talbot, you will probably use Junction 41. For many residents of the town, it was their route to and from work. Yet, unbeknownst to many residents, the Welsh Assembly had decided to temporarily close the junction at peak times in order to speed up traffic on the M4. The first that some people knew about the closure was when they set off for work that morning and found access to the motorway blocked by a barrier. One resident found out about the road closure not from a news outlet but from graffiti he had seen sprayed on the walls of the M4. The Romans were well known for using graffiti to communicate, though you could be forgiven for assuming that communications technology had moved on since then.

When Howells spoke to Port Talbot residents as part of her research shortly after the closure, she found them justifiably angry. Just like the residents of Grenfell Tower, they felt that nobody was listening to them. Many had signed a petition to object to the road closure, but it just seemed to disappear. One resident described feeling as if the petition had "been chucked in the bin", Howells reported. "Who signed a petition in this room? All of us. Nobody's heard anything about the petition." Coupled with their sense of impotence was a disorienting confusion, a sense of not knowing what was happening or even who to speak to if you did. The anger and frustration spilt over onto other issues – protests over the local power station, plans to redevelop a school site, the closure of magistrates' courts. The younger residents talked about turning to vandalism and violence to get heard. One suggested dismantling the barrier themselves: "I'd be very tempted to go up there [to Junction 41] with a disc cutter and just open it up myself and then drive on it." Another proposed a riot: "Need a revolution really but it's going to take violence for people to listen to it . . . a bit of a riot. The town's upset," he went on, "they're just going to riot one day, everyone's just going to blow. I think everyone's going to get so angry they're just going to go." It was getting to that stage, another agreed. Without adequate local news, without knowing what local authorities were doing, and without any shared local channel through which to speak to authority, the community had lost trust in that authority, had become alienated and despondent, and was willing to consider anything – including violence – to get noticed.

Disturbed by the vacuum in local news, Howells had herself tried to help plug the news gap. With some other ex-journalists she started an online-only news site, the *Port Talbot Magnet*, and ran it on a shoestring for five years. Eventually, unable to cover costs, isolated, and increasingly harassed when the site covered controversial local issues, Howells closed the *Magnet*. She still follows news in the town closely, though most now travels by word of mouth or social media. A consequence of this is that every unexplained event – the death of a local resident, a police cordon around the local school – is followed by a surge of rumours and outlandish theories. "The original incident . . . is quickly blown up into something quite dramatic that bears little resemblance to reality. I know of local councillors who spend hours online, answering questions or correcting false assumptions."[62]

★

By 2017 many journalists, though still using Twitter, were losing faith in its usefulness. "The little blue bird has flown," journalist Matthew Clayfield wrote in the *Guardian*. "Since the Boston bombings four years ago, Twitter's value as a news source has gradually but inexorably faded."[63] Clayfield and others complained that the platform had become a cacophony of voices, many choosing to believe their own versions of events, even when these had been thoroughly debunked. Journalists, particularly women, were subject to Twitter mobs and lynchings, leading its chief executive in 2015, Dick Costolo, to confess to employees that "we [Twitter] suck at dealing with abuse and trolls on the platform and we've sucked at it for years."[64] Despite acknowledging the problem, trolling continued to grow.[65] Yet even as Costolo and his successor, Jack Dorsey, struggled to deal with harassment, it was becoming apparent that their service was also awash with bots.

During the 2016 US presidential election campaign, researchers found that a third of pro-Trump tweets and a fifth of pro-Clinton ones came from bots.[66] Many journalists, especially in the US and Britain, were still addicted to Twitter (one comparing it to crack), but they were now more conscious of its shortcomings.[67] Whatever its faults, the service had triggered huge changes in the culture and practices of journalism. Journalism was faster, lighter and more agile, if more skittish. It fitted with the definition Noah Glass had alighted on back in 2006: "Agitation or excitement; flutter". Journalists could use the platform to gather quotes and pictures or to reach eye-witnesses without leaving their desks. News organizations could cover news from anywhere in the world without sending a reporter out of the office. Though as quickly as attention focused on one thing, it moved onto another.

As for the public, in 2016 Jack Dorsey claimed that Twitter was the 'people's news network'.[68] Except for most people it wasn't. Though Twitter had shown it had incredible assets – its openness, its speed, its breadth, its access to sources – for most of the public it was simply too much. Too boisterous, too visceral, too fleeting. A small proportion of people posted the vast majority of the tweets. Much of the dialogue on the network was either exclusionary or aggressive. And it was increasingly used primarily as a means of self-promotion.

Twitter's growth having stalled by 2015, the number of Twitter users then crept slowly upwards over the next few years. It was not that people were rejecting Twitter in favour of print newspapers or even legacy news websites, but rather that Facebook, Instagram, Snapchat and Slack performed similar functions to Twitter, without the hard work or the risk of public humiliation. Neither had Twitter, or social media generally, lived up to some of the lofty hopes about 'citizen journalism'. It could be extremely useful in gathering first responses to natural disasters, accidents or freak events, but for the day-to-day stuff, the meat and drink of news reporting, it was sporadic, scattered and random. Ironically, despite the vast cornucopia of news available via social media, people said they felt less informed. A report published by the Knight Foundation in 2018 found that "most Americans believe it is now harder to be well-informed and to determine which news is accurate."[69]

Meanwhile, local news reporting continued to melt away. Courts, councils and public services started to realize that, without journalists coming to their cases and meetings, no-one was telling the public what they were doing. The British courts service set up a special initiative to try to increase court reporting. Various efforts were made to fill the gap. In the UK, the BBC committed to subsidizing local 'public interest' reporters – though even in the time it took them to work out how do this, more journalists had been let go by publishers than the subsidy replaced. Google started a European Digital News Initiative to support innovative news projects. In the US the Knight Foundation continued the efforts it had originally started in the mid-twentieth century to support journalism and promote 'informed and engaged communities'. And there were, in the US, UK, Canada, Australia and elsewhere, lots of individual attempts to create new digital news operations – including ones that served tiny, ultra-local, areas. These were, for the most part, earnest and well-meaning operations, run out of bedrooms and garages, with hardly enough money to cover hosting costs. Some, like the local Isle of Wight news site *On the Wight*, took off and grew. Others, like the *Port Talbot Magnet*, toiled for a few years and then reluctantly folded.

By 2018, across various democracies, you could point to whole cities or regions where there were 'news deserts': places where few, if any, dedicated reporters regularly ventured. In the US, as Philip Napoli and his colleagues at Rutgers University discovered, these often correlated with areas that were poorer or more remote. Newark, a city of 300,000 in New Jersey, in 2015 had less than a tenth of the local news sources dedicated to the 19,000 residents of wealthier Morristown, twenty miles away.[70] In Britain in 2015, over half of parliamentary constituencies – 330 out of 650 – were not covered by a dedicated daily local newspaper.[71] Whole areas, such as the eastern part of Northamptonshire, had no local daily paper and no regular local digital news services. Even large cities had lost their dedicated news outlets. At the beginning of October 2017, the *Makedonia* newspaper in Thessaloniki, Greece, closed down. Its competitor, *Aggelioforos*, had already shut in 2015, meaning that by 2018 Greece's second largest city had no newspaper of any significant size dedicated to reporting it.[72]

Into the reporting vacuum stepped public authorities and PR professionals. By 2015 in the UK, there were about the same number of communications staff at public authorities as there were local journalists. Local councils employed 3,400 communications staff; the police employed over 775; and central government 1,500.[73] This did not include communications staff at other authorities, hospitals, schools or commercial organizations. The dominance of communications professionals over journalists had become even more pronounced in the US. In *The Death and Life of American Journalism*, Robert McChesney and John Nichols found that the number of people employed in public relations in the US doubled between 1980 and 2008, while the number of journalists dropped by a quarter, making almost four PR people for every journalist. Social media accelerated this process. "In the shift from old to new media," the *Washington Post* reported in 2015, "the White House has essentially become its own media production company," posting more than 400 videos to YouTube and 275 infographics in the first half of the year alone.[74]

These official reports were, however well intentioned, essentially propaganda. Worse, for the most part they were dull propaganda. Public authorities are not wont to criticize themselves. When they report on their own performance their reports are, at best, plainly factual, and at worst, gnomic and misleading. This is more often a consequence of what they leave out rather than what they put in. Embarrassing details are quietly overlooked; internal arguments are airbrushed from minutes; resignations go unremarked upon. For the general public these releases, deprived of context and interpretation, and presented with as much flair as your average company annual report, might as well be published in ancient Greek.

To have a chance of being noticed, especially in the hubbub of social media chatter, political communication needs personality. This is especially the case for digital media natives, who look for online cues as to what is noteworthy and worth paying attention to. In practice this means looking at what other people – especially opinion formers – say and do. When academics from Gothenburg University studied the news habits of sixteen- to nineteen-year-olds in Sweden, they were struck by the importance of opinion leaders for how they navigated news. The opinion leaders, they wrote, "are perceived [by young people] as central or even crucial to the news-gathering process".[75] In politics on Twitter, those gaining the most attention – and having the greatest influence – were those making controversial claims, decrying the status quo, hurling personal insults and picking fights. Enter Donald Trump, stage right.

Trump's decision to join Twitter, in March 2009, was not politically motivated. Trump saw it as a way to promote his new book, *Think Big*. For the first couple of years, as journalists Peter Oborne and Tom Roberts chart in their analysis of Trump's tweets, the posts were about commercial self-promotion.[76] It was only after mulling another presidential run in 2011 that he found his distinctive political voice. Out came the controversial claims ("Made in America?" he tweeted on 18 November 2011. "@BarackObama called his 'birthplace' Hawaii 'here in Asia'") along with frequent tweets disparaging Washington politics inside the beltway: "It's easy to see why Americans are sick of career politicians and both parties." These were coupled with personal insults aimed at the president – "@BarackObama played golf yesterday. Now he heads off to a 10 day vacation in Martha's Vineyard. Nice work ethic" – and taunts aimed at media commentators and public figures: "Bob Beckel, a commentator for FOX is bad for the @FoxNews brand: @BobBeckel is close to incompetent."

Donald Trump was not the only politician to benefit from the transformation in the public's news consumption habits. Like him, India's Narendra Modi used Twitter to bypass mainstream media and speak directly to the people, presenting himself as the voice of a silent majority. "If you want to listen to Modi," one analyst of his tweets wrote in 2015, "you go to his social media feed – whether you are a citizen, a print reporter or a television channel."[77] Like Trump, Modi focused public attention on himself – rather than on the state or party – in what communications scholar Shakuntala Rao has called "selfie nationalism".[78] As Rao documents, through his ubiquitous and constant presence on social media, Modi has shown himself as the 'people's prime minister' who represents *janashakti* (people's power). In practice, this has meant ignoring the boring aspects of governance – the legislative process, the judicial system, the implementation of policy – and focusing on attention-grabbing new initiatives, illustrations of power in action (such as photographs of meetings with international leaders) and demonstrations of nationalism and religious devoutness (exclusively playing to the Hindu majority). Tellingly, Modi does not tweet links to news stories – mainstream media is to be bypassed and ignored, not promoted.

Other political leaders may not have Narendra Modi's forty million-plus followers, but have cultivated a similar style of personalized communication using Twitter and other social media. Turkey's Recep Tayyip Erdoğan, who said "I don't like to tweet, schmeet" and blocked the service in Turkey in 2014, joined in 2015 and gained over twelve million followers in the subsequent three years. Mexico's Enrique Peña Nieto, with seven million followers in early 2018, was an early adopter, and used the platform to spar with Donald Trump about who would pay for a wall between Mexico and the US. The social media service that had once seemed disruptive and democratizing was now being used to enhance the strength and voice of leaders in government.

Many of us are choosing to hear politicians speak for themselves, rather than through the filter of traditional media. We are letting public figures we know and like – not just political figures but actors, models, singers, TV personalities and commentators – point us to what they think is important and shape our news agenda. We are expecting news to find its way to us, rather than the other way round. Often it does, or at least the big news stories do. And increasingly that is what the news is composed of – big news stories to which we all flock temporarily, then move on. As we follow first one big story and then the next, distracted along the way by viral videos and listicles, we fail to notice that the foundation beneath these big stories, the multiplicity of smaller news stories, local stories, important but dull stories, complex and obscure stories, awkward and uncomfortable stories, have been disappearing. We only notice when something unexpected or terrible happens, something like the Grenfell fire, and then we blame the big news media organizations for failing to warn us. The more self-critical amongst them then go into paroxysms of self-flagellation. We – the media elite – "are in breach", Channel 4's news anchor, Jon Snow, told his august Edinburgh audience in 2017, of our obligation "to be aware of, connect with, and understand the lives, concerns, and needs of " those not in the elite.

But *Channel 4 News* is never going to have a journalist dedicated to covering a single London borough, just like the *New York Times* can never have enough journalists to connect regularly with those in Wisconsin, Michigan and Ohio who feel ignored and disconnected. The failure is at another level, a local and provincial level. Here, though everyone may have a voice on social media, we have lost – and continue to lose – the collective voices of poor, marginalized or remote communities, the powerless people most in need of society's attention. Where these communities correspond with political boundaries, they have lost their channel to speak together to their elected representatives.

Our news has become Twitterized. It is nimble, light-footed, fleeting and ephemeral. Sometimes there are roots beneath it; often there are none. Mostly we do not know as we flutter, moth-like, from one bright light to the next. As we flit from filament to filament we inadvertently pick up news – some true, some false, some straight, some spun – and pass on what we like or what excites us. It is a precarious and unstable news ecosystem that falls far short of the obligations democracy places on it. Yet this is the trade we have made. To move on from the plodding, worthy, flawed but necessary professional reporting we have relied on for the last couple of hundred years, to the unbearable lightness of Twitter.

Part 3

ALTERNATIVE FUTURES

7
PLATFORM DEMOCRACY

It is a pity that so many of the experts or technologists who are called in to attempt the solution of some of these [political] problems feel that they know best what order should be attached to these attempts, and feel that politics impedes, rather than clears the way, for the use of their techniques.

Bernard Crick, *In Defence of Politics*

On the morning of 30 January 2018, as the temperature hovered around freezing in New York, online retail giant Amazon released a joint statement with Warren Buffett's Berkshire Hathaway and investment bank JPMorgan Chase. The three organizations announced they would be forming a new company that would develop 'technology solutions' to give their US employees "simplified, high-quality and transparent healthcare at a reasonable cost".[1]

This announcement, accompanied by typically uninformative corporate statements by the respective company heads, sparked huge excitement in the media and convulsions in the US healthcare sector. The three behemoths were going to "team up to try to disrupt health care", the *New York Times* declared.[2] "The ambitions are thrilling," *The Atlantic* exclaimed. These three companies "are going to fix healthcare – somehow".[3] The *Financial Times*, which led its front page with the news, pointed to the immediate economic impact of the statement. It "wiped billions of dollars from the market value of the [health] sector's biggest participants" – especially health insurers and drug makers.[4]

Despite the scant details about what exactly the three planned to do, there was plenty of hope that they would revolutionize an industry that, all agreed, was desperately in need of it. Of the three companies involved, almost all of this hope rested on Amazon. "Amazon could think big", Chunka Mui wrote in *Forbes*, "by simply applying the standard operating principles and capabilities that it has perfected for retail." And *Fortune* magazine argued: "What will make this different ... is that patients will make real and frequent choices with this instantly available data: For lack of a better verb, they'll 'Amazon' it."[5] Some even saw Amazon as the only chance of rescuing American healthcare. Four months before the announcement, Amitai Etzioni, sociologist and George Washington University professor, had written a plaintive open letter to Amazon's chief executive, Jeff Bezos. "You are needed to disrupt the health care sector," Etzioni wrote. "Only you have the vision, ambition, capital, and computing power this mission requires."[6] After the announcement was made there were a handful who were less sanguine about the magical powers of Amazon to solve America's spiralling healthcare costs, but even amongst these there were few who thought it could do worse than the government.

Despite the giddy excitement surrounding the news, Amazon was already involved in healthcare. It had partnered with the American Heart Association in 2016 to use its phenomenal cloud computing capacity to support medical research.[7] In mid-2017 CNBC reported that Amazon had set up a "secret skunkworks lab" to look into how it might store people's medical records electronically, and enable remote diagnosis of patients.[8] The online retailer also employed a pharmacy team and was reported to be exploring the potential of handling mail-order prescriptions.[9] And anyway, focusing all this attention on Amazon ignored the fact that

Amazon was itself playing catch-up with other big tech platforms. Google and Apple had got there first.

In 2014, when Google paid £400 million for an obscure British company that had never even launched a product, people were understandably curious as to what it did. The company, called DeepMind, was set up in 2010 by two childhood friends, Demis Hassabis and Mustafa Suleyman, and machine learning expert Shane Legg. Of the three, Hassabis was quickly labelled the resident genius. Growing up in north London, he had, by the age of seventeen, reached the level of chess master, designed a video game that went on to sell millions of copies, and done well enough in his exams to get into Cambridge University. The inventor of the World Wide Web, Sir Tim Berners-Lee, called Hassabis one of the smartest human beings on the planet. His company's aim fitted with his reputation. He, Suleyman and Legg wanted to 'solve intelligence'. To do this they planned to build a machine that could not only learn, and become cleverer, but could apply its learning to problems it had not come across before. They wanted, in other words, to build a machine that could think like a human (and then exceed one). By 2014 they had got far enough that Google was willing to spend hundreds of millions on acquiring them. Two years later *The Economist* was calling them "Google's hippocampus".

Although DeepMind first made headlines when its artificial intelligence beat the grand master of the board game Go, it soon began to focus much of its attention on healthcare. "Preventative medicine is the area I'm most excited about," Suleyman told *Wired* editor David Rowan in 2015. "There's huge potential for our methods to improve the way we make sense of data." [10] All DeepMind needed was the medical data itself. It did not have long to wait. A month after the *Wired* interview was published, the Royal Free Hospital in London approached DeepMind and proposed they collaborate. That November, the Royal Free started passing medical data from millions of its patients to the artificial intelligence company. The eventual hope, as expressed in an understanding between DeepMind and the Royal Free at the beginning of 2016, was that theirs would be a "broad ranging, mutually beneficial partnership" leading to "genuinely innovative and transformational projects".[11] Initially, DeepMind's ambitions were relatively narrow. It planned to integrate various different medical data streams to help doctors manage kidney disease. Yet Suleyman made clear that its ultimate aspirations were much grander. At a packed meeting during 2016's NHS Expo in Manchester, Suleyman explained how DeepMind wanted to use its algorithms to "tackle some of society's toughest social problems", especially in healthcare where they sought to "make much better predictions" and where he set out a vision of a "truly digital NHS".[12]

While DeepMind beavered away in its brand new offices in King's Cross in London in 2016, across the ocean another Alphabet/Google subsidiary was preparing to launch a similarly ambitious data-driven health venture.* In spring 2017, Verily Life Sciences announced that it would be collecting the personal health information of ten thousand US volunteers over the next four years. It would track each volunteer using a special watch, combined with bed sensors to monitor their sleep, backed up by regular in-person visits. Their objective was to figure out what normal health is (for someone of a particular age, gender etc.), to make it easier to see when we are deviating from it. Verily expressed its ambitions in similarly sweeping rhetoric to DeepMind. "We've mapped the world," the company said (presumably referring to cartographers and explorers since Columbus and Magellan); "now let's map human health." Should the project work, then it could transform predictive and preventative healthcare – as long as

---

* Google created a holding company called Alphabet in 2015 for all its diverse ventures (Google itself included).

people are willing to track themselves constantly, by wearing a health watch, attaching health sensors, or ingesting a health device.[13] Everything comes in threes, the saying goes, and so with Alphabet/Google health ventures. Along with DeepMind and Verily there was Calico, a company that distinguished itself from its healthcare colleagues at Alphabet by aspiring to tackle ageing. What Mark O'Connell, in his book on transhumanism, calls the "modest problem of death".

Apple too was deeply committed to healthcare by 2018. As much as Amazon's initial ambitions in the sector were vague and constrained, and Alphabet's boundless, Apple's were both audacious and pragmatic. It too wanted to let its users collect and integrate their own personal health data. It too wanted them to benefit from preventative healthcare and early diagnoses. And it too wanted to enable large-scale medical research via its platform. It just wanted this all to happen on Apple devices and under Apple's aegis. Since 2014 Apple had been building an end-to-end healthcare service for its users, and a research and development platform for researchers and entrepreneurs – through 'HealthKit', 'CareKit' and 'ResearchKit'. It even applied for a patent to turn the iPhone into a diagnostic device.[14] "Health care", the company's chief executive, Tim Cook, said in September 2017, "is big for Apple's future."[15]

★

Why, in 2018, were three of the world's largest and most innovative companies going head to head in a race to transform healthcare? Putting to one side the financial incentive – that this was a global industry worth something like $7 trillion a year – each clearly believed there was an opportunity to do what they had done to many other sectors: disrupt it. Just as they had done with retail, music and information, respectively, Amazon, Apple and Google figured they could give people access to healthcare in a way that was more efficient, more responsive, more personalized and cheaper. In the same way as people now made their own holiday arrangements online rather than visiting a travel agent, why not give people the same degree of choice and freedom when it came to healthcare? Indeed, these platforms believed they could perform a double service: they could not only make healthcare more accessible, they could also – with the personal data they gathered – make it smarter.

The reason these organizations were convinced they could do things better, smarter and cheaper in healthcare – apart from a dash of hubris – is because they are technology platforms. We use the word 'platform' constantly now, but rarely actually define what it means or why it should make these companies different. A tech platform is a digital space in which people can produce and exchange goods and services. The economist and Cambridge University professor Diane Coyle compares a platform to a bazaar.[16] The bazaar has its origins in Persia, where it helped solve a perennial human dilemma. How do you connect merchants and customers in the same place at the same time? Answer: you set a space aside where, at a consistent and regular time, merchants set up their stalls, such that people know where to come and when. Online bazaars, or platforms, work in a similar way but without the constraints of space and time. You can go to a tech platform anytime, from anywhere. So, unlike their physical counterparts they can potentially cater to millions of stallholders and customers simultaneously. The problem – for both the bazaar and the digital platform – is how to get both to turn up. If either or both fail to show then the whole thing collapses. Bazaars can at least count on a certain amount of human traffic within the town. Tech platforms do not have this advantage. Instead, they give their services away for free, or at very low cost, and try to grow as fast as they can. Once they reach a certain size, with enough stallholders and customers, they can then take advantage of the network effect. This is when it makes sense for people to be there because everyone else is there too.

Tech platforms have another advantage over bazaars. They know who you are, and follow you – while you are there, and even after you leave. This way they can tailor their services for you, and keep offering you things they think you might like – a bit like a persistent carpet salesman pestering you as you walk down the street (and round the corner, and into your home ...). Unlike ancient bazaars, Google, Facebook, Amazon and other digital platforms are corporate entities, who not only run the space, but write the rules, manage the security and set the rates. Think more private shopping mall than public square.

When it comes to healthcare, the big tech platforms already have many advantages over other health providers. They have millions (in some cases billions) of people who visit them every day. They know a phenomenal amount about these people – and have the capability to know lots more. And, they can deliver personalized services to each of these people on the basis of what they know about them. As a consequence, the big tech platforms – and many of their investors – can imagine a future in which each of them becomes our main gateway to healthcare. In this virtual world, each of us collects our own personal health data and stores it on one of these platforms. We can then use a combination of apps and services on the platform to self-diagnose, or to warn us when we stray from our usual healthy baseline (Beep! Beep! Your blood pressure is unusually high!).* This way, outside surgery, emergency or chronic care, many of us will be able to avoid visiting a doctor or hospital almost entirely. At some stage, platforms like Amazon must be calculating, we will also be able to order our

---

* One self-diagnosis skin cancer app – Skinvision – claimed to have over one million users by early 2018.

medicines online and have them delivered to our door, so we do not even need to walk to the pharmacy.

On top of the convenience and early warning system, there are the potential upsides of platform healthcare for medical research. If one puts aside some of the more absurd and outlandish claims (one of which led *Time* magazine to ask mischievously in 2013, "Can Google solve death?"), there is growing evidence to suggest that, with their capacity to store and analyse big data and through their development of machine intelligence, these organizations may be able to advance medical research and understanding. The American Heart Association's partnership with Amazon is geared towards leveraging its cloud storage and processing power to "accelerate discovery in cardiovascular health". Amazon's cloud hosts the Cancer Genome Atlas, a multi-year international project aimed at increasing our knowledge of the molecular basis of cancer.[17] Apple's ResearchKit makes it much easier, and less expensive, to recruit research volunteers. A study of Parkinson's disease, started in 2015, was able to sign up over nine thousand people for free via the iPhone ResearchKit.[18] By comparison, it cost around $800 to recruit less than a thousand people for a similar study in 2010.[19] And Alphabet's DeepMind, after reviewing thousands of retinal scans, announced in February 2018 that it had been able to create artificial intelligence software capable of spotting eye disease faster than a human.[20] This could make the difference between keeping your sight and going blind.

In their rush to discover new diagnoses and to beat their competition, however, these platforms risk making mistakes and – directly or indirectly – harming patients' rights. Julia Powles, research fellow at New York University, and *Economist* journalist Hal Hodson showed that when the Royal Free started feeding medical data to DeepMind in 2015, for example, it had not sought the agreement of the patients themselves, or even notified them.[21] The platforms also assume that there will be a medical diagnosis to illness, and minimize or ignore the social causes of ill health. The eight-year-old boy with persistent headaches may be helped by painkillers, but if the problem is stress or tensions at home, then sending aspirin in the mail is unlikely to be much help.

Yet even beyond this, if these platforms succeed in their healthcare ambitions, and successfully disrupt the sector, then the way our societies care for the sick in the future will be fundamentally different than it is today. This future will be built around individual quantified selves and the platforms on which these quantified selves live. It is a future in which our healthcare relationship is less with the state (particularly in the case of countries with a national health service like the UK), or with a specific medical institution or doctor, and more with a healthcare platform – like Apple, Google or Amazon. There are, of course, many social and economic implications of this, but there are also political ones. You cannot vote out a healthcare platform. There is no democratic equivalent to a peaceful transition of power from one healthcare platform to another. You can leave a platform, though leaving might come with a pretty high price tag. Going from one healthcare platform to another may – if you are lucky – just be a hassle, but leaving entirely could leave you, and your quantified self, stranded. You would be free of the platform, but unable to access many of the healthcare services available to others.

Stay within a health platform and you ought to be able to access most of these (though, naturally for commercial organizations, there will be tiered services). Yet you will inevitably have to sacrifice elements of privacy and lose a degree of freedom or agency. Decisions made by the platform, for example, will be made for various reasons – commercial, legal, regulatory, reputational – though not for democratic ones. Plus, since you will be recording yourself constantly – so you can be alerted if you veer off your health baseline – you will be discouraged, or even punished, for doing things that negatively affect your health. This has started already. The health insurer Aetna committed to giving away half a million Apple Watches to its customers in 2018. The aim, Aetna said, was to bundle watches into corporate wellness programmes to encourage its customers "to live more productive, healthy lives". Once the health device is on, it will keep track of today's workout but also the one you missed yesterday, the extra glass of wine and the late night ice cream sundae. The latter could add to your weight and to the cost of your insurance. It is a short step from encouragement to incentives, such as discounts for those who reduce their alcohol or calorific intake (and corresponding penalties for those who do not). "This is only the beginning," Aetna's chairman and CEO said in 2016. "We look forward to using these tools to improve health outcomes and help more people achieve more healthy days" – and penalize them for unhealthy ones, he might have added.[22]

Democratic governments can, and will, step in and try to control this, though there are strong financial and social incentives pulling them in the direction of platform healthcare. It is rare to find a democratic government that does not want to save money on health. The prospect of increasing preventative care through self-monitoring, of enabling self-diagnosis and in-home diagnosis and treatment, and of having automated AI diagnostics as an alternative to manual human analysis, will be very attractive to cash-strapped administrations. Especially if it means reducing the need for state-funded hospital buildings, care institutions and doctors' surgeries. At the same time, it may be beyond the power of many democratic governments to choose which direction healthcare takes. If enough people decide to self-track and to entrust their personal health data to a platform, then, before long, network effects will kick in and the government will risk angering and alienating a large number of its voters if it tries to intervene.

Still, this may be underestimating the politics, the emotiveness and the sheer complexity of healthcare. As Donald Trump said in

2017, "Nobody knew health care could be so complicated." No doubt different democracies will encourage and discourage, inhibit and allow, regulate and deregulate platform healthcare. Though some, particularly those like the US that discourage government intervention, will go further and faster in this direction than others. Were healthcare the only public service that the tech platforms were seeking to transform, then democratic politics might emerge relatively unscathed. But it is not just healthcare. There is a corresponding revolution happening in the way children learn.

★

When Mark Zuckerberg visited a Summit school in Sunnyvale, California, in 2014, it was at the prompting of his wife, Priscilla Chan.[23] Chan had been so impressed by her earlier visit to the school that she told her husband he simply had to come and see it for himself. He did, and was equally bowled over. It looked "more like a Google or a Facebook than a school", the chief executive of Summit Public Schools told the *New York Times*, where "students with laptops often zoom around on caster chairs."[24] The school had been set up by a group of Silicon Valley parents in response to what they saw as America's broken education system. "What happened to the American public high school," they asked, "and what can we do to fix it?"[25] Their answer was 'personalized learning', an approach in which children follow their own paths and learn at their own pace. Necessarily the approach relies heavily on technology. Which is why, when Zuckerberg offered to help, the chief executive, Diane Tavenner, did not ask for money but for technical expertise. The Facebook head duly provided a team of engineers who, overseen by Zuckerberg, developed a 'Personal Learning Platform', or PLP, for Summit. This was able both to capture data and to be used as a resource from which teachers and students could access projects, curriculums and assessments.[26]

"We're starting small," Zuckerberg wrote when he announced the partnership, "but planning to grow this program to offer personalized learning technology for free to many more schools." Two years later, 330 schools across forty US states were using the Summit Learning Program.[27]

One can see why the Summit approach appealed to Zuckerberg. Apart from looking like a start-up, children had to show personal initiative and direction – just like entrepreneurs – and personal data and technology sat at the heart of the model. From his perspective, and that of his wife, it accelerated learning, and looked like it had the potential to scale. "This is not the kind of thing you can change overnight," Zuckerberg said in a Facebook Live talk at the end of 2016. "But if you take a five-, ten- or fifteen-year time frame, it's possible to help teachers at schools around the country, and eventually the world, to do personalized learning."[28] This was also personal for Mark Zuckerberg and his wife. In their letter to their newborn daughter, shared with the world, they wrote about their "moral responsibility to all children in the next generation" and their hope their daughter would "learn and experience 100 times more than we do today".[29] In 2017, the Chan–Zuckerberg Initiative (CZI) took over responsibility for the Summit Schools Program.[30]

The Facebook founder was far from the only tech entrepreneur to be excited about personalized learning. Microsoft founder Bill Gates was similarly enthused. "I wish I'd had a system like that when I was in school," Gates wrote in 2016.[31] So taken was he that his foundation partnered with that of the Zuckerbergs to invest $12 million in a personalized learning initiative. In fact, the personalized, technology-focused, data–driven approach appealed to lots of Silicon Valley tech entrepreneurs. Reed Hastings, the founder of Netflix, invested $11 million in an AI maths platform called Dreambox, via a charter school, which personalizes maths lessons for students.[32] Silicon Valley venture capital firms Andreessen

Horowitz and Peter Thiel's Founders Fund, along with Mark Zuckerberg and other members of the West Coast technocracy, invested $100 million in AltSchool, experimental schools started by an ex-head of personalization at Google, Max Ventilla. Ventilla prefers the term 'student-centred learning' but his approach is much the same. Give each child a tablet or computer, let them move through projects at their own speed, and capture data on everything they do. These tech investors are scathing about the current approach to education. Ventilla refers to it as 'the factory model'.[33] Gates calls America's high schools 'obsolete'. They bring with them not just money, but ideas, methodologies, zeal – even a new vocabulary of learning. The student curriculum becomes 'playlists'. Using computers and tablets as part of the lesson becomes 'blended learning'. Studying on a computer outside class becomes a 'flipped classroom'. As with much else that these successful businessmen do, the tech leaders evangelize about their new approach and its potential to transform learning. They also share an unsettling determinism about the future of education. They all appear to believe that technology, and tech devices, will be at the heart of learning, and that tech platforms will form the foundation on which this future is built. For them, it is not a question of whether education will be based on platforms, it is simply a question of which ones.

By 2018, one platform had already taken a commanding lead – Google. Up to 2012 Google had not focused its attention on education. Its search engine and other products were widely used, but it had not sought to differentiate between its services in schools and elsewhere. Then, between 2012 and 2017 it colonized more than half the schools in America, in addition to many others in democracies across the globe. Natasha Singer, a journalist at the *New York Times* who has spent years investigating Silicon Valley's inroads into education, found that the majority of America's schoolchildren were using Google's education apps by mid-2017, and a similar proportion were using Google-powered Chromebooks.[34] Another study estimated two thirds of school districts were using Google Classroom or G-Suite (Google's collection of cloud and collaboration tools such as Google Drive, Docs and Sheets).[35] "'Between the fall of 2012 and now,'" Singer says, quoting a former New York chief information officer, "'Google went from an interesting possibility to the dominant way that schools around the country' teach students to find information, create documents and turn them in." Central to Google's success was going directly to teachers and students. As they had so successfully done in other areas, Google bypassed the existing intermediaries – like the state and school district – and went direct. Other education technology platforms and services did the same, each one seeing teachers and students as their best marketeers.

Wade through all the rhetoric and marketing-speak, and the vision that these tech companies have for the future of education is radically different from that which exists today. In their vision, the way children learn is different. The way teachers teach is different. The classroom is different (if there is a physical classroom at all). And the way children are tracked and assessed is different. Learning is self-directed, self-motivated and data-driven, much of it via a computer or tablet. Lessons become 'projects', and are often turned into games – or 'gamified' – to increase children's interest and participation. Google's ClassCraft – used in more than twenty thousand schools according to its website – turns the curriculum into an interactive 'epic adventure' in which children choose to be fantasy characters and go on quests. Teachers morph into 'mentors' or overseers who allocate short bursts of focused attention on individual children and track the class from a central data dashboard. The founder of AltSchool sees teachers becoming more like 'data detectives' rather than pedagogues. Schools become less places where you are taught than places where you have access to learning materials, to learning advisers and to other children. Initially, this will still require a physical classroom, but once most lessons are done through individualized projects via an app on an electronic device, this too could be superfluous. From a distance, a single teacher could guide many more children, located anywhere. Eventually, if lots of teachers are providing the same advice on a regular basis, then this too could be pre-recorded and 'scaled'. Fundamental to this imagined future is personal learning data, an electronic education record that captures everything from how you perform, to how quickly you learn, to how much initiative you show, and how you behave. Some of the data recorded at AltSchools includes film footage of classes, audio recordings, and motion-tracking and facial- and speech-recognition software. The vision is of a whole education ecosystem where you live your virtual educational life. And the ecosystem is run on the platform.

It is possible that this blended and personalized approach to education could substantially enhance and accelerate learning, though the research to date is, at best, conflicted. A 2017 study by the RAND Corporation, commissioned by the Gates Foundation itself, was hardly glowing. "There is suggestive evidence", it concluded, "that greater implementation of P[ersonalized] L[earning] practices may be related to more positive effects on achievement." This was followed immediately by the qualification "However, this finding requires confirmation through further research."[36] A slightly earlier study, by Data & Society's Monica Bulger, was even less convinced by its merits: "The realities do not point to a binary conclusion of whether personalized learning is beneficial or not, but rather a complex story in which technology developers are applying successful marketing tactics … to education."[37] Kentucky teacher Tiffany Dunn was not far off the mark when she told industry journal *Education Week*, "I'm not aware of any research that says sticking a child in front of a computer for hours on end does them any good."

Then there is the question of what happens to all that personal data. "Schools' and students' use of technology offers a potential treasure trove of data about students", the National Education Policy Center writes, "that private companies, their partners, and their customers can exploit."[38] The platforms themselves have bent over backwards to reassure schools and parents that they are keeping the data private and not using it for advertising or other commercial purposes, though there is understandable anxiety, especially amongst parents, that they may change the rules after the fact. Leonie Haimson, who co-chairs a parents' privacy campaign group, has claimed that the Summit schools altered their criteria for who they share data with, and altered the terms of consent. In 2017, Haimson writes, the CZI-backed Summit schools "claimed the right to access, data-mine and redisclose their children's data ... without asking if parents agreed to these terms".[39] Summit says that it "does not and will not sell student personal information".[40] Even if they do not sell data, or even access to data, the platforms will use it to gain knowledge about how people behave and progress, and to figure out what works and what does not – so they can be in a strong position to provide the platform for education in the future.

Parts of the contemporary debate about technology in the classroom reflect arguments that have dogged public education since it began. Whether to give children the skills they need to get a job, or whether to give them the knowledge and understanding to get the most out of life. Yet other aspects of the debate are quite new, such as the effects of 'datafication' on children. In 'The Datafied Child', academics Ben Williamson and Deborah Lupton describe how many humans are now datafied from before they are born – when their parents share scans of them *in utero*. The authors refer to these pictures, and all the other measurements of children which are subsequently captured – particularly during their education – as 'biocapital'. Biocapital, they suggest, can turn each measurable aspect of the child "into a form of value that can be exchanged by them for rewards such as upgrades and personalized features, transforming classrooms into little digital economies and calculative spaces where personal data have exchange value and utility".[41] It represents, in other words, another step on the road towards turning our personal data into an alternative currency, only in this case, a kids' currency.

Modern democracies were designed in part to help resolve arguments about how we should educate our children, as well as allowing for flexibility and diversity through devolved approaches. We may not have this democratic luxury if education shifts to tech platforms. We may find ourselves 'baked in' to a particular approach to education – a data-intensive, personalized approach that relies on the tools, services and data storage of a particular platform. We may not even enjoy the freedom to decide the platform in which we invest our educational futures, since – thanks to the network effect – our peers, teachers and local schools may have already decided for us. It will be a brave parent who chooses to opt out of a data-driven system, if by opting out it means their child has less chance of gaining entry to the college of their choice, or of entering the career they aspire to. Just as in healthcare, we may find our quantified, virtual identities become as materially important to who we are and what we do as our physical, real selves. Health and education may be the most obvious areas in which commercial platforms are disrupting public services, but they are far from the only ones.

*

In the summer of 2017, San Francisco-based transport platform Lyft started trialling a new service, called Lyft Shuttle, in its home town. The company said it would provide "a fast, affordable way to commute". For a low standard fare, the Shuttle would pick people up and drop people off at specific locations along fixed, frequently used routes in the city. The initial reaction to the launch was less than effusive. "Lyft just came out with its biggest innovation yet," *Mashable* reported, "buses."[42] Yet some residents, who had suffered through years of poor transport options in San Francisco, were grateful for an alternative. Lyft Shuttle, though awfully similar to a public bus service, differed in a couple of important ways. It would only work at peak times, and only on routes where there was high demand. It would, in other words, cherry-pick. It was also just one of a number of shared-transport experiments that Lyft was trying across the US. Its carpooling service – Lyft Line – launched in 2015, and it piloted a car service in Centennial, Colorado, in 2016 to ferry people to local train stations – subsidized by the local authority. Yet Lyft's attempts to complement – or cannibalize – public transport services were dwarfed by those of its giant competitor, Uber. Uber had already tried mashing together buses with carpooling in Seattle and Toronto (UberHop – shuttered after seven months). It had its own separate carpooling service (uberPOOL) in thirty US cities by mid-2017. And it was working with various town and city authorities to provide subsidized transport alternatives – in Altamonte Springs and Pinellas Park, Florida; Summit, New Jersey; Innisfil, Ontario; and in Philadelphia, Atlanta and Cincinnati. Some of these experiments failed and were quickly shut down, leading people to write them off as misguided flops. But this misses the point. Silicon Valley tech companies were doing what Silicon Valley tech companies do – experimenting; or throwing lots of spaghetti at the wall and seeing what stuck.

Uber and Lyft both saw public transport as the Next Big Thing, and the race was on to 'reinvent' and 'reimagine' it (euphemisms for 'disrupt', which fell into disuse after 2016). If Uber's deal in Altamonte Springs worked – where the company was shuttling people to bus and train stations at a reduced rate (with a subsidy from City Hall) – then it could take it to lots of other towns. If Lyft's Shuttle worked, then it could roll it out to other American cities. Paralleling the efforts of these two big tech transport platforms were a jostling crowd of smaller tech initiatives. A platform called Via claimed to be "re-engineering public transit" in New York City, Chicago and Washington, DC. Another called Swiftly was working with over forty cities to use "big data and predictive algorithms to transform how public transportation systems operate". Heaven forbid there should be any sector of life where Alphabet/Google was not competing. So sure enough, in transport too, Alphabet had a substantial and growing role. Alphabet's satnav app, Waze, provides real-time traffic-sensitive directions, and had – by 2018 – been downloaded more than 100 million times. As a consequence Waze (and by extension Alphabet) had reached a level of penetration in some cities that gave the company better real-time knowledge of traffic than any public authority.*

For many US city authorities, partnering with these tech companies is an opportunity to save money. The subsidized Uber cars in Pinellas Park, for example, took the place of two local bus services at a quarter of the cost. Civic leaders can also sell platform public transport to the public as a more efficient, personalized service. "It's about convenience and control," Altamonte's city manager told journalist Spencer Woodman.[43] For some towns, it is a for-profit transport service or nothing. In Arlington, Texas, the public voted to put money into the Texas Rangers stadium rather than into public transport. So the city contracted Via to set up a micro-transit service.† As tech firms move into public transport,

---

* Alphabet/Google also has a stake in both Lyft and Uber.

† No tech platform transformation is without its own obtuse vocabulary and acronyms, and public transport is the same. Transport platforms are 'Transportation Network Companies' (TNCs). For-profit bus services are 'micro-transit' services. And the whole transformation – the tech-driven shift from car owning to using whatever transportation your chosen tech platform tells you to – is referred to unhelpfully as 'Mobility-as-a-Service' (MaaS).

critics worry this will lead to the decline of publicly owned transport services, and worse provision for the poorest and the most in need of help. Or, as the Greenlining Institute's Hana Creger put it succinctly, "Uber and Lyft's effort to disrupt public transportation will hurt the environment and screw the poor."[44]

The ultimate prize is not to run a micro-transit service in Pineallas Park, Florida, or even somewhere as big as New York City. The ultimate prize is to be the platform of choice for all the transport in a city – or even a whole country (bearing in mind most Silicon Valley companies are also investing in self-driving cars). Sooner or later, these companies figure, we will all plan our movements via our phones. We will plug in where we want to go (or the platform will work it out), and our phone will tell us the fastest, cheapest and most convenient ways of getting there. Some of these options will be provided by the platform itself (like Lyft Shuttles), others by separate public or private companies (though the platform will profit somehow). Ultimately, for the platform, the data is the key. The more data it has, the more knowledge it has about who is moving where and how, and the more comprehensive travel information it can give to people and share – on its own terms – with authorities and other organizations (such as advertisers). Eventually, this data could form the basis for any transport decision – from someone deciding how to get to work, to a transport authority choosing which bus routes to drop or keep, to an ambulance trying to find the quickest way to the hospital. If a civic authority is not collecting, organizing and analysing this data itself, it will quickly become very reliant on whoever is.

As platforms rapidly colonize health, education and transport, so they move more gradually into other areas of public life. In energy, each of the big tech platforms is investing in sustainable energy solutions to power their own ever-growing needs, with the potential for powering those of the rest of us. Amazon has been building wind and solar farms across the US – in Indiana, North Carolina,

Virginia, Ohio and beyond – enough to power 240,000 homes annually, or a city equivalent to Atlanta. At the same time services like Alphabet's Nest are trying to change the way people consume energy at home. In housing, the short-term rental platform Airbnb offers short-term social housing through OpenHomes, and has been exploring the future of home design and urban planning through a division called Samara.[45] In law enforcement, the secretive security tech platform Palantir supports what is being called 'big data policing'. Palantir partners with police departments, like the one in Los Angeles, to produce real-time data dashboards that record criminal activity, direct police responses, and predict future crimes. "Police can identify the street corner most likely to see the next car theft," Andrew Guthrie Ferguson, author of *The Rise of Big Data Policing*, writes, "or the people most likely to be shot."[46] Soon there will be few public services where the tech platforms are not active.

The frustration, for super-platforms like Alphabet and Amazon, is that public services are siloed into departments. Life is not like that. Crime can affect health. Schools rely on good transport networks. Transport requires energy solutions. From the platforms' perspective it would be so much more efficient if all the data could be merged together, everything that we do captured in one central, omniscient, data centre. Our personal data combined with digital maps, schools, healthcare facilities and police stations. If only they could find a place where they could take control of all the data. Initially, this would need to be relatively small, perhaps a town or a neighbour-hood within a city. And they would have to build almost everything from the ground up – so that all the elements were wired together and could talk to each other. Once this experiment was up and running, they could scale it nationwide. In 2015, Alphabet set up a subsidiary, Sidewalk Labs, to think about how this might work in a city. In 2017 it was given a chance to experiment on one.

★

On Tuesday, 17 October 2017, Canada's prime minister, Justin Trudeau, the mayor of Toronto and Alphabet executive chairman Eric Schmidt jointly announced a partnership between Toronto and Sidewalk Labs to develop the eight-hundred-acre Eastern Waterfront district of the city.[47] Starting with a twelve-acre plot at Quayside, Toronto Sidewalk planned to turn the area into the world's first data-driven, technology-centric urban space.

It would, they claimed, be a "global hub for urban innovation". Sidewalk's proposals included self-driving taxibots, demand-priced parking, garbage robots, data-driven social services, modular buildings and a "programmable public realm". More importantly, every road, every building, every street sign and every public vehicle would be connected – constantly emitting and receiving data. The eventual aim was to merge "the physical and digital realms, creating a blueprint for the 21st-century urban neighbourhood" (according to Sidewalk's 'vision').[48] As ever with platform experiments, Quayside Toronto was meant to be a testbed, a trial whose successful features could be rolled out to the district and beyond – "what happens in Quayside", Sidewalk said, "will not stay in Quayside." Google's sister company saw its venture in global terms. "The world sits on the cusp of a revolution in urban life," and Quayside was, it believed, the place to start this revolution. Less than a month after the Toronto announcement, news broke that Bill Gates had bought 25,000 acres of land in Arizona, where he too planned to build a smart city. The space, to be called Belmont, was literally a blank slate – just desert and scrubland, without a building, or person in sight.

For Alphabet and Gates, the smart city – or platform city – is the future. They see these spaces as safer, cleaner, healthier, more sustainable and more efficient. The platform city will – they believe – raise up whoever is on it. Everyone will be better able to find the cheapest, fastest and most convenient route to their destination. Everyone will be in a stronger position to prevent or respond to sickness and disease. Everyone's learning – adults' too – will be personalized and responsive, and every achievement (and failure) recorded. All of those on the platform will benefit from its networked intelligence and behave more 'smartly' as a result.

This assumes, of course, that the platforms themselves function smoothly, which is far from certain given their track record of abandoned, aborted and misguided experiments (remember Google Buzz, Google Wave and Google Glass?). Similarly, it assumes that their belief in the inherent benefits of technology is justified. In sectors like education this is highly debatable. In another decade or so we may discover, for example, that personalized, device-based education actually retards learning, curtails curiosity and impedes socialization. We may find that rather than becoming 'smarter' on a platform, people's capacity to think independently diminishes. On top of which, one thing we know for sure is that our futures will be uneven. Not every city or neighbourhood will be smart. Not every platform will be equal. And for those who are not on a platform? Will they simply have to put up with worse public services, inferior infrastructure and poor health?

Once authorities come to rely on these commercial platforms to help them function, the platforms will acquire significant power. This power may be separate from, or complementary to, that of the authorities with which they work. Being omniscient, the platforms can watch for any deviant behaviour, and punish those who transgress (or pass on this responsibility to the authority concerned). Anyone who has felt the wrath of Google after breaching its terms and conditions will know that once ostracized by the platform it is very hard to return. In general, though, this power will more likely be used to prompt, prod and nudge. In London in 2017, for example, the transport authority (TfL) asked for Waze's help in dealing with traffic problems in the Blackwall Tunnel under the Thames. TfL knew that a major cause of blockages was people running out of fuel mid-tunnel. Since Waze had almost two million UK users,

TfL thought it might be able to divert drivers low on fuel before they got there. As Waze knows where drivers are, and knows where petrol stations are, it was able to tell them to reroute to a petrol station before they got to the tunnel.[49] Six months later it had rerouted over four hundred cars. To some this will seem like a positive and constructive application of technology, to others like the first step towards Orwellian super-surveillance.

Whether these public service platforms lead to Shangri-La or Jeremy Bentham's Panopticon (the all-seeing prison) – or somewhere in between – one thing is certain. They will not be democratic – at least not in the sense of the twentieth-century model of liberal democracy that many of us have grown up with. As citizens increasingly live their lives through platforms – using them to manage their health, their education, their transport and their energy – so they will rely on them more and more, and on government less and less. As a result, the platforms will gain what legal scholar Frank Pasquale calls 'functional sovereignty'. The democratically elected government will, ostensibly, remain in charge and people will be able to vote parties in and out of office. But those in government will have decreasing power to effect change.

The platforms will emphasize their belief in democracy and democratic values, but will not themselves behave democratically. "For all its democratic ethos," the journalist Ken Auletta writes, "its belief in 'the wisdom of crowds', at Google the engineer is king, held high above the crowd."[50] As at Google, so at other successful Silicon Valley tech companies. Not only is the engineer king, but the philosophy of the engineer – using data as the guide to decision-making, doing things quickly – even recklessly – then learning from mistakes. Larry Page, Sergey Brin, Jeff Bezos, Tim Cook, Mark Zuckerberg, Bill Gates, Satya Nadella were not democratically elected to run their companies and do not call for regular public votes on company decisions. Peter Thiel, the billionaire venture capitalist who invested in many of Silicon Valley's most successful start-ups, and went on to support and advise President Trump, wrote that "the companies that create new technology often resemble feudal monarchies rather than organizations that are supposedly more 'modern'."[51] Decision-making, for them, is strictly utilitarian. Decisions should be data-led and should generate the maximum value for the greatest number. There is nothing to suggest the same philosophy would not inform their approach to public services. When applied to domains like health, education and transport this translates into lots of people getting left out. Based on the numbers, the platform will simply not be able to justify serving them.

Many of those in Silicon Valley see a data-driven approach to public services as a positive step forward. They see the current services, and democratic governance generally, as inefficient, wasteful, short-termist, lumbering and sclerotic. This comes out clearly in a fascinating chapter in Steven Levy's biography of Google, *In the Plex*. Levy writes about a gaggle of Googlers who joined Barack Obama's campaign in 2007, some of whom went on to work in his administration. Obama convinced them that government could be run like Google, driven by data and populated by innovators and entrepreneurs. Yet, when they went to Washington, they found it impossibly bureaucratic, monstrously slow and, well, political. Katie Stanton, who had led the Google Election Team, joined the administration as director of citizen participation. She quickly, Levy writes, became frustrated and despondent. "I didn't meet one engineer," Stanton told Levy. "At Google I worked with people far smarter and creative [*sic*] than me, and they were engineers, and they always made everyone else look good. They're doers. We get stuck in the government because we don't really have a lot of those people." Stanton's criticisms of government have been echoed by others within Silicon Valley. Yet what is, for Stanton, slow and bureaucratic administration provides, for others, the necessary checks and balances to prevent harm, to preserve rights or to protect vulnerable groups. What a venture capitalist would view as evidence of sclerotic decision making a civil rights campaigner would view as democratic protection of basic freedoms. What an engineer would see as an inefficient process an elected representative would see as means by which to reach broader consensus.

There have been, before Silicon Valley even existed, plenty of others who saw technology as the answer to society's ills, from French revolutionaries in the eighteenth century to Soviet technologists in the twentieth. The British political theorist Bernard Crick wrote the most cogent critique of this technologically determinist approach, while he was teaching at the London School of Economics in the early 1960s.[52] One of the greatest threats to politics, Crick wrote, came from those who sought to apply "scientific knowledge to the administration of society." "Technology holds that all the important problems facing humanity are technical, and that therefore they are all soluble on the basis of existing knowledge or readily attainable knowledge." If all you have is a hammer, Maslow's dictum states, everything looks like a nail. The technologist craves certainty and uses data as a way of distinguishing the right from the wrong answer. Though, as Crick points out, there are rarely right and wrong answers in politics; human life is far messier than that. The scientist wants to engineer this messiness from the system. Yet to remove it would be to remove discussion, to eliminate deliberation and to obviate dissent. All the messiness that makes politics, politics. To the engineer, "the whole state, then, is seen as a factory producing goods for society." Compare this to what Katie Stanton said about her time in the Obama government: "I feel like I'm a vegetarian trapped inside a sausage factory and it's kind of ugly on the inside."

Yet for all its promise of a healthier, brighter and happier life, the vision conjured up by twenty-first-century Silicon Valley technologists of the perfect tech city bears plenty of similarities to science fiction dystopias. *We*, a novel written in 1920 by Yevgeny Zamyatin, describes a twenty-sixth-century society, the United State, in which everything is based on logic, reason and openness. A 'table of hours' determines exactly where everybody should be at every hour of the day. Moral problems are resolved mathematically, by 'scientific ethics'. Residents are obliged to be healthy, to live in transparent glass-walled houses, and to have sex at a set time with the curtains closed. Nobody is *one*, in the United State, but '*one of*', and everyone enjoys 'a mathematically faultless happiness'. There is no freedom, but that is because freedom and happiness are believed to be incompatible. Behaviour is governed by the Bureau of Guardians, and the State overseen by the Well-Doer. "It is pleasant to feel that somebody's penetrating eye is watching you from behind your shoulder," the narrator – called D-503 – writes, "lovingly guarding you from making the most minute mistake." George Orwell came across *We* in 1946, shortly before writing *Nineteen Eighty-Four*. Though Zamyatin was Russian, Orwell did not believe the novel was directed at any particular country but rather at the aims of industrial civilization. "It is in effect a study of the Machine, the genie that man has thoughtlessly let out of its bottle and cannot put back again."[53] It is certainly not inevitable that democracies will go in the platform direction. Of those that do, some will shift faster than others. However, whatever the future of platform democracy, like the Machine, it cannot be put back in its bottle.

8

SURVEILLANCE DEMOCRACY

Pansophism: universal wisdom or knowledge or pretension thereto
Merriam-Webster Dictionary

Tembhli, a remote rural village in northern Maharashtra, about 250 miles north of Mumbai, is rarely visited by high-powered politicians or prominent dignitaries. But on Wednesday, 29 September 2010, it found itself hosting not just the Indian prime minister, Manmohan Singh, but the president of Congress, Sonia Gandhi; the chief and deputy chief ministers and the governor of Maharashtra; and the head of the recently established Unique Identification Authority of India, Nandan Nilekani. It was this last figure, the least well known of the distinguished group, who was the reason behind the visit, and who would subsequently play the most important role in its aftermath. Nilekani and the politicians were there to give out the first ten 'unique identifiers' to residents of Tembhli. These ten people received their own twelve-digit number, a number that would, from that day forward, distinguish each of them from every other Indian citizen, and indeed – combined with their biometric data – from every other citizen in the world. "With this," Sonia Gandhi said, "Tembhli has got a special importance in the map of India. People of Tembhli will lead the rest of the country. It is a historic step towards strengthening the people of our nation."[1]

Governments of all stripes are prone to exaggerated rhetoric, but in this instance, Gandhi was proved right when she proclaimed that "starting from this tiny hamlet, the scheme will reach more than a billion people of this country." Despite the change of government in 2014, by April 2016 a billion Indians had been allocated their unique identifier. By 2018 the number had exceeded 1.1 billion, out of a total population of just over 1.3 billion. It was, in the words of a Harvard Business School report, a "hugely ambitious project", "the largest-scale project of its kind in the world".[2] Aadhaar, as the project was called, was "unique in its scale and ambition".[3] Each Aadhaar identifier included not just a twelve-digit number, but all ten fingerprints, iris scans from both eyes, and a photograph of each person's face (with the potential for facial recognition later). By combining the number with one element of biometric data, the government believed, it could ensure that every Indian citizen had a single, verifiable, machine-readable identity. With this verifiable identity a citizen could open a bank account, receive welfare or pension payments, pay tax, apply for a driving licence, or receive healthcare, regardless of literacy. In a country known for its administrative torpor and tortuous bureaucracy, where – in 2013 – only forty per cent of children's births were even registered, such a scheme had the potential to let India leapfrog other democratic countries into the digital era, and make government not just digitally enabled but digitally empowered.

Yet this, for critics of the scheme, was one of its many flaws. "Aadhaar marks a fundamental shift in citizen–state relations," Pranesh Prakash from India's Centre for the Internet and Society wrote in the *Hindustan Times*, "from 'We the People' to 'We the Government'."[4] Civil society activists objected to the government's enhanced power, and the relative unaccountability of the body running Aadhaar, headed by Nandan Nilekani until 2014. "In effect," tech developer and activist Kiran Jonnalagadda wrote, "they are beyond the rule of law."[5] Others had practical objections.

Biometric identification often did not work. A database of this size and importance was bound to attract hackers. Leaks were inevitable. Indeed, the *Tribune* newspaper in January 2018 revealed that it had been able to buy a service, for 500 rupees (less than $10), that gave it access to any of up to one billion Aadhaar details.[6] Yet such objections were written off as 'scaremongering' and Aadhaar critics as "activists of the upper crust, upper class, wine 'n cheese, Netflix-watching social media elite".[7] On top of which, despite an Indian Supreme Court judgment in August 2017 that affirmed the fundamental right of Indians to privacy, by early 2018 Aadhaar had achieved such momentum as to appear unstoppable. If the government was able to navigate the various legislative challenges to the scheme, then there was also a queue of other nations keen to adopt something similar.

Modern states, both democratic and non-democratic, have been fascinated by the potential of citizen data since it first became possible to collect, store and use large quantities of it, from the early nineteenth century onwards. Knowing the citizen enhances the ability of the state to make rational judgements on their behalf, about where to build a road, how to improve hygiene, or how to ensure safety and security (not to mention how to tax). "Quantification", New York University anthropologist Sally Merry writes, has an "aura of objectivity".[8] Yet, prior to our digital era, states ran up against two obstacles in trying to gain anything more than basic knowledge about their citizens. The first was practical. Keeping track of people – even how many there were and where they lived – was fraught with complexity. Capturing more detailed information was even harder, even in political systems that championed close surveillance. After the establishment of the People's Republic of China in 1949, for example, Mao Zedong's communist government insisted that a secret dossier called a *dangan* be kept on each individual, which, in addition to basic information, catalogued their activities, their attitudes, and evaluations of their character. Yet this had to be abandoned as inoperable during the decade of the Cultural Revolution (it was subsequently reinstated for employees). In communist East Germany, Erich Honecker's government kept intimate files on anyone it considered suspicious, files that were constantly updated with reports from a huge network of government informers. The material in these files, the writer Timothy Garton Ash found when he studied his own, could be both fantastically banal and "chillingly accurate", but it was also, necessarily, erratic.[9] The second obstacle to state omniscience, from the perspective of democracy, is ideological. Intimate and unrestricted knowledge of the citizen by the state jeopardizes individual autonomy, compromises privacy, and gives authorities much greater power over their citizens.

Security and welfare prompted India's great Aadhaar experiment. A conflict in 1999 between India and Pakistan in Kashmir, in which a number of Pakistani soldiers were able to pose as Kashmiri militants, sparked the project's first phase – the development of a national population register and a multi-purpose identity card.[10] The next phase had to wait until 2008, when the coalition government became increasingly concerned about the 'leakage' of welfare payments – to false claimants and duplicate claims. But it was not until the appointment of Nandan Nilekani as chairman of the Unique Identification Authority of India in 2009 that it gained its twenty-first-century digital dimension. Nilekani is India's equivalent of Gates, Page, Brin or Bezos. Born in India's Silicon Valley, Bangalore, he co-founded the Indian software and digital services giant Infosys. Like his US West Coast counterparts he has a vision of the future, a vision in which technology plays a central part. After he stepped down as chief executive of Infosys in 2007 he wrote a book, *Imagining India*, in which he set out his dream for India's future. We "can use technology for governance", Nilekani said in a 2009 TED Talk he gave to promote his book. "We can use technology for direct benefits. We can use technology for transparency, and many other things."[11] But, also like his West Coast counterparts, Nilekani and his team were conscious that democratic governments were fickle, and that new initiatives often became politicized. To protect against this they proposed establishing Aadhaar as an independent organization outside the ambit of any particular ministry, and building the identification plan not simply as a database but as a platform. "When we designed the system," Nilekani told an audience at Harvard in 2014, "we designed this to be a platform."[12] What this meant in practice was that, from the start, it was designed as a basis on which government services – and, crucially, commercial services too – could build. *Aadhaar* means 'foundation' in Hindi, and that is what it was designed to be.

Despite Nilekani's efforts, his ambitious programme was almost scuppered by the first change of administration. Though used by the government for benefit transfers, Aadhaar had not yet taken off by the time politicians started campaigning for the 2014 election. Worse, a retired judge had launched a legal action against the scheme, saying it violated Indians' fundamental right to privacy. The leader of the BJP, Narendra Modi, was scathing about Aadhaar on the campaign trail. "It is a political gimmick with no vision," he said in April of that year. Yet after Modi swept to power at the election he met Nilekani and had a radical change of heart. Rather than close the programme he decided to expand it. He would use it as both a virtual and a rhetorical platform to fight endemic corruption in the Indian welfare system, and to turn India into a model for twenty-first-century digital government. In October 2014, Modi announced that he would use Aadhaar to help provide access to universal healthcare. The following year his government decided to link Aadhaar to the National Population Register (NPR), creating a 'mother database' from which departments could find fraudsters, identify migrants and reward genuine beneficiaries. Later that year Modi linked it to his scheme to ensure all Indians have access to financial services.

From the government's perspective, the great thing about the Aadhaar platform was how it could streamline government, just as Nilekani had intended. There was no need for all that arduous form-filling. All the bureaucracy that existed simply to distribute welfare and administer state services could be reduced to a central core. And everything could be tracked. It was not surprising, therefore, that government by Aadhaar was accelerating, with more and more services being linked to the unique identity. And though technically the scheme was voluntary, it was becoming increasingly difficult to function in India without it. By mid-2017 you needed Aadhaar to open a bank account, to access your pension, to pay your taxes, to get a mobile phone number, to apply for a passport, to register your marriage, to apply for a scholarship, to book a train journey. From July 2017 children in state schools could not get their lunch without Aadhaar (yes, it was for children as well as grown-ups). Internet platform firms saw the potential of linking to it too. Amazon started asking people to key in their Aadhaar number to trace lost packages. Facebook encouraged people to use Aadhaar to confirm their real world identity. Microsoft launched Skype Lite, integrating Aadhaar so that interviewers could verify the identity of interviewees.[13]

Aadhaar was moving at such a pace that it did not even have legislative backing until 2016, when the government rushed an Aadhaar Bill through Parliament as a money bill, avoiding the upper house. Nor had the courts decided whether the scheme breached Indians' fundamental right to privacy. The Supreme Court did not rule on this until 2017. Yet, as Facebook had discovered to its cost, virtual platforms do not magically solve all the practical problems of the physical world, and can make them worse.

*

As the government pushed Aadhaar towards every interaction the state had with the citizen, evidence mounted of failures in the system.

In the north-eastern state of Jharkhand, an eleven-year-old girl died of starvation after her family stopped receiving their government food ration. Their ration card, the Hindu Centre for Politics and Public Policy reported, "was not linked to Aadhaar".[14] The centre also reported on data, taken from the government's websites, showing that in Rajasthan, where receiving rations was dependent on Aadhaar authentication, between a quarter and a third of people with ration cards did not receive rations between September 2016 and July 2017. In some ration shops, after having spent hours trying and failing to get their fingerprints read by the biometric machines, people lost their temper and smashed the machines on the ground.[15]

Across India there were reports of machines not recognizing fingerprints, or only recognizing them after multiple attempts. Old people's prints turned out to be more difficult to read, as were those of manual workers and fishermen. Since the system presumes guilt rather than innocence, the burden of proof lies with the citizen, not with the state. To claim a ration, apply for a scholarship or buy a train ticket, you have to prove who you are before receiving it. The obligation lies with the citizen to prove she is not a fraud. Even if she is not, and the failure is not with her but with the system, she pays for the system's failure, not the government. To dispute a decision made by the machine means going to the nearest large town – often many miles away – and convincing an official that the problem is with the machine or the digital record, not with you. It is not surprising that some people wrecked Aadhaar machines in their rage.

While the system was found to reduce agency in citizens, it empowered those in positions of authority. Central government was able to make public services conditional on authentication by Aadhaar (despite repeated court rulings that Aadhaar be voluntary, not mandatory). This conditionality could then be extended to the level and type of public services available to individuals. In fact, it had to be for many services – distinguishing pensioners from non–pensioners, for example. Yet in this conditionality, there is plenty of scope for harm and abuse. In 2017 the independent media site *Scroll.in* reported a rising number of HIV-positive patients who were dropping out of treatment programmes because they were required to use their Aadhaar numbers and were fearful of their condition becoming public.[16]

Equally, while Aadhaar itself did not provide any information about caste, ethnicity, religion or language, once it was linked to other databases, most notably the National Population Register, then it became possible to identify people by group. Formal group identification by the state has an ignominious history. During the apartheid era in South Africa, the penultimate number on the South African identity card indicated race. In the Rwandan genocide in 1994, anyone who had 'Tutsi' on their identification was liable to be killed. In Nazi Germany in 1938, every Jewish citizen had 'J' stamped on their ID cards and passports. In India, where political and reli-gious divisions are closely intertwined, there is good reason to be anxious about new opportunities for group identification.

Thanks to Aadhaar, companies started to build services using unique identification. A series of 'trust platforms' emerged, built on top of Aadhaar, where employers – and others – could access and authenticate people's identity. A company called TrustID advertised itself as "India's first, unique and comprehensive online verification platform". Through TrustID an employer could check whether a potential employee had any criminal or civil convictions, or whether that person had a good or bad reputation (based on a news search and social media profiling). The company even encouraged women to check up on potential husbands they had found via marriage websites.[17] Other international companies integrated Aadhaar into existing services. This is similar to the way in which companies work with platforms like Facebook to profile, and target, individuals based on their personal information – except in this instance doing it via the government. All the same questions about trust, privacy, freedom and power arise, with even greater political potency. The state and private companies are in partnership to track citizens constantly and to gather as much data as they can on them – data that they can then use for commercial or political purposes. This opaque, asymmetrical knowledge of the citizen seems like the reverse of what was intended by democratic transparency, especially in the absence of strong privacy and data protection. "Totalitarian states often do this against the wishes of their citizens," Pratap Bhanu Mehta, the president of the Centre for Policy Research, writes, yet "in our democracy, our consent is being mobilized to put an imprimatur over more control and arbitrariness."[18]

In August 2017, the Supreme Court of India came to a unanimous 9–0 decision that Article 21 of the Indian Constitution did guarantee a fundamental right to privacy. As such, it was not lawful for the government to make it mandatory for people to identify themselves using a unique identifier like Aadhaar, except in specific circumstances. To some this looked like a huge blow to the grand project. The Supreme Court decision "raises serious questions about Aadhaar", lawyer Adarsh Ramanujan argued in India's *Financial Express*, and appeared to send "a direction to the central government to create a regime to ensure that privacy rights are not trammelled by other private parties".[19] The judgment was about privacy broadly, and did not refer to specific cases like Aadhaar, but was seen as the basis from which future challenges to the scheme could be launched. The Modi government, however, appeared to carry on regardless. In October it linked Aadhaar to driving licence applications. By mid-December, the government had made Aadhaar mandatory if citizens wanted to access any of 140 government services.[20]

Nandan Nilekani, who had stepped down as chair of Aadhaar in 2014 in order to become a candidate for the Congress party, railed against those who criticized the scheme. There was, he claimed, an "orchestrated campaign" to malign the system.[21] "I think this so-called anti-Aadhaar lobby is really just a small bunch of liberal elites who are in some echo chamber," he told an Indian business news channel.[22] Anyway, Nilekani argued, it was too late for the naysayers to stop it. Too many people were now enrolled. It was too integral to the provision of services. Others saw attacks on Aadhaar as political, arguing that Congress was using it for political gain prior to the 2019 election, and that this would backfire. "Aadhaar today is not just a number," the editor of India's *Economic Times* wrote. "The Congress envisaged it as a means of identity but the Modi government has taken it to a different level. It has become a weapon in the hands of the poor and a powerful tool to fight entrenched black money interests. It is now a symbol of anti-corruption, anti-black money drives, a symbol of efficient allocation of welfare benefits."[23]

*

While virtual identities, government tracking and the limits of privacy were becoming increasingly conflicted political issues in India, two thousand miles to the south-east there was a country where citizens seemed to embrace surveillance as the route to the future. Since Singapore's prime minister, Lee Hsien Loong, set out his vision of Singapore as the first truly 'smart nation' in November 2014, the country had been racing to connect everything. "We should see it [smartness] in our daily living," the prime minister said, "where networks of sensors and smart devices enable us to live sustainably and comfortably." These sensors – wires buried beneath roads and within buildings, cameras on street corners, GPS devices on buses, trains and taxis – read and record everything from traffic movement to environmental conditions to crowd density. The government calls it E3A – 'Everyone, Everything, Everywhere, All the Time'.[24] By 2020 every car in Singapore has to have a built-in GPS that communicates location and speed not just to the driver but to the authorities. This way the authorities can reduce congestion, alert people to parking spaces, and even charge them automatically for the space. If drivers ignore the advice, they can be penalized. As *Computerworld* reported, "Drivers will be dinged financially if they don't heed the advice, and be rewarded if they do."[25]

Yet virtual interconnectedness in Singapore is going far beyond traffic and commuting. As more than eighty per cent of Singapore residents live in government-owned property (under temporary leaseholds) the government is able to connect homes up too. The minister in charge of the Smart Nation programme – Dr Vivian Balakrishnan – described how, on one housing estate that is already sensored up, this means that, in "partnership with private companies, authorities are able to measure energy draw, waste production and water usage in real time".[26] In layman's terms this translates to the local authority knowing when you have just flushed the toilet. For vulnerable people, particularly the elderly, motion sensors capture their movements in the home and text their family where they are and when ("Your mum is in the kitchen").[27] And the Singaporean government is already ahead of Google and Apple when it comes to digital healthcare. Physiotherapy patients can stick on body sensors and film themselves doing exercises. A specialist can then look at the data and check how they did.[28] The plan even borrows terms more suited to Silicon Valley start-ups – talking about the nation becoming a 'living laboratory' for smart approaches to life. Presumably, this means Singaporean citizens are the living lab rats. Just like Nandan Nilekani's Aadhaar in India, the Singaporean government is developing its Smart Nation as a platform, so that separate public services, and private corporations, can build on top of it. Healthcare companies can build for-profit physiotherapy apps, and car insurance companies can build on the GPS data, all of them benefiting from smart tracking and citizen surveillance.

Politically, the plan is pitched as fundamental to the nation's future well-being. "Smart Nation is for all of us, young and old," the prime minister said at the 2017 National Day Rally.[29] It is also seen, within government at least, as essential to the country's survival. In an influential 2014 essay in *Foreign Policy*, Shane Harris attributes Singapore's decision to invest heavily in big-data surveillance to the terrorist attack in Bali in 2002 and to the outbreak of SARS in 2003. The respiratory disease, as well as killing thirty-three people and leading to an economic slowdown and the temporary closure of all schools, re-emphasized the island's vulnerability to unexpected crises and attacks. Surveillance technology and big data were seen as a way both to better anticipate future shocks and to respond more effectively. As a consequence, Singapore became a "laboratory not only for testing how mass surveillance and big-data analysis might prevent terrorism, but for determining whether technology can be used to engineer a more harmonious society".[30] The surveillance and Smart Nation programme builds on five decades of Singapore's history as a managed society. Since it gained independence in 1965, and given its small size and lack of natural resources, Singapore's government has been highly strategic in using the assets it has to maintain its economy and autonomy. This means, primarily, its location and its five and a half million inhabitants. Yet despite its particular aptitude for big-data surveillance, its Smart Nation programme is being closely observed by many other governments and policy makers as a potential model to imitate. If not entire nations, then it could certainly show other cities how they might become more environmentally sustainable, more economically efficient, more technologically interconnected and more socially ordered.

However, even if Singapore is successful in creating the first truly digital nation, it will do so at the cost of any vestige of democratic politics. This is an initiative designed, delivered and dictated by the government, a technocratic government of engineers (Google would approve). Singapore has "a society with a leadership that embraces the engineering ethos", Vivian Balakrishnan has said.

"Almost half of our cabinet consists of engineers. Our Prime Minister is a mathematician. He studied computer science almost four decades ago in Cambridge, and he can still code. In other words, we get it."[31] It is not a programme that provides much room for dissent. Ostensibly, Singapore is a representative democracy, though de facto it has become a one-party state. The same party has been in power since independence in 1965. The various means of open public discussion and opposition have been systematically and efficiently cut off. In 2017 Singapore lay at number 151 in the World Press Freedom Index, below Russia and Mexico. Since 2013, any website with over fifty thousand unique viewers each month has had to apply for a licence (at a cost of US$40,000) – which can be refused or revoked if the government objects to its content.[32] Should a publication or journalist publish anything considered to be of a "seditious tendency" – such as "to excite disaffection against the government" – they are liable for prosecution under the Sedition Act, and up to three years in prison, more for a second offence. Civil protest and peaceful assembly have become almost impossible. Any 'cause-related' – political – assembly requires a police permit, and these are regularly rejected. "The definition of what is treated as an assembly", Human Rights Watch reported, "is extremely broad, and includes one person acting alone."[33] The political environment, the civil rights organization writes, "is stifling".

Since there is no constitutional right to privacy protection for citizens, there is nothing to stop the authorities using all the personal data they gather for greater social monitoring and control. According to the US State Department this is exactly what they do. Security and law enforcement agencies, the State Department reports, have "extensive networks for gathering information and conducting surveillance and highly sophisticated capabilities to monitor telephone, e-mail, text messaging, or other digital communications intended to remain private". They do not even need to get a warrant. This surveillance extends to personal posts on social media. Li Shengwu, the prime minister's nephew, was taken to court in 2017 for a Facebook post in which he wrote that "the Singapore Government is very litigious and has a pliant court system."[34] By contrast, Singapore does have strong data protection legislation, though this fits with the government's commitment to encourage business and protect against fraud, rather than with any concern for citizens' privacy.

The majority of Singaporean citizens do not seem to be unhappy with their political situation. Citizens voted the ruling party back into office in 2015 (with eighty-three of eighty-nine seats and seventy per cent of the vote). The country has enjoyed extraordinary economic success, with average incomes per head of over \$50,000.[35] It is increasingly interconnected, data-rich and data-driven. Yet the cost of this has been political freedom, personal privacy and individual agency. The citizens have become depoliticized. Should you object to limits on what you can do – sexual relations between men, for example, are illegal in Singapore – then you have virtually no avenue through which to voice your dissent or to press for change. Become too vocal and you will face a fine or imprisonment. Interconnectedness, personal data and 'smartness' are enabling and enhancing constraints on citizens' rights and depoliticization. The Enlightenment philosopher Immanuel Kant wrote that happiness was not an adequate basis for a state, and any government that tried to govern on this basis would necessarily become autocratic. "Nobody can coerce me to be happy," Kant wrote, since happiness is subjective. "A government that was erected on the principle of benevolence towards the people, as a father's towards his children ... [would be] the worst conceivable despotism."[36]

Not everyone in Singapore is pleased with the direction the city state is taking. In mid-2017, in a highly unusual public display of discord, the prime minister's brother and sister announced they were leaving the island indefinitely because they felt threatened by their brother's "misuse of his position" to pursue a personal agenda.

Surveillance and the constant oversight by the state were, they said, central to their decision to leave. "We feel Big Brother omnipresent," they wrote. "We fear the use of the organs of state against us." Yet, by contrast, the prime minister himself believed Singapore was not moving fast enough. It did not yet have a biometric ID scheme, and there were not enough e-payments being made via mobile phones. Lee Hsien Loong looked enviously across at China, where the platform revolution was moving at breathtaking speed. "China has gone the furthest with e-payments," Lee told the audience at his 2017 National Day address:

> Indeed, in major Chinese cities, cash has become obsolete. Even debit and credit cards are becoming rare. Everyone is using WeChat Pay or Alipay and these apps are linked to your bank account . . . You can buy snacks from a roadside stall . . . You can pay for a taxi ride. You can even tip the waiter at a restaurant. So when visitors from China find that they have to use cash here, they ask: how can Singapore be so backward?

Nor was it just about electronic payments; China was leading the development of artificial intelligence, facial recognition, e-commerce and digital healthcare.

This was a long way from where China started its relationship with the World Wide Web. Back in the 1990s, when there was a comfortable consensus that no government could control the internet, and when John Perry Barlow could declare that "Governments of the Industrial World" had "no sovereignty" in cyberspace, the Chinese government was amongst those most anxious about the threat it posed to its political system. It became more worried still after the wave of protest and revolutions spread through North Africa and the Middle East during 2011. Like Vladimir Putin, Chinese leaders saw protestors carrying signs thanking Facebook, and heard the claims of Hillary Clinton and others about the inherently democratizing effects of the internet, and believed their own government could be next. Yet, towards the end of the second decade of the twenty-first century, the Chinese government realized that, if a state has the will – and is willing to harness the power of commercial partners – then not only can it tame the web domestically, it can use it to enhance authoritarianism and autocracy. Indeed, it gives a state the potential to create a more centralized and controlled society than the world has ever known. There are many aspects to this control, and none of them are yet complete, but over two decades the Chinese government has built up an arsenal that would make any twentieth-century totalitarian state extremely jealous.

*

When delegates arrived for the 19th National Communist Party Congress in Beijing in October 2017, censorship of public communication about the event had already been going for over a year. On WeChat, the Chinese messaging app with almost a billion users, people were unable to talk about the Congress, or about those who were speaking there, or about the issues they were planning to discuss. It was not that they could not write 'Belt and Road Initiative' or 'leaked information', but if they sent a message containing those phrases, it would never reach the intended recipient. It would just disappear.

We know this thanks to research done prior to and during the Congress by Toronto University's Citizen Lab. Researchers sent messages to different phones – some registered in China and some not – and watched what made it through and what did not.[37] This way they could see what was actually missing. We do not know exactly who blocks the keywords and phrases, though every internet communications company in China employs its own cadre of censors in order to comply with strict government guidelines. Harvard

China specialists Gary King, Jennifer Pan and Margaret Roberts estimated that, in 2013, each internet content provider "employ[ed] up to 1,000 censors", and that this was boosted by between 20,000 and 50,000 internet police or *wang jing*.[38] These are all part of the Great Shield, a domestic surveillance programme started in 1998, two years after John Perry Barlow's Declaration of the Independence of Cyberspace. Unlike its less sophisticated twentieth-century counterparts, however, the Chinese programme does not aim to censor all political discussion. Criticisms of local politicians, allegations of low-level corruption, and general grumbles about political issues are seen as helpful to the Party (which is recording them all).[39] However, criticism of Party leaders or any sign of coordinated political action will trigger censorship and police action. The Great Shield is complemented by the Great Firewall, which prevents those in China from accessing many international websites and services (including Facebook, YouTube and the *New York Times*).

Sometimes, during big political events like the removal of presidential term limits, censorship is not enough, especially if masses of people are sending and publishing posts. For this reason, the Chinese government also uses what has been called the '50 Cent Party' (due to an early belief that they were paid fifty cents per post) to deluge social media with positive comments, and to distract people from contentious political news. Gary King and his colleagues have calculated that the Chinese government, and those working on its behalf, "fabricates and posts about 448 million social media comments a year".[40] The government's overall approach to control of digital communication has been described by Margaret Roberts as "fear, friction and flood".[41] Instil fear, by picking on a few high-profile campaigners or protestors and making an example of them, as a warning to others. Create friction, by making it awkward and difficult to access censored material or to discover what really happened – for example by using a virtual private network (VPN) to read foreign sites. And flood, by generating a torrent of adulatory and irrelevant posts around political events in order to steer people away from criticism or controversy.

Central to the success of the Chinese government's approach has been the enrolment of commercial internet companies to its cause. It does this with both stick and carrot. Internet companies have to impose censorship, monitor and inform on their users, and limit their users' ability to access 'incorrect ideas'. Even foreign internet platforms in China have to abide by the same rules. In 2017 Apple agreed to remove over six hundred VPN apps from its app store in China, so that people within the country could not use them to reach international sites. In early 2018, it handed control of its cloud services in China to a local corporation, giving the Chinese government access to the data in Apple's cloud in China.[42] Some of the largest Chinese internet companies have willingly and enthusiastically collaborated with the government, knowing that their future prosperity may well depend upon it. Alibaba, China's Amazon, has partnered with Chinese local government in healthcare, for example, using blockchains to secure patient data, through its healthcare platform, Ali Health.[43] Baidu, China's Google, is working with China's airport security to use facial recognition software to identify airline crew and, in future, passengers.[44] There is even a police station on Alibaba's campus, so that employees can report possible crimes directly to the police and give the police access to personal data for their investigations.[45]

Two of China's largest internet companies have gone further still and are helping the government create the largest state surveillance and social control experiment ever attempted – the already notorious Social Credit System. This scheme's "inherent requirements", the government set out in its original proposal in 2014, "are establishing the idea of a sincerity culture, and carrying forward sincerity and traditional virtues". To do this, it will use "encouragement to keep trust and constraints against breaking trust as incentive mechanisms". The aim, the government said, was to raise "the honest mentality and credit levels of the entire society".[46] Having set out its aim, the government decided to let commercial companies figure out how to put the scheme into practice – to see how it might work before the government took over and, if successful, make it mandatory in 2020. Alibaba, through its financial arm, Ant Financial, launched the first initiative, called Sesame Credit, in 2015. Tencent, which owns WeChat and instant messaging service QQ, launched a similar initiative in early 2018, though this was quickly withdrawn for further development at the request of the government.[47]

Ostensibly, the Social Credit System is a financial credit scheme for a country which has never had an equivalent to credit scores like those in the US. Yet, in practice, the scheme gives each citizen a running score, on a scale between 350 and 950, of how obedient and well behaved they are. As Rachel Botsman, who describes the scheme in her book *Who Can You Trust?*, writes, "Sesame Credit is basically a 'big data' gamified version of the Communist Party's surveillance methods." Scores are calculated based on everything from what you buy to how you spend your time and who your friends are – all of which is recorded thanks to the ubiquity of the Alibaba platform and its mobile-phone payment service, Alipay. Your score then has both virtual and real-world consequences. Mara Hvistendahl, who lived in China for a decade and went back for a visit in 2017, discovered that Sesame Credit scores already spanned huge areas of public life.[48] Securing a loan, renting an apartment, hiring a bike, booking a flight, finding a hotel room, could all be affected by your score. If you have a low score, or worse, are on the 'List of Dishonest People', then you become a member of the digital underclass. Escaping from this underclass, like improving a bad financial credit score, can be painful and arduous – and made worse if your friends desert you for fear of harming their own scores. These companies, and by extension the Chinese government, can do this because Chinese citizens' digital lives are – as for most of us – becoming synonymous with their real lives.

China's Great Firewall, its Great Shield, its 50 Cent Party and its nascent Social Credit System, are all justified in the pursuit of social stability and so that the Communist Party can maintain rule. They have led to a vast expansion in the powers of the state and, by extension, those of some of the large commercial platforms like Alibaba and Tencent. They have also enrolled the Chinese people in their programme of digital social control, creating not just paranoid citizens – who must now worry constantly about their social credit – but a nation of watchers and informers, all consciously or unconsciously observing and recording one another through their digitally enabled daily lives. The opportunities for dissent in China, already scarce, are becoming virtually non-existent. Except where this dissent or disapproval is state sanctioned – reporting on misbehaviour or misconduct for example. Reading the proposal for the Social Credit System, it appears that the Chinese state sees citizens almost as rats in a Skinner box, who – thanks to its new digital levers – it can direct and control through operant conditioning. The state will "launch mass activities for moral judgment, conduct analysis and evaluation of instances where there was a lack of sincerity and credit was not stressed, and guide people towards sincerity and trust-keeping, morality and upholding courtesy". Singapore is not at the same stage as China, but admires China's technological leadership, and is en route to total information awareness. In India, while democratic politics remains open, robust and highly contested, with Aadhaar the means has been created by which the state can amass much greater political and social control over its citizens.

*

In New Delhi in January 2018, India's prime minister, Narendra Modi, met with the leader of the Philippines, Rodrigo Duterte. At the meeting they discussed, amongst other things, the potential of taking Aadhaar to the Philippines. Duterte appeared keen to import the system to help him "fight corruption", and Modi "assured the Philippine President of all possible assistance in rolling out unique identification numbers for citizens of the Southeast Asian nation".[49] In addition to the Philippines, twenty other countries were reported to be interested in Aadhaar.[50] Indonesia, Malaysia, Sri Lanka and Singapore were all exploring whether Aadhaar would work domestically.[51] Thailand introduced biometric checks for mobile banking and, from December 2017, required them for mobile phone SIM cards. "This is not aimed at tracking users," the regulator said, "but enhancing security, especially in case of mobile payments."[52] These moves towards unique digital identification and platform governance are, in part, defensive. These countries are worried that if they do not take control of citizens' data then transnational tech platforms will. At the same time, they cannot help but see it as a great way to improve government efficiency and drag citizens into the digital economy. They do not make explicit whether they are also keen on enhancing the power of the state.

Singapore wins international prizes and accolades for its 'smart city' innovations. It won three awards at *Le Monde*'s SmartCities 2017, including for the 'ultimate public transport system'.[53] There has even been a Lee Kuan Yew World City Prize since 2010, to "facilitate the sharing of best practices in urban solutions that are easily replicable across cities".[54] While not every city is taking the same approach as Singapore, there is a growing consensus that the smart city is the future, and that Singapore is a leading smart city, from which many others are learning. Media coverage of its Smart Nation initiative is invariably wide-eyed, positive and uncritical. A BBC report from 2017 focused on the efficiency and convenience of the technology and its potential for saving lives. The only criticism referenced in the report was that the project "needed to speed up".[55] Those that do critique Singapore's direction focus on the threat to personal privacy. "Singapore's 'city brain' project is ground-breaking – but what about privacy?" is typical. And privacy is clearly threatened – if not abolished – by the project, especially in its ultimate form. But few talk about the power it will give to the Singaporean state. Once Singapore has a data-friendly biometric identity scheme like Aadhaar, hooked up to its ubiquitous city and home sensors, then the state can know everything that its citizens are doing, all the time. Like a pansophist god. The distinction that Aristotle originally made, between the public sphere of political activity, and the private sphere of the home, will be extinguished.

Reimagining the state as a digital platform represents an even greater threat to liberal democracy than imagining commercial tech platforms like Google and Amazon taking over the functions of the state – especially if the state as platform collaborates closely with commercial entities, as it does in China with companies like Alibaba and Tencent. Once the state's primary relationship with its citizens is through its digital platform, then its executive powers will be immeasurably enhanced, and those of the citizen – particularly as regards their autonomy and agency – diminished. The datafied citizen, just like the datafied child, can be told what they can and cannot do, where they can and cannot go, what they can and cannot have. They can be nudged, prodded, incentivized and gamified. Power over digital identity gives government height-ened control – or a heightened sense of control – over its citizens: over their movements, over the welfare they receive, over the services they can access, and over their rights. This enhanced executive power can be used positively, to distribute welfare more widely, to ensure universal healthcare, to provide access to credit. Equally, the power can be abused: to deny access, to suppress dissent, to segregate groups. Either way, power is more centralized, more operable and more opaque.

Once the state has defined and datafied its citizens, this enables and encourages official discrimination, and a harsh and unforgiving meritocracy. Pity those to whom the state accords limited rights, or no rights at all. Immigrants and other non-citizens are liable to suffer most in the datafied state, lacking any data history, any earned reputation or any social credit. They will be unpersons. Yet even those who do have richer digital identities will be subject to official discrimination. Authorities will discriminate on the basis of data histories – those who have committed a crime in the past will be more liable to police attention; those with a chequered driving licence will be stopped more often; those with a poor credit record will find it harder to get loans. The discrimination will be justified, the authorities will argue, because it is based on data. Indeed, they may have no choice but to discriminate if the algorithm tells them to. Yet, as well as pre-supposing that our pasts define our futures, this datafication of citizens will solidify existing inequalities. It will lead to "a particularly cruel form of inequality", in the words of sociologist Ralf Dahrendorf, since it will be that much harder to free yourself.[56] There will also be data-driven injustice. The Indian journal *Scroll* has been reporting a series of just these types of injustice in its Identity Project. One tells the story of Santosh Devi, a goatherd with two young children in Rajasthan, whose Aadhaar card was accidentally associated with the wrong name. The local authorities said they were unable to change it, meaning that though her family is below the poverty line, she cannot buy subsidized grain, and is unable to properly feed her children.[57]

The digitally tracked citizen will not be as free to protest, oppose or dissent as her analogue ancestor. In some countries, like Singapore and China, opposition and dissent are already highly circumscribed and will become both legally and socially unacceptable if social credit systems take hold. In more democratic countries, as people become more aware that authorities and private companies are constantly gathering personal information and adding it to their profile, and that this profile will determine their prospects, then many will temper their activities accordingly.

If they think their political activities are being monitored and recorded, this will affect their behaviour too. During protests in the Ukraine in 2014, for example, protestors in Kiev were sent a text message from authorities: "Dear subscriber," it read, "you are registered as a participant in a mass riot." We know who you are, and will be watching you, the authorities were telling marchers.

Once all citizens and services are digitally linked and centralized, there will be fewer checks and balances on the executive. The careful separation of powers, which the philosopher Montesquieu thought were essential for protection against despotism, which the framers of the US Constitution spent so long discussing and perfecting, are compromised and jeopardized by the centralization of citizen data in the state. The use of citizen data to make predictions, as with predictive policing, compromises the power of the judiciary to limit executive authority and law enforcement. Politics becomes frozen by automation and algorithms. Or as scholars Jathan Sadowski and Frank Pasquale write of society in smart cities, "The *body* politic mummifies into a very different type of social organization: a leviathan *machine*."[58] Nor are journalists capable of keeping the state accountable. Surveillance democracy makes it impossible for them to offer their sources anonymity or protection.

At the end of 2016, the *Times of India* went back to Tembhli and spoke to Ranjana Sonawane, the first person to receive an Aadhaar number back in September 2010. The paper asked Sonawane how her new digital identity, and access to cashless banking, had helped her since then. "I am finding it difficult to survive," she said. "I feel all governments use the poor just for politics and actually work for the rich. Getting daily work has become difficult because farmers say they are not getting cash from banks and cannot give us work. I wanted to go to the Sarangkheda fair to set up a toy shop there, but couldn't because I have no money to travel."[59] In Tembhli, the unique ID scheme had not even made life simpler or more affluent, never mind what it was doing to democracy.

9

DEMOCRACY REHACKED

On a huge hill,
Cragged and steep, Truth stands, and he that will
Reach her, about must and about must go

John Donne, *Satire III*

Only the cockiest of politicians would travel to Athens, to the spot where democracy was invented, to relaunch European democracy. Emmanuel Macron was nothing if not cocky. Yet not only did the freshly elected French president choose Athens, he chose to give his speech outside, in the evening, with the spectacularly lit Acropolis in the background. It was here, Macron told his audience in September 2017, "that the risk of democracy was taken, the risk that puts the government of the people into the hands of the people in the belief that respectable law is better decided by as many as possible and not as few". We, Macron continued, "should ask ourselves: what have we done with our democracy?"[1] Having accused his fellow Europeans of letting democracy wither, the president challenged them to "rediscover the meaning of sovereignty, democracy and culture". To jog their memory, Macron pointed to the legacy of Pericles – the "first citizen of Athens", namechecked André Malraux, the revered French author of *La Condition Humaine*, and gave a nod to the great German philosopher Hegel. Few politicians could get away with such lofty rhetoric, but Macron was seen by many – himself included – as the potential saviour of liberal democracy after the convulsions of the previous few years. He would soon bring forward a "roadmap to build the future of our Europe over the next decade". Citizens would be central to this democratic renewal, integrated into the process of reform through a whole series of 'democratic conventions'. For the many people who were worried about politics' authoritarian turn and were desperate for a new narrative, Macron offered hope.

Six months later, when Macron came forward with these plans for democratic renewal, reformists were desperately disappointed. David Van Reybrouck, the Belgian author of *Against Elections: The Case for Democracy*, and Claudia Chwalisz, author of *The People's Verdict*, together condemned the plans as "archaic, elitist and out-of-touch with the latest developments in democratic innovation". They would, the pair wrote, essentially "amount to Guy Verhofstadt and Daniel Cohn-Bendit philosophizing with Jacques Delors over a glass of cognac on what Europeans want".[2] What Macron had proposed that had so disillusioned these and other reformists was essentially an online questionnaire coupled with a collection of local, town hall meetings. Renamed 'citizen's consultations', rather than the more ambitious-sounding 'democratic conventions', the findings from the questionnaire and meetings would be fed back to Brussels, where they would be digested and considered. The whole process, whose new structure meant it would inevitably be dominated by a distinctly unrepresentative group of people – would be purely advisory, not binding.

Still, at least Emmanuel Macron acknowledged the scale of the challenge, even if his vision for democratic renewal lacked substance and he fluffed its execution. Other democratic leaders either failed to recognize the extent of the crisis or were too distracted by internal divisions to think about reform. In Britain, Prime Minister Theresa May was frantically trying to figure out what Brexit meant, while papering over widening rifts within her own party. In the US, government officials and Congress could not work out what Donald Trump would do that day, let alone over the next year. In Germany, Italy and Spain, mainstream political parties were collapsing and new populist alternatives pushing their way into power.

These and other democratic governments were ignoring mounting evidence of rising disenchantment with the way in which politics was done and how democracy worked. They were discounting, for one, repeated surveys showing high levels of public discontent. "Publics around the globe", the Pew Research Center found in a global review of public attitudes in 2017, "are generally unhappy with the functioning of their nations' political systems", and this general unhappiness included many living within democracies.[3] Over half of Americans said they were unhappy with their democracy, as did a majority in southern Europe, the Middle East and Latin America. Even more startling was the degree of democratic dissatisfaction amongst young people. Research by Yascha Mounk, who lectures on political theory at Harvard, and Roberto Stefan Foa, from Melbourne University, found that across mature democracies, young people were far less likely to believe that it was essential to live in a democracy, and were more open to authoritarian forms of government. In the US, Britain, the Netherlands, Australia and New Zealand, four in ten millennials or fewer said they were committed to living in a democracy – a much lower proportion than the generations before them. This scepticism about democracy extended, Foa and Mounk's research found, to liberal institutions – with citizens "growing more disaffected with established political parties, representative institutions, and minority rights". Accompanying this disaffection was an increasing desire across many countries for a strong leader "who does not need to bother with elections".[4]

Democratic governments had also, for the most part, ignored the demands of waves of protestors across the globe between 2011 and 2013, who were incensed at what they called 'actually existing democracy'. Occupy protestors in hundreds of cities across scores of countries railed against the corruption and perversion of democratic politics by financial elites and the political class. Paolo Gerbaudo, a political sociologist at King's College London, attended protests in the US, Spain, Egypt, Greece and elsewhere and spoke to many participants. Their aim was not, Gerbaudo found, to overturn democracy, but to reclaim it. "They call it democracy but it is not" was one of the slogans he saw in Spain. "Democracy, where are you?" read a banner in Paris's Place de la Republique.[5] As the leading scholar of the networked society, Manuel Castells, wrote of these movements, they "do not object to the principle of representative democracy, but denounce the practice of democracy as it is today".[6] This is why protestors experimented with alternative ways in which to involve people in political deliberation and come to collective decisions. Some of these might best be described as unconventional, like the repeat-after-me human microphone. Others harked back to models first tried in ancient Athens, while yet others piggybacked off the latest tech. The Occupy protests eventually petered out, but not because democratic governments decided to institute radical reform, and much of the anger and frustration remained latent, some of it being channelled towards new parties or populist causes.

The public's growing disillusionment with democracy was presaged and mirrored by a rising collection of intellectual critiques and calls for radical reform. What we are witnessing, professor of political theory Simon Tormey wrote in 2015, is 'The End of Representative Politics', where people are bypassing and subverting established structures and conventions, and opting instead for the immediate or 'subterranean' politics of Twitter storms, flash mobs, cyber-protests, 'buy-cotts' and direct action.[7] People do not wait for elections, they act. John Keane, an Australian scholar who has traced the travails of democracy from the sixth century BC through to the twenty-first AD, believes that the "decline of representative politics has been coming for a generation".[8] For David Van Reybrouck, the Belgian writer and historian who was so disheartened by Emmanuel Macron's proposals for EU reform, democracies have become unhealthily fixated on elections. "Free and fair elections", he writes, have "become an Ikea kit for democracy – to be assembled by the recipient, with or without the help of the instructions enclosed".[9] They should be junked and instead, he suggests, we should return to the central principle of Athenian democracy, drafting by lot or 'sortition'.

While some applaud the shift away from conventional political expression towards the politics of the street, for others this shift justifies going the other way, and investing more power in the authority of experts. Jason Brennan, a political scientist at Georgetown University, proposes the revival of epistocracy, or rule by political experts.[10] While scholars argue heatedly about the state of politics, and even more vociferously about what could or should come next, there is a growing consensus that democracy is at a critical juncture, an inflexion point, an existential crisis. As the eminent late Polish philosopher Zygmunt Bauman told *El País* in 2016: "We could describe what is going on at the moment as a crisis of democracy . . . People no longer believe in the democratic system because it doesn't keep its promises."[11]

To be fair, some of those in positions of authority were themselves despondent at democratic dysfunctionalism and urged political reform. In Britain the former leader of the Liberal Democrats, Nick Clegg, made his party's participation in the 2010 coalition government conditional on a referendum on voting reform (which he lost). At the European Parliament, Guy Verhofstadt, ex-prime minister of Belgium, pressed for reform of the EU and for a more federal Europe, similar to the United States, though even these efforts were frequently written off as self-interested or technocratic. For the most part, finding a successful politician who wanted root and branch reform was as rare as finding a truffle in the desert. Rather than expand participative democracy in Europe after the end of the Cold War, the author and journalist Edward Luce argued, those in power made a conscious effort to manage and control the masses. "Oikophobia is real," Luce wrote in his perceptive 2017 book, *The Retreat of Western Liberalism*. "The feelings of the elites have become progressively more sceptical of democracy since the fall of the Berlin Wall." It took Brexit and Trump, and subsequent electoral shocks, to provoke much wider reflection and reassessment of whether democracy was functioning as it should.

Though even then, some of those assessing the health of democracy concluded that 2016, and particularly the election of Donald Trump to the presidency, was anomalous. For Steven Levitsky and Daniel Ziblatt, two Harvard professors who wrote about 'how democracies die' in the shadow of Trump's victory, democracy in the US is at risk, but internationally America is an outlier. As such, wider predictions of democracy's imminent demise are, they believe, premature. "Prior to Donald Trump's election," they write, "claims about a global democratic recession were exaggerated." As evidence, they point to the persistence of democratic governments across much of the world, and say that "for every Hungary, Turkey and Venezuela" that slides backwards, "there is a Colombia, Sri Lanka or Tunisia" which goes the other way. Hence, the argument goes, to claim that democracy is in global crisis after the US election is simply to extend American political defects and psychoses to a global stage. Looking at various democratic indices, Levitsky and Ziblatt appear to be right. According to the 2016 Lexical Index of Electoral Democracy, more than two thirds of countries in the world held contested elections.[12] A separate study, the Global State of Democracy 2017, found that "democracy overall has made considerable progress over the last forty years."[13] Still, these studies contrast starkly with others such as the Economist Intelligence Unit's 2017 Democracy Index, which "records the worst decline in global democracy in years". Necessarily, each assessment depends on different criteria and different time frames. The world is a big place and it is hard to make all-encompassing global claims.

And yet, there is one glaring omission from Levitsky and Ziblatt's thesis. Entirely missing from their analysis is the communications revolution. There are lots of lessons from history, and assessments of formal and informal constraints on the US presidency, but – if one takes out the references to a few Donald Trump tweets – it is as if the internet, social media and tech platforms had not happened. This is like a life insurance company calculating someone's life expectancy based on their diet, without taking into account that they are living in a warzone. And Levitsky and Ziblatt's omission is also made by most democratic governments. For most democratic governments the communications revolution is something that – when it comes to politics – they can for the most part ignore. Of course, they are conscious of what a big deal it is economically. Yes, they recognize it is changing the way people relate to each other socially. But politically? It is a means of public engagement and a way in which to make government services more 'e'-fficient, but does it justify a transformation of democratic politics?

★

To ignore or deny the scale of political disruption brought about by the communications revolution carries with it huge democratic risks. It ignores, for example, the extent to which this revolution has already played havoc with democratic checks and balances. The extent to which the 'scarecrow' function of the press – the bedrock of independent local reporting that was meant to keep authorities honest – is broken: when whole regions or cities have no dedicated independent media, then it is hard to say democratic accountability is functioning as it should. The extent to which the channels through which a community can speak collectively to those in authority, and to their elected representatives, are in terminal decline: the residents of Grenfell Tower could blog and tweet as much as they liked, but without a local independent news outlet, no-one in authority heard them. The extent to which a public sphere characterized by certain unspoken rules – respect, temperateness, civility, an aspiration to the truth – has been blown wide open: when the president of the United States trolls other politicians and celebrities, publicly insults other heads of state via Twitter, and undermines the legitimacy of the judiciary ("this so-called judge"), it pushes the boundaries of the public sphere way beyond their twentieth-century limits. If people have lost trust in the main sources of public information and communication, if they lack a collective voice to speak to power, and if they have lost respect for the legitimacy of those in authority, then it is hard not to conclude that democracy is in a fragile state.

Liberal democracy is also premised on the idea that the citizen is protected from the state, and – for the most part – can live their life free from intrusion by the state. In US terms, this is spelt out in the Fourth Amendment, which provides for "the right of the people to be secure in their persons, houses, papers, and effects, against unreasonable searches and seizures". Yet, in our data-drenched world, unless there is explicit and concrete data protection, the state can know – or can find out – almost anything about its citizens. On top of which, those citizens may never know when the state is watching them.

Authoritarian governments have certainly not been in denial about the extent to which the communications revolution and tech platforms have upended politics. The Communist Party of China was the first to recognize the dangers of the internet to its power, and then turn these to its advantage, but other authoritarian regimes followed its lead. Iran's theocratic government, unnerved by the use of Twitter in its 2009 elections and by the Arab Spring in 2011, announced it would build a national internet, a 'halal internet'. Despite scoffs from those who saw this as the equivalent of the Dutch boy sticking his finger in a leaking dike, by the end of 2017 Iran had constructed its state-controlled National Internet Network, or NIN. All five hundred websites on the NIN had been carefully screened by the state. The government made sure that accessing these domestic approved sites was faster and cheaper than accessing foreign websites (many of which – like Twitter, Facebook and YouTube – were blocked).[14] It also structured the NIN so that people would be guided to government-sanctioned news and information, and away from services or information of which the government disapproved. But the biggest enhancement of the Iranian regime's power would come from the next phase of the NIN when, as with Aadhaar in India, every Iranian would be required to use a single, unique identifier to get online. President Rouhani, like Xi Jinping in China, was coming around to the view that the web, once domesticated, could give the state even greater control over its citizens than it had before. Russia was taking a similar route, introducing a law in 2015 requiring that any personal data about Russian citizens be stored on servers located within Russia. Ostensibly, it could justify this move towards 'data sovereignty' by claiming it could not protect its own citizens' data outside Russia. Yet in practice, since Russian citizens lacked data protection from the state, the government and security services were free to spy on everything their people did. China passed a similar law in June 2017, obliging all companies to keep data gathered in China within China, unless explicitly sanctioned by regulators.

Authoritarian governments without the money or capacity to nationalize the net adopted alternative methods to police and suppress digital dissent, to distort debate, and to limit political freedom online. In Sudan after 2011, as criticism of the government grew on social media, the ruling National Congress Party established a Cyber Jihadist Unit (CJU) to wage domestic "online defence operations".[15] Its efforts intensified after the revolts of the following year, with the unit tracking online discussions, deliberately spreading misinformation and discrediting opponents. After Sudanese soldiers raped more than two hundred women and girls in North Darfur in November 2014, for example, the CJU launched disinformation campaigns and tried to vilify those who reported on the atrocity.[16] In Vietnam, the government in Hanoi admitted in 2013 that it had followed China in employing almost a thousand online "public opinion shapers" to push positive government propaganda.[17] In Turkey, after the Gezi Park protests in 2013, the government set up a six-thousand-strong social media team to promote the government and attack opponents. Similar to Vladimir Putin's covert online army, they used a mixture of distraction, harassment and personal smears. Some of this was only discovered after a hacker group, RedHack, released 57,623 emails between the most senior figures in government, dating back to 2000.[18] Ironically, commercial technology, built to make web advertising possible, proved particularly helpful to authoritarian governments. It gave them the ability to track citizens as they moved and interacted online, and shifted across different platforms and devices. When combined with data localization, this gave these governments even greater capacity to suppress protest, marginalize opposition and limit dissent.

While democratic governments have been in denial about the scale of disruption, resourceful political campaigners and insurgent political parties have been busy taking advantage of the new political freedoms the platforms bring. "Thank God for the internet, thank God for social media, thank God for Facebook," Matteo Salvini, the leader of the Italian far-right party Lega, said after the

2018 Italian election. Salvini's populist party had just stunned observers by winning almost eighteen per cent of the national vote, four points higher than Silvio Berlusconi's Forza Italia. Yet this was still over a dozen points shy of M5S, or the Five Star Movement, a party that had sprung directly from the net and lived much of its life on it. Five Star used a combination of dominant social media services like Facebook, plus its own bespoke platform – fittingly called Rousseau – to organize, to survey members, to run internal votes and to fundraise. From its launch via Beppe Grillo's blog in 2009 it was able to propel itself, by 2018, to becoming the most popular party in Italy. Or take Spain's Podemos, itself partly inspired by Five Star. It was started in 2014 by a group of Spanish academics led by the pony-tailed political scientist Pablo Iglesias, building on the 15-M or Indignados protest movement. Within three months it won eight per cent of the vote in the European elections and five seats in the European Parliament.[19] A year after its formation the party was the second largest in Spain based on membership.

Across Europe, parties and campaigns that devoted their money and effort to new digital campaign methods saw remarkable returns on investment. In Reykjavik, after Iceland's devastating financial collapse following 2008, only one party initially took platform politics seriously, and that one was started as a joke. The Best Party (named so that you would think it was the best party), was set up in 2009 in protest at the mess made by other politicians. Unlike the other parties it took advantage of the newly established Shadow City platform to promote its policies – "based on the best of all other policies", it said – which included free towels at public swimming pools, a polar bear display at the zoo, and free flights for women.[20] Its leader, Jón Gnarr, was, like Beppe Grillo in Italy, a comedian. Then, to most people's astonishment, Gnarr was elected mayor of Reykjavik in 2010. In Britain, in 2016, the official Leave campaign in the Brexit referendum claimed to be the first "in the

UK to put almost all our money into digital communication, then have it partly controlled by people whose normal work was subjects like quantum information". Though it is impossible to quantify what difference knowledge of quantum information made, the gamble paid off and, to widespread astonishment, Britons voted fifty-two per cent to forty-eight to leave the EU. In the following year's general election campaign the British Labour Party ignored mainstream media and focused its attention on social media. With the help of the grassroots campaign group Momentum it grew its share of the vote from the low- to mid-twenties at the start of the campaign to forty per cent in the election itself six weeks later. Even Emmanuel Macron founded a new party from scratch with the benefit of big data and intelligent voter-targeting. In the year before the 2017 election the French leader ran a big listening exercise across France – 'La Grande Marche' – that had the double benefit of discovering what political issues people most cared about, and capturing data for the subsequent presidential campaign. And Donald Trump, who initially dismissed data-driven campaigning as 'mumbo-jumbo digital stuff', came to believe it was crucial to his 2016 victory.[21] So crucial indeed that he made his 2016 digital director, Brad Parscale, his 2020 campaign manager.

Yet outside elections, democratic governments continued to treat the communications revolution as though it was marginal to the way politics functioned, and emerging digital disruption as something for the tech titans to sort out. In the UK, the government published a Digital Charter in 2018 that used cookie-cutter clichés which could have been written in 1998. "The internet is a powerful force for good," it asserted. "It serves humanity, spreads ideas and enhances freedom and opportunity across the world." Apart from being politically anaemic, the Charter gave 'the internet' itself agency, presenting an unhelpful determinist perspective which most people had moved beyond after 2011. At the 2018 World Economic Forum in Davos, the British prime minister, Theresa May, spoke at length about the power of technology, but saw problems in the online world as social, not political. As such they could be solved by regulating for safety, and by pressuring the platforms to intervene. "These companies have some of the best brains in the world," May told a half-empty room in Davos. "They must focus their brightest and best on meeting these fundamental social responsibilities."[22]

In the US, there were no signs that President Trump was anxious about the disruptive democratic effects of communications technology on politics. Rather, as he said when he gathered eighteen tech leaders at the White House in mid-2017, he saw advances in tech simply as a way in which to shrink government, make its services more efficient and boost the economy.[23] For Trump himself, the chief benefit of the communications revolution seemed to be being able to tweet. Meanwhile, politics continued to migrate online, and the disparity between the opportunities for people to participate and represent themselves digitally, and the limits to participation and representation in the institutions of democracy, grew ever larger.

*

It is not as though there has been any lack of global experiments in doing democracy differently in the digital age. There have been, and continue to be, literally thousands of initiatives aimed at changing the way in which people come up with new political ideas, set the political agenda, participate in policy-making, debate legislation, spend public money, monitor political representatives and vote. Some have been around a long while and involve millions of people – for example, petitioning and collective action platforms, like Avaaz, which was launched back in 2007 and boasts over 46 million members. Other initiatives involve building practical civic tools to make it easier for citizens to engage with authorities and their political representatives. MySociety, a non-profit social enterprise started in the UK, has developed sites such as TheyWorkForYou, WhatDoTheyKnow and EveryPolitician, to enable citizens, journalists and political campaigners to find out more about their elected representatives. And there is a growing collection of nascent national projects that aim to include people in the formation of policy and legislation – such as Parlement & Citoyens in France, LabHacker in the Brazilian Chamber of Deputies, and the Rahvaalgatus platform in Estonia. These are complemented by a vast array of incredibly useful electoral tools that provide basic information like where and how to vote, and a growing army of digital democracy volunteers (such as tiny civil society groups like Democracy Club in the UK, run on a shoe-string by a handful of committed coordinators). Yet something that characterizes almost all these experiments, no matter how well meaning and how innovative, is how marginal most still are to mainstream politics. Many started outside conventional political channels (deliberately), but have remained there ever since. That is not to say they have not had impact – many have; but they have yet to change the way established democratic politics is done. People still draw a cross on a piece of paper and put it in a ballot box. Members of Parliament in Britain still walk through separate doorways to vote. Public money is still allocated by central governments and voted through by parliaments. Though this is not true everywhere.[24] There are cities and even nations experimenting with new democratic methods. A few are even taking some risks.

Imagine letting schoolchildren tell you how to spend €10 million. Irresponsible? The mayor of Paris did not think so. In 2017 Anne Hidalgo let Parisian primary and secondary pupils vote on how the city's schools budget ought to be allocated. Almost seventy thousand took the chance to vote, "with 82% of elementary schools and 55% of colleges mobilized" according to Pauline Véron, who is in charge of the programme.[25] Paris, along with other cities including Madrid, Barcelona and Reykjavik, has been experimenting with 'participatory budgeting' since 2015. Five per cent of the city's investment budget, or around €100 million a year, is allotted through this process.[26] Outside Europe, involving the public in the allocation of city budgets dates back long before 2015. The southern Brazilian city of Porto Alegre started using a pre-digital version of participatory budgeting in the 1980s, and since then over 120 Brazilian cities have adopted it.[27] And digital tools have made participation easier and outcomes much clearer. In Reykjavik, almost sixty per cent of the city's residents have used the Better Reykjavik platform since 2010, to suggest ideas for what the city should do, and thousands have participated in deciding how to spend €3 million of the city's annual budget through Better Neighbourhoods.[28] Since 2017 they have also been using it to crowdsource education policy.

Yet, outside participatory budgeting, and beyond the innovations of start-up and insurgent political parties, experiments in reinventing democracy have been, for the most part, peripheral and tangential to the functioning of mainstream democratic politics. Why is this? For one thing, it appears that many incumbent politicians are yet to be convinced that the current system is broken. Why institute major reforms if the current system still works? It may be a little rickety, but that is an argument for incremental change, not root and branch upheaval. And even if a growing number of young people are unconvinced of the system's efficacy, a majority still believe in democracy – if perhaps more in the ideal than the actuality.[29] There are also understandable and justifiable historical reasons why democratic representatives are anxious about rushing towards greater democratization. As the histories of the French and Russian revolutions show, charging towards full-blooded democracy can as easily lead to chaos and autocracy as to a free, open and diverse society. In 1791 Maximilien Robespierre spoke passionately in favour of citizens' rights and against the death penalty. "Free countries are those where the rights of man are respected and where, consequently, the laws are just," he told the Constituent Assembly. Where countries use the death penalty, it is "proof that the legislator is nothing but a master who commands slaves and who pitilessly punishes them according to his whim." Three years later, as a leading member of the Committee of Public Safety, Robespierre set about killing off political enemies in a reign of terror, claiming that terror "is less a distinct principle than a natural consequence of the general principle of democracy". The effects of greater democratization depend on circumstances and context. Democracy, Bernard Crick writes in *In Defence of Politics*, "not merely stabilizes free regimes, it makes stronger unfree regimes, and it has made possible totalitarianism".

So, cautiously and reticently, democratic governments have dipped their toes in reform rather than plunged in. Though this sounds sensible in theory, in practice it has often been worse than not experimenting at all. Tokenistic trials, tentative schemes and poor execution have led to limited participation, low awareness and greater public cynicism. Government experiments in re-engineering democracy have suffered from three particular problems, perhaps best described as: the 'Justin Bieber law', the 'middleman paradox' and the '*Field of Dreams* dilemma'.

The Justin Bieber law states that, if a government makes a superficial commitment to public participation, then the public will participate superficially. The White House petition site is a great example of this. In September 2011, the Obama administration launched 'We the People', an online petition site intended to be "your voice in the White House". If a petition managed to gain enough signatures within thirty days of being posted, then the White House promised to respond. Though the number of signatures was first set at 5,000, within a month this was raised to 25,000, and within eighteen months to 100,000.[30] If the aim of this was to lower the proportion of petitions the White House had to respond to, then it was fantastically successful, reducing it from forty-four per cent to two per cent.[31] Even this small number effected little change in government. The Pew Research Center went through every petition submitted between 2011 and 2016 that reached over 150 signatures – almost five thousand in total – and found that only one "was instrumental in creating a significant piece of legislation", and one other in changing President Obama's position on an issue. The fifth most popular petition during those five years, gaining 273,968 signatures, was to 'Deport Justin Bieber and revoke his Green Card'.[32] Hence, the Justin Bieber law.

The 'middleman paradox' was conceived by two academics in Vienna in 2005. Harald Mahrer and Robert Krimmer were trying to figure out why so few e-democracy proposals made it through the Austrian parliament or government, and why even those projects that did make it through progressed substantially more slowly than others. After interviewing over two hundred parliamentarians, and examining public statements about digital projects, they found that the "vast majority of Austrian politicians are very actively opposing e-democracy", mainly because they saw it as a direct threat to themselves. As one politician told them, "At the end of the day it is a question of power. More citizens' participation leads to a loss of power for the members of the political elite." This led the study's authors to conclude there was a 'middleman paradox': "the very same parliamentarians who would be responsible for introducing new forms of citizens' participation for political decision-making are explicitly and implicitly opposing these reforms."[33] Just as, given a choice, turkeys are unlikely to vote for Christmas, so politicians are unlikely to vote for their own diminishment.

In the 1989 movie *Field of Dreams*, Kevin Costner plays an Iowa farmer who hears a disembodied voice telling him, "If you build it, he will come." After ignoring it for a while, Costner decides he has figured out what it means, and cuts down his cornfield to build a baseball stadium. Despite the farm's isolated location, and friends telling him he is crazy, sure enough, he – or rather they – do come. Democratic innovators are not always so lucky. In Brazil, the Chamber of Deputies built an e-Democracia portal to draft bills collaboratively with the public. Although 37,000 Brazilians registered on the site and made over one thousand suggestions, only six per cent of deputies used it. In the UK, between 2010 and 2013, the government piloted an online initiative to let people comment on proposed legislation. Three bills went through the pilot; none of them gained much new public input. One of them received comments from just twenty-three organizations. They built it, but people did not come. This is the perennial dilemma when re-engineering democracy: not knowing if people will participate. Or if only an unrepresentative group will participate. Or if everyone will participate and the system will be over-whelmed. If you do not build it at all, of course, then you do not run that risk. So the easy option is not to build it at all.

There is also a strong undercurrent of anxiety about greater democratization, and about whether giving more power to the people necessarily leads to either a stronger democracy or better decision-making. This anxiety is cogently voiced by Christopher Achen and Larry Bartels in their 2016 book, *Democracy for Realists*. The book, which was almost two decades in the making, presents copious evidence to show that the 'folk theory of democracy', where rational voters make informed decisions, does not hold up to scrutiny. Most citizens ignore politics most of the time. When they do pay attention, at elections, they tend to base their vote not on an informed retrospective analysis of the performance of the party in power, but on a combination of what is happening at the time of the election (however irrelevant it is), past loyalties and social identity. The authors were particularly struck by the influ-ence of a string of New Jersey shark attacks on the 1916 US presidential election. If citizens are given a greater say outside elections, for example through initiatives and referendums, the evidence suggests that, following myopic self-interest or swayed by electoral entrepreneurs, they make similarly irrational and ill-informed judgements.

This is particularly obvious when citizens are asked to vote on narrow, complicated issues about which they have limited knowledge, like water fluoridation or multiple vaccinations, though it also comes across strongly where citizens are given the chance to decide if they would like to pay more or less tax. Even when citizens say they value public services highly, and even when it has implications for public safety, if given a vote, they tend to vote for cheaper public services. Achen and Bartels estimate, for example, that reductions in fire protection services in California in the 1980s, as a consequence of the popular tax reform of 1978, hampered the services' ability to protect against, or deal with, the terrible fires of 1991 that destroyed more than three thousand homes. "Direct democracy", the authors write, "had overruled the judgment of fire professionals, with horrific results."[34]

Achen and Bartels follow a long line of those who, since the advent of modern democracy, have questioned the efficacy or wisdom of direct democracy, especially in its purest form – from Montesquieu's *Spirit of the Laws*, in which the French baron advocated that any balanced system of government had to have checks on power – including checks on the power of the majority – through to James Madison, who asked in the *Federalist Papers* whether in critical moments there did not need to be "some temperate and respectable body of citizens, in order to check the misguided career, and to suspend the blow meditated by the people against themselves, until reason, justice, and truth can regain their authority over the public mind", and on to Alexis de Tocqueville, who, though so enamoured of US democracy, made clear his anxiety about the dangers of the tyranny of the majority. The majority "exercise a prodigious actual authority, and a power of opinion which is nearly as great; no obstacles exist which can impede or even retard its progress, so as to make it heed the complaints of those whom it crushes upon its path".[35]

Yet, as Achen and Bartels themselves acknowledge, these are not arguments against reform itself, but against bad reform. They show the danger of empowerment for empowerment's sake, or reform based on false or misguided theories. They are also strong arguments against those who have blithely assumed that the internet and social media are inherently democratizing, without questioning whether this is true or what it actually means. If there is one thing we have learnt from the past decade, and especially from the stories of countries like China and Singapore, it is that neither the internet nor social media is inherently democratizing. Both are enormously powerful communications tools that can transform politics. How they transform politics depends on their context, on how they are structured and how they are used. An authoritarian government can use technology to quash dissent. A democratic one can ensure that technology enables and even encourages dissent. There is no technologically pre-determined platform future for democratic societies, no matter what the sages of Silicon Valley say. Neither is it inevitable that smart technology and personal data will enhance state power. For the moment, at least, the future is up for grabs. It depends on what each democratic society and its representatives decide to do.

Up to now, many have simply accepted that tech platforms like Google and Facebook, which were built to do specific jobs like search the web or connect with friends, have come to perform so many others – including fundamental civic functions like informing people's vote, delivering the news and giving people a public voice. Yet entrusting such vital democratic functions to these organizations seems pretty strange. As Mark Zuckerberg himself has said, "If you had asked me, when I got started with Facebook, if one of the central things I'd need to work on now is preventing governments from interfering in each other's elections, there's no way I thought that's what I'd be doing, if we talked in 2004 in my dorm room."[36] He is right. To steal Zuck's own turn of phrase, it is a "pretty crazy idea" to think that these communications platforms should necessarily serve the needs of democracy. They work well for some public services – such as emergency communications in the aftermath of natural disasters – but are terrible for others – like distinguishing between credible and less credible news. On top of which, because of their business models, they are intrinsically liable to be gamed. No matter how hard they try to serve the needs of democracy, they will always fall down on this.

Which is why it is strange to see democratic leaders and policy makers telling the platforms to *take responsibility*. The tech giants should, Theresa May has said more than once, "do more in stepping up to their responsibilities".[37] Not only are they ill equipped to do any such thing, the danger, for liberal democracy, is that they should do so: that Google, Amazon, Apple, Facebook and other commercial platforms do take more responsibility for engineering the public sphere, for providing public services, for helping government work more efficiently. Many citizens may then find themselves living in a for-profit platform democracy. Alternatively, some democratic governments will go the other way and try to take much greater control of our virtual world, creating their own state platforms built on big data and unique digital identities like Aadhaar, linked in one enormous spider's web across government and commercial services. If they are successful, this will hugely enhance and centralize their power, and their citizens will find themselves living in surveillance or pansophic democracies, better described as authoritarian in all but name.

It is up to democracies themselves – up to their citizens, to civil society and to their elected representatives – to reinvent democracy for the digital era. To do so conscious of the changes wrought by the communications revolution, but trying to turn these changes to the advantage of democracy, rather than letting it be warped by them. To figure out how technology and platforms can give more power to people – not power for the sake of power, but power so that people can participate constructively, power so that people can be heard, power so that people can actually change things. There are countries and communities where citizens and civil society have taken the lead, and where elected representatives have followed. Where technology has been used to enhance participation and strengthen the democratic process, including deliberation and compromise, without being naïve about the dangers. These start to give us an inkling of where democratic politics could go next.

*

In 2012, lying in a hospital bed, Chia-liang Kao decided to 'fork the government' (meaning to create another version of existing digital services).[38] Frustrated with Taiwan's lack of transparency and engagement, he, and a group of self-proclaimed netizens, built an online alternative to the government's site that was more open and more useable. Like lots of other civic tech initiatives, g0v.tw, as it was called, might have remained useful but marginal had it not been for a political crisis two years later that propelled it into the mainstream. In March 2014, angry at a proposed trade deal, a hundred students occupied the main legislative assembly hall and refused to leave. Thousands of others then flocked to the parliament building in support of this 'Sunflower Movement'. The peaceful occupation, which continued for over three weeks, was distinguished by its remarkable use of communications technology. The protestors broadcast their activities online to people across Taiwan. This may not have been possible without the help of Audrey Tang.

If there were such a thing as a gov tech rockstar, Audrey Tang would be one. She is described variously as a 'brilliant programmer', a 'coding genius' and a 'genius hacker' whose tech talks are rapturously received. Born in 1981, Tang taught herself to program, quit school at fourteen, launched her first start-up shortly after, worked with Apple and other tech companies, changed gender, retired at thirty-three, and became a civic hacker. When the Sunflower Movement protest began Tang was able to help the protestors broadcast live via YouTube. Without the broadcast, mainstream media reports that violent 'mobsters' had broken in would have seemed credible. Once the protests had finished (and achieved their aim), the government invited Tang to help them change how they worked. In 2016 they asked her to join them. She refers to herself as the minister for hacking, and still claims to be an anarchist.

What is fascinating about what Tang and others have done in Taiwan is how they have used technology in the service of democracy, rather than let it shape democracy. They have looked at where there are problems with how democracy works, and figured out fixes. Take Uber, for example. Like most governments across the world, Taiwan did not know what to do when the platform taxi service arrived in 2013. Should they treat it like existing services? Should Uber drivers be regarded as employees or self-employed? Should Uber be banned? Rather than pushing it through the normal policy-making process, they decided to do an open, live consultation using a deliberation platform called pol.is. Some 4,500 people participated over four weeks, eventually cohering around seven recommendations (such as not being allowed to undercut the standard taxi fare). The government then met with Uber to discuss the recommendations in a live-streamed meeting. Unlike in most other countries across the world, Uber accepted almost all of them.[39] "I see Uber as an epidemic of the mind," Tang said. "You don't negotiate with a virus. All you can do is inoculate people – by deliberation."[40]

Equally, Tang has recognized that although technology has given lots of people a public voice, democratic governments are yet to find new ways in which to listen – which has made her determined to experiment with innovations in 'scalable listening', or listening to lots of people at once. Or take legislation and planning: most people find legalese impenetrable, and this deters them from commenting on proposals for new laws, even if they are given a chance (as with the UK parliament's pilot of a public reading stage for bills). So Tang has experimented with other ways of communicating text, such as using virtual reality simulations.[41] The integration of technology and democracy in Taiwan is still young, and many of the experiments still nascent, but already it shows how differently things can be done. One aspect where Taiwan has yet to innovate is around the digital identity of the citizen and her relationship with democratic government. To find the country that has gone furthest in rethinking this aspect, you have to travel five thousand miles west of Taipei to the Baltic state of Estonia.

On 20 August 1991, the 76th Guards Air Assault Division of the Soviet Union arrived in Tallinn ready to take control of Estonia's communications. They had been sent by coup leaders in Moscow who were trying to derail Mikhail Gorbachev's reforms of the USSR. Estonian citizens, who by this time had been demonstrating for independence for years, blocked access to the radio and television buildings. That night, the Supreme Council of the Republic of Estonia voted to make the country independent. Two days later, Iceland was the first country to recognize this independence officially.[42] A fortnight before Estonia's declaration, Tim Berners-Lee posted on a newsgroup that he was making the World Wide Web publicly available for the first time. From the moment that Estonians started to build their new nation, they baked in data and the web. At the same time, they did so in the acute knowledge of their vulnerability as a nation, aware of the looming security threat from the east, and viscerally conscious of the dangers of Soviet-style big government. Jump forward twenty-five years, and

Estonia had successfully turned itself into the most digitally enabled, digitally secure, and digitally comfortable, nation in the world. Yet, unlike authoritarian countries such as China, it has managed to do this this while centring control with the citizen, not with the state. From the beginning, Helen Margetts and Andre Naumann of the Oxford Internet Institute write, the country's aim was "to develop a citizen-centric and inclusive society" with the emphasis on the "citizen as principal".[43] They wanted to see the citizen as a subject, not as an object of government.[44] So while almost all citizens have an electronic ID, they also own their own public data. Though government services are incredibly efficient – it famously takes five minutes to file your taxes – no departments are allowed to duplicate your personal data or coordinate their knowledge of you. And while authorities can check your data if they have justification and cause, you are notified when they do, and for what purpose. The state, in other words, is more transparent than the citizen. The whole system is based on open standards but secured through encryption, accessible but decentralized, and efficient but not intrusive.

*

There is an old joke in which a tourist is lost and stops to ask a local for directions. "Well, I wouldn't start from here," the local replies. The same could be said for most democracies by the close of the second decade of the twenty-first century. Given the chance, when redesigning their information systems, most would be better off starting from the position of Estonia in 1991. But they are not there, they are here. Here, when it comes to politics in the digital world, is a mess. And the digital world has now spilt into, and become inextricably linked with, the real world. It is a world dominated by gargantuan transnational tech platforms, whose aims sometimes support democratic politics and sometimes undermine it. It is a world where authoritarian governments have worked out how to 'tame' the internet such that it enhances their power. It is a world where democratic societies are only belatedly starting to realize quite how much their politics has been disrupted.

Remaking things will not be easy. It will mean recognizing that there is an unsustainable discrepancy between our capacity to represent ourselves and the ways in which we are represented in democratic politics. It will mean acknowledging that this discrepancy is undermining the legitimacy of established democratic processes, particularly elections, and if they are not reformed this will only get worse. It will mean accepting that the media systems through which citizens gain their political information, and by which authorities are held accountable, are broken. And, it will mean recognizing that the market currency of the web, personal data, while problematic commercially, can corrupt democratic politics.

If we are going to create a new digital democracy, we should start by coming to terms with the scale of the task. As with tackling climate change, it will not take months, or years, but decades. We should also be honest about what we know and don't know. Every time a group of politicians interrogates a Silicon Valley executive, it ends up looking like a YouTube video on how a platform works. In part this is a generational issue, though that is no excuse for governments not to learn. At the same time, we should stop treating software engineers like a priesthood. Just because someone can write an algorithm does not mean they get how politics works. This goes especially for the high priests themselves, the Zuckerbergs, Pages, Brins, Cooks and Bezoses. However smart and talented they are, their creations have grown beyond their understanding and their control. It is tough to see a healthy future for liberal democracy in a world entirely dominated by a handful of commercial tech superpowers. We need a digital sphere that is less centralized, digital civic spaces and public services that do not rely on personal data tracking and ad tech, and a digital democracy that starts – like in Estonia – with the citizen at its centre.

Given how hard it will be for democracy to evolve, it is tempting to reject digital innovations entirely; to try to go back to a world of pens and paper (and typewriters, as the Russian government has done). But sticking our heads in the sand is not going to make the web, tech giants, AI, big data and platform politics go away. And change may be difficult, but it is not impossible. As Taiwan, Estonia and other countries and communities have shown, democracy can evolve, and technology can be used to renew democratic processes. Democracy can be rehacked, but only if there is the will to do it.

ACKNOWLEDGEMENTS

'book?' This is almost certainly the first and last time that I'll receive an email with such a remarkably pithy offer in the subject line. The email was from Alex Christofi at Oneworld, who subsequently became the editor and publisher of this book. I am immensely grateful to Alex for not only proposing I write this book, but for all his advice and support throughout. His ideas and suggestions have been hugely helpful, and I could not have completed it without his support and encouragement. And I should extend this thanks to all the others at Oneworld.

An eclectic mix of people have very kindly read, commented and offered advice on various chapters, most notably my wife Jojo, my colleague Gordon Ramsay (not the chef), my brother-in-law Nick Kettlewell, Brian Cathcart, Sam Robertshaw and others. I'm very grateful to all of them, and to all those I interviewed for the book. Thank you, too, to Annabel Merullo and Laura McNeill at PFD, and to King's College London, where I teach and do research.

This book relies on a great stack of journal articles, books, news reports, op-eds, think tank studies, industry assessments and primary data. Fortunately, most of these are in the public domain, and I've tried to point to all those that are directly from the text. I'm grateful to the many authors and researchers whose work helped inform the book, even if I do not have the space to thank them all here.

Eighteen months ago I bought a pig. You could put this down to an unconventional mid-life crisis, but really it was my failure of imagination. My wife had gone away for the weekend and I was struggling to find ways to entertain our four small children. Thanks to a quick search on the internet I discovered there was a litter of piglets for sale not far from us. Thinking it was a good way to spend Saturday morning we all bundled in the car and set off. A couple of hours later we arrived home with a pig in a basket.

I have various regrets about my spontaneous purchase. Failing to plan where Pigpig (as she came to be called) would live was probably uppermost. Equally, I should have better prepared my startled but welcoming wife. But one thing I do not regret is buying Pigpig. There are few things more grounding than a pig. She is about as far from virtual as it is possible to go. For those, like me, who find themselves getting lost worrying about our political future in the age of superpower tech platforms, AI-enabled political campaigns and a data-fuelled state, I recommend getting a pig. Few things can bring you back to earth quicker. A final thank you should go to Pigpig.

NOTES

Chapter 1: Individuals: the Freextremist Model

1 Konstantin von Hammerstein, Roman Höfner and Marcel Rosenbach, 'Right-wing activists take aim at German election', *Der Spiegel*, 13 September 2017.

2 Karsten Schmehl, Saba MBoundza, Jane Lytvynenko and Ryan Broderick, 'Trolls are trying to hijack the German election by copying Trump supporters', *Buzzfeed*, 4 September 2017.

3 Jacob Davey and Julia Ebner (2017), 'The Fringe Insurgency: Connectivity, Convergence and Mainstreaming of the Extreme Right', Institute for Strategic Dialogue.

4 Richard Barbrook and Andy Cameron, 'The Californian ideology', *Mute*, 1 September 1995.

5 Steven Levy (1984), *Hackers: Heroes of the Computer Revolution*, New York: Dell.

6 Fred Turner (2006), *From Counterculture to Cyberculture: Stewart Brand, the Whole Earth Network, and the Rise of Digital Utopianism*, Chicago: University of Chicago Press.

7 John Perry Barlow, 'A Declaration of the Independence of Cyberspace', 8 February 1996, Electronic Frontier Foundation, www.eff.org/cyberspace-independence (accessed 16 May 2018).

8 John Perry Barlow, 'Is cyberspace still anti-sovereign?' *California Magazine*, April 2006.

9 Michael Bernstein, Andrés Monroy-Hernández, Drew Harry, Paul André, Katrina Panovich and Greg Vargas (2011), '4chan and /b/: An Analysis of Anonymity and Ephemerality in a Large Online Community', *Proceedings of the Fifth International AAAI Conference on Weblogs and Social Media*, Menlo Park, CA: AAAI Press.

10 Christopher 'moot' Poole, 'The case for anonymity online', TED Talk, February 2010.

11 Chris Poole, interview, Fimoculous, 18 February 2009, http://fimoculous. com/archive/post-5738.cfm (accessed 16 May 2018).

12 Whitney Phillips (2015), *This Is Why We Can't Have Nice Things: Mapping the Relationship Between Online Trolling and Mainstream Culture*, Cambridge, MA: MIT Press.

13 Ryan M. Milner (2016), *The World Made Meme: Public Conversations and Participatory Media*, Cambridge, MA: MIT Press.

14 Jessica L. Beyer (2014), *Expect Us: Online Communities and Political Mobilization*, New York: Oxford University Press.

15 Parmy Olson (2012), *We Are Anonymous: Inside the Hacker World of LulzSec, Anonymous, and the Global Cyber Insurgency*, New York: Little, Brown.

16 Gabriella Coleman (2014), *Hacker, Hoaxer, Whistleblower, Spy: The Many Faces of Anonymous*, New York: Verso.

17 Adam Clark Estes, 'The hacks that mattered in the year of the hack', *The Atlantic*, 28 December 2011.

18 Coleman, *Hacker, Hoaxer, Whistleblower, Spy*.

19 Josh Constine, 'The future of memes: 4chan hits 22m monthlies, unveils new API', *TechCrunch*, 6 September 2012, https://techcrunch.com/2012/09/05/ 4chan-api/ (accessed 16 May 2018).

20 Josh Constine, 'TechCrunch's picks: the 10 best startups from Y Combinator's S12 Demo Day', *TechCrunch*, 22 August 2012, https://techcrunch. com/2012/08/21/best-of-yc-demo-day/ (accessed 16 May 2018).

21 Southern Poverty Law Center, 'Andrew Anglin', https://www.splcenter. org/fighting-hate/extremist-files/individual/andrew-anglin (accessed 16 May 2018).

22 Marcus Dysch, 'Neo-Nazi gave out internet abuse tips in campaign against MP', *The JC*, 30 October 2014.

23 Ethan Chiel, 'Meet the man keeping 8chan, the world's most vile website, alive', *Splinter*, 19 April 2016.

24 'The international alternative right', Hope Not Hate, 2017, https://alterna- tiveright.hopenothate.com (accessed 16 May 2018).

25 Joshua Green (2017), *Devil's Bargain: Steve Bannon, Donald Trump and the Storming of the White House*, London: Scribe UK.

26 Joseph Bernstein, 'The disturbing misogynist history of Gamergate's good- will ambassadors', *Buzzfeed*, 30 October 2014.

27 For the cultural background to #Gamergate, and a good explanation, see Angela Nagle (2017), *Kill All Normies: Online Culture Wars from 4chan and Tumblr to Trump and the Alt-Right*, Winchester: Zero.

28 Milo Yiannopoulos, 'Feminist bullies tearing the video game industry apart', *Breitbart*, 1 September 2014.

29 Chiel, 'Meet the man keeping 8chan, the world's most vile website, alive'.

30 Allum Bokhari and Milo Yiannopoulos, 'Why online anonymity frightens progressives', *Breitbart*, 27 October 2015.

31 Ben Schreckinger, 'World War Meme', *Politico Magazine*, March/April 2017.

32 Jeff Giesea (2015), 'It's Time to Embrace Memetic Warfare', *Defence Strategic Communications*, 1:1, 67–75; supplemented by Skype interview.

33 Abby Ohlheiser, '"We actually elected a meme as president": how 4chan celebrated Trump's victory', *Washington Post*, 9 November 2016.

34 Gabriel Emile Hine, Jeremiah Onaolapo, Emiliano De Cristofaro, Nicolas Kourtellis, Ilias Leontiadis, Riginos Samaras, Gianluca Stringhini and Jeremy Blackburn (2016), 'Kek, Cucks, and God Emperor Trump: A Measurement Study of 4chan's Politically Incorrect Forum and Its Effects on the Web', *Proceedings of the Eleventh International AAAI Conference on Weblogs and Social Media*, Menlo Park, CA: AAAI Press.

35 Josh Harkinson, 'Meet Silicon Valley's secretive alt-right followers', *Mother Jones*, 10 March 2017.

36 Nausicaa Renner, 'Memes trump articles on Breitbart's Facebook page', *Columbia Journalism Review*, 30 January 2017.

37 Michael Barthel, Galen Stocking, Jesse Holcomb and Amy Mitchell, 'Seven-in-ten Reddit users get news on the site', Pew Research Center, 25 February 2016, http://www.journalism.org/2016/02/25/seven-in-ten-reddit-users-get-news-on-the-site/ (accessed 16 May 2018).

38 Jason Koebler, 'How r/the_donald became a melting pot of frustration and hate', *Motherboard*, 12 July 2016.

39 'Let's all have a Town Hall about r/all', Reddit, 16 June 2016, https://www.reddit.com/r/announcements/comments/4oedco/lets_all_have_a_town_hall_about_rall/ (accessed 16 May 2018).

40 As reported in Schreckinger, 'World War Meme'.

41 See 'Podesta emails MAGAthread', Reddit, 17 October 2016, https://www.reddit.com/r/The_Donald/comments/57vefh/podesta_emails_magathread/ (accessed 16 May 2018).

42 See 'DNC planning to fake Trump "assault" scandal all the way back in May', Reddit, 14 October 2016 https://www.reddit.com/r/The_Donald/comments/57iv9k/dnc_planning_to_fake_trump_assault_scandal_all/; and 'New James O'Keefe video: rigging the election', Reddit, 17 October 2016 https://www.reddit.com/r/The_Donald/comments/57y384/new_james_okeefe_video_rigging_the_election_video/ (both accessed 16 May 2018).

43 Andrew Couts and Austin Powell, '4chan and Reddit bombarded debate polls to declare Trump the winner', *Daily Dot*, 27 September 2016.

44 CNN/ORC International poll, 26 September 2016, available at http://i2.cdn.turner.com/cnn/2016/images/09/27/poll.pdf; 'Voters nationally say Clinton won debate 51/40', Public Policy Polling, 26 September 2016, available at https://www.publicpolicypolling.com/wp-content/uploads/2017/09/PPP_Release_PostDebatePoll_92616.pdf (both accessed 16 May 2018).

45 Donald J. Trump, @realDonaldTrump, Twitter, 27 September 2016, https://twitter.com/realDonaldTrump/status/780796008854876160 (accessed 16 May 2018).

46 Andrew Marantz, 'Trolls for Trump', *New Yorker*, 31 October 2016.

47 Shane Dixon Kavanaugh, 'Trump fans dox "anti-Trump" journalists', *vocativ*, 18 October 2016.

48 'Anti-Semitic Targeting of Journalists during the 2016 Presidential Campaign', Anti-Defamation League, 19 October 2016, available at https://www.adl.org/sites/default/files/documents/assets/pdf/press-center/CR_4862_Journalism-Task-Force_v2.pdf (accessed 16 May 2018).

49 Johan Galtung and Mari Holmboe Ruge (1965), 'The Structure of Foreign News: The Presentation of the Congo, Cuba and Cyprus Crises in Four Norwegian Newspapers', *Journal of Peace Research*, 2:1, 64–90.

50 'Transcript: Hillary Clinton's full remarks in Reno, Nevada', *Politico*, 25 August 2016; Hannah Kozlowska, 'Hillary Clinton's website now has an explainer about a frog that recently became a Nazi', *Quartz*, 13 September 2016.

51 Alice Marwick and Rebecca Lewis, 'Media Manipulation and Disinformation Online', Data & Society Research Institute, 15 May 2017, available at https://datasociety.net/pubs/oh/DataAndSociety_MediaManipulationAndDisinformationOnline.pdf (accessed 16 May 2018).

52 Sam Sanders and Paulina Firozi, '#MemeOfTheWeek: Ted Cruz and the Zodiac killer', NPR, 26 February 2016.

53 Schmehl et al., 'Trolls are trying to hijack the German election'.

54 Ian Lavery MP, public hearing, Review of Intimidation in Public Life, 14 September 2017.

55 Sir Patrick McLoughlin MP, chairman of the Conservative Party, submission to Review of Intimidation in Public Life, 8 September 2017.

Chapter 2: Plutocrats: the Mercer Model

1 Cecil Gauert, '*Sea Owl* – the personal and enchanting 62m feadship', *Boat International*, 18 February 2017.

2 'Hmmm. We can't see missile launchers …', *Yachting*, 6 June 2013.

3 The author wrote to Robert Mercer but did not receive a reply.

4 As based on public records and reports of their views. These include but are not restricted to (in alphabetical order by author): ACL, 'Robert L. Mercer receives the 2014 Lifetime Achievement Award', Association for Computational Linguistics, 14 October 2014; Nicholas Confessore, 'How one family's deep pockets helped reshape Donald Trump's campaign', *New York Times*, 18 August 2016; Lawrence Delevingne, 'Have Mercer! The money man who helped the GOP win', CNBC, 4 November 2014; Matea Gold, 'The Mercers and Stephen Bannon: how a populist power base was funded and built', *Washington Post*, 17 March 2017; Rosie Gray, 'What does the billionaire family backing Donald Trump really want?', *The Atlantic*, 27 January 2017; Max Kutner, 'Meet Robert Mercer, the mysterious billionaire benefactor of Breitbart', *Newsweek*, 21 November 2016; Sebastian Mallaby (2011), *More Money than God: Hedge Funds and the Making of a New Elite*, London: Bloomsbury; 'Jane Mayer on Robert Mercer & the dark money behind Trump and Bannon', *Democracy Now!*, 23 March 2017; Jane Mayer, 'The reclusive hedge-fund tycoon behind the Trump presidency', *New Yorker*, 27 March 2017; Zachary Mider, 'What Kind of Man Spends Millions to Elect Ted Cruz?', *Bloomberg*, 20 January 2016; Kenneth P. Vogel and Ben Schreckinger, 'The most powerful woman in GOP politics, *Politico*, 7 September 2016; Vicky Ward, 'The blow-it-all-up billionaires', *Highline*, 17 March 2017; Jim Zarroli, 'Robert Mercer is a force to be reckoned with in finance and conservative politics', NPR, 26 May 2017.

5 As documented in Jane Mayer (2016), *Dark Money: How a Secretive Group of Billionaires Is Trying to Buy Political Control in the US*, London: Scribe UK.

6 'ACORN Prostitution Investigation – James O'Keefe and Hannah Giles – Part 1', Push Back Now/YouTube, 10 September 2009, https://www.youtube.com/watch?v=9UOL9Jh61S8 (accessed 17 May 2018).

7 Donald Lambro, 'BREITBART: The politicized art behind the ACORN plan', *Washington Times*, 21 September 2009.

8 'House votes to strip funding for ACORN', Fox News, 17 September 2009.

9 Scott Harshbarger, Proskauer, 2009 (report since removed from the web).

10 See 'Acorn Investigation', Project Veritas, https://www.projectveritas.com/acorn/ (accessed 17 May 2018).

11 'Internet 2009 in Numbers', Pingdom, https://royal.pingdom.com/2010/01/22/internet-2009-in-numbers/ (accessed 17 May 2018).

12 Rebecca Mead, 'Rage machine: Andrew Breitbart's empire of bluster', *New Yorker*, 24 May 2010.

13 Joshua Green (2017), *Devil's Bargain: Steve Bannon, Donald Trump and the Storming of the White House*, London: Scribe UK.

14 James Rainey, 'Breitbart.com sets sights on ruling the conservative conversation', *Los Angeles Times*, 1 August 2012.

15 Amy Mitchell, Jeffrey Gottfried, Jocelyn Kiley and Katerina Eva Matsa, 'Political Polarization and Media Habits, Section 1: Media Sources – Distinct Favorites Emerge on the Left and Right', Pew Research Center, 21 October 2014.

16 Leslie Kaufman, 'Breitbart News Network plans global expansion', *New York Times*, 16 February 2014.

17 See, for example, Kristin Tate, 'Report: lice, scabies, disease at children's immigration shelter on Texas airbase', 2 June 2014; Kristin Tate, 'Illegal immigrants treated better than homeless in US', 17 June 2014; Caroline May, 'Report: more than half of Central American immigrants on welfare', 8 July 2014; Ben Shapiro, '8 reasons to close the border now', 8 July 2014; Brandon Darby, 'Leaked CBP report shows entire world exploiting open US border', 3 August 2014; Matthew Boyle, 'Experts: Ebola could cross unsecured US border', 8 August 2014; Breitbart News, '"Border States of America": New documentary to highlight insecure border, rampant lawlessness in America', 13 October 2014; Tony Lee, 'Professor: Illegal immigrants make "American Dream" more difficult for all', 1 December 2014.

18 Stanley Cohen (1972), *Folk Devils and Moral Panics: The Creation of the Mods and Rockers*, London: MacGibbon & Kee.

19 Keegan Hankes, 'Breitbart under Bannon: how Breitbart became a favorite news source for neo-Nazis and white nationalists', Southern Poverty Law Center, 1 March 2017.

20 Alexis C. Madrigal, 'What Facebook did to American democracy', *The Atlantic*, 12 October 2017.

21 Clare Malone, 'Trump made Breitbart great again', *FiveThirtyEight*, 18 August 2016.

22 Breitbart News, 'Politico: Breitbart audience 18.7 million "conservative fire-brands"', *Breitbart*, 10 July 2015.

23 Joshua Green and Sasha Issenberg, 'Inside the Trump bunker, with days to go', *Bloomberg*, 27 October 2016.

24 Green (2017).

25 Brian Montopoli, 'Propaganda clothed as critique', *Columbia Journalism Review*, 23 March 2005.

26 Vogel and Schreckinger, 'The most powerful woman in GOP politics'.

27 Media Research Center, 'Battle Tested, Battle Ready: 2015 Annual Report'.

28 Rob Faris, Hal Roberts, Bruce Etling, Nikki Bourassa, Ethan Zuckerman and Yochai Benkler, 'Partisanship, Propaganda, and Disinformation: Online Media and the 2016 US Presidential Election', Berkman Klein Center, 16 August 2017.

29 'Alexander Nix, CEO, Cambridge Analytica – Online Marketing Rockstars Keynote OMR17', OMR/YouTube, 10 March 2017, https://www.youtube.com/watch?v=6bG5ps5KdDo (accessed 17 May 2018).

30 Josh Meyer, 'Cambridge Analytica boss went from "aromatics" to psyops to Trump's campaign', *Politico*, 22 March 2018.

31 SCL Elections, 26 January 2013; see https://web.archive.org/web/20130126021428/http:/sclelections.com/ (accessed 17 May 2018).

32 Steve Paulson, 'Former presidential advisor reveals how Obama changed the campaign', Wisconsin Public Radio, 16 September 2015.

33 'Data Brokers: A Call for Transparency and Accountability', Federal Trade Commission, May 2014. Consumers are "largely unaware that data brokers are collecting and using this information" (p. iv).

34 Mike Allen and Kenneth P. Vogel, 'Inside the Koch data mine', *Politico*, 8 December 2014.

35 Jon Ward, 'The Koch brothers and the Republican Party go to war – with each other', Yahoo!, 11 June 2015. Includes 'all-out war' quote.

36 See, in particular, Bert N. Bakker, Matthijs Rooduijn and Gijs Schumacher (2016), 'The Psychological Roots of Populist Voting: Evidence from the United States, the Netherlands and Germany', *European Journal of Political*

Research, 55:2, 302–20; Claudio Barbaranelli, Gian Vittorio Caprara, Michele Vecchione and Chris R. Fraley (2007), 'Voters' Personality Traits in Presidential Elections', *Personality and Individual Differences*, 42:7, 1199–1208; Christopher A. Cooper, Lauren Golden and Alan Socha (2013), 'The Big Five Personality Factors and Mass Politics', *Journal of Applied Social Psychology*, 43:1, 68–82; Alan S. Gerber, Gregory A. Huber, David Doherty, Conor M. Dowling and Shang E. Ha (2010), 'Personality and Political Attitudes: Relationships across Issue Domains and Political Contexts', *American Political Science Review*, 104:1, 111–33; Alan S. Gerber, Gregory A. Huber, David Doherty and Conor M. Dowling (2012), 'Personality and the Strength and Direction of Partisan Identification', *Political Behavior*, 34:4, 653–88; Robert R. McCrae and Oliver P. John (1992), 'An Introduction to the Five-Factor Model and Its Applications', *Journal of Personality*, 60:2, 175–215; Jeffery J. Mondak (2010), *Personality and the Foundations of Political Behavior*, New York: Cambridge University Press.

37 Aina Gallego and Sergi Pardos-Prado (2014), 'The Big Five Personality Traits and Attitudes towards Immigrants', *Journal of Ethnic and Migration Studies*, 40:1, 79–99.

38 Jeffery J. Mondak and Karen D. Halperin (2008), 'A Framework for the Study of Personality and Political Behaviour', *British Journal of Political Science*, 38:2, 335–62.

39 See Michal Kosinski, Sandra C. Matz, Samuel D. Gosling, Vesselin Popov and David Stillwell (2015), 'Facebook as a Research Tool for the Social Sciences: Opportunities, Challenges, Ethical Considerations, and Practical Guidelines', *American Psychologist*, 70:6, 543–56, supplemented by telephone interview with David Stillwell, 11 October 2017.

40 Michal Kosinski, David Stillwell and Thore Graepel (2013), 'Private Traits and Attributes are Predictable from Digital Records of Human Behavior', *Proceedings of the National Academy of Sciences*, 110:15, 5802–5; see also Wu Youyou, Michal Kosinski and David Stillwell (2015), 'Computer-Based Personality Judgments Are More Accurate than Those Made by Humans', *Proceedings of the National Academy of Sciences*, 112:4, 1036–40.

41 Frances Stead Sellers, 'Cruz campaign paid $750,000 to "psychographic profiling" company', *Washington Post*, 19 October 2015.

42 Sasha Issenberg, 'Cruz-connected data miner aims to get inside US voters' heads', *Bloomberg*, 12 November 2015.

43 Arron Banks (2016), *Bad Boys of Brexit*, London: Biteback.

44 Arron Banks, @Arron_banks, Twitter, 30 January 2017, https://twitter.com/arron_banks/status/826092291467132928?lang=en (accessed 21 May 2018).

45 Tom Hamburger, 'Cruz campaign credits psychological data and analytics for its rising success', *Washington Post*, 13 December 2015.

46 Ronald Radosh, 'Steve Bannon, Trump's top guy, told me he was "a Leninist"', *Daily Beast*, 22 August 2016.

47 Jerome Taylor, 'Google chief: my fears for Generation Facebook', *Independent*, 17 August 2010.

Chapter 3: States: the Russia Model

1 See Alexander Smith, 'Vladimir Putin to Megyn Kelly: even children could hack an election', NBC News, 2 June 2017.

2 For reports on various alleged Russian hacks in Europe see Anna Sauerbrey, 'Will the Russians hack Germany, too?', *New York Times*, 21 July 2017; 'Russia hacked Danish defense for two years, minister tells newspaper', Reuters, 23 April 2017; 'Norway institutions "targeted by Russia-linked hackers"', BBC News, 3 February 2017; Kim Willsher and Jon Henley, 'Emmanuel Macron's campaign hacked on eve of French election', *Guardian*, 6 May 2017.

3 For details about the Internet Research Agency see the indictment of February 2018 (Case 1:18-cr-00032-DLF) filed by the Robert Mueller inquiry into alleged Russian meddling in the 2016 US election. The January 2018 minority staff report prepared for the Senate Committee on Foreign Relations, titled 'Putin's Asymmetric Assault on Democracy in Russia and Europe: Implications for US National Security', contains further information about alleged interference across the world.

4 For reports on RT and *Sputnik* see Henry Meyer, Carol Matlack and Stefan Nicola, 'How the Kremlin's disinformation machine is targeting Europe', *Bloomberg*, 16 February 2017; Simon Shuster, 'How Russian voters fueled the rise of Germany's far-right', *Time*, 25 September 2017; Finian Cunningham, 'Who gains from poisoning a Russian exile in Britain?', *Sputnik*, 8 March 2018.

5 For a selection (from many) of Russian denials see Will Worley, 'EU referendum: Vladimir Putin says David Cameron called vote "to blackmail Europe"', *Independent*, 17 June 2016; Michel Rose and Denis Dyomkin, 'After talks, France's Macron hits out at Russian media, Putin denies hacking', Reuters,

29 May 2017; Neil MacFarquhar, 'Denmark says "key elements" of Russian government hacked defense ministry', *New York Times*, 24 April 2017; Mary Ilyushina, Emma Burrows and Hilary Clarke, 'Kremlin dismisses Mueller's indictment of 13 Russians', CNN Politics, 19 February 2018.

6 'The latest: France says no trace of Russian hacking Macron', Associated Press, 1 June 2017.

7 For the full description of this episode in Cold War history see Ladislav Bittman's two autobiographical accounts in *The Deception Game: Czechoslovak Intelligence in Soviet Political Warfare* (1972), Syracuse, NY: Syracuse University Research Corporation; and *The KGB and Soviet Disinformation: An Insider's View* (1985), Washington, DC: Pergamon-Brassey.

8 Major General Oleg Kalugin, quoted in Max Holland (2006), 'The Propagation and Power of Communist Security Services *Dezinformatsiya*', *International Journal of Intelligence and CounterIntelligence*, 19:1, 1–31.

9 Jacues Ellul ([1962] 1965), *Propaganda: The Formation of Men's Attitudes*, New York: Knopf.

10 Examples of these and other KGB activities can be found in Christopher Andrew and Vasili Mitrokhin (2000), *The Mitrokhin Archive, vol. 1: The KGB in Europe and the West*, London: Penguin (notably Chapter 14, 'Information Warfare'); Herbert Romerstein (2001), 'Disinformation as a KGB Weapon in the Cold War', *Journal of Intelligence History*, 1:1, 54–67; Holland (2006); and in Ladislav Bittman's books and various Congressional reports from the period.

11 Cited in Thomas Boghardt (2009), 'Soviet Bloc Intelligence and Its AIDS Disinformation Campaign', *Studies in Intelligence*, 53:4.

12 See Steve Rosenberg's BBC reporting, 'Russia PM Vladimir Putin accuses US over poll protests', BBC News, 8 December 2011.

13 For the development of Russian attitudes to the internet see Sergey Sanovich (2017), 'Computational Propaganda in Russia: The Origins of Digital Disinformation', Working Paper 2017.3, Computational Propaganda Research Project, University of Oxford; Bruce Etling, Karina Alexanyan, John Kelly, Robert Faris, John Palfrey and Urs Gasser (2010), 'Public Discourse in the Russian Blogosphere: Mapping RuNet Politics and Mobilization', Research Publication 2010-11, Berkman Center, Harvard University; Karina Alexanyan, Vladimir Barash, Bruce Etling, Robert Faris, Urs Gasser, John Kelly, John Palfrey and Hal Roberts (2012), 'Exploring Russian Cyberspace: Digitally-Mediated Collective Action and the

Networked Public Sphere', Research Publication 2012-2, Berkman Center, Harvard University.

14 For reports on Medvedev's Silicon Valley visit and attempts to cultivate something similar in Russia see Peter Henderson, 'Russian president tweets, tours Silicon Valley', Reuters, 23 June 2010 and similar; plus James Appell, 'The short life and speedy death of Russia's Silicon Valley', *Foreign Policy*, 6 May 2015. Responses to Medvedev's Facebook post quoted in Kevin O'Flynn, 'Dmitry Medvedev Facebook message against Russian protesters backfires', *Telegraph*, 11 December 2011.

15 'Information Security Doctrine of the Russian Federation, Approved by President of the Russian Federation Vladimir Putin on September 9, 2000', available at https://info.publicintelligence.net/RU-InformationSecurity-2000.pdf (accessed 21 May 2018).

16 Reported by Micah L. Sifry, 'Hillary Clinton launches "21st century state-craft" initiative by State Department', TechPresident blog, 13 May 2009.

17 Sam Dupont, 'Secretary Clinton announces "Civil Society 2.0"', NDN blog, 3 November 2009.

18 Josh Halliday, 'Hillary Clinton adviser compares internet to Che Guevara', *Guardian*, 22 June 2011.

19 Richard Sakwa (2014), *Putin Redux: Power and Contradiction in Contemporary Russia*, Abingdon: Routledge.

20 For a translation of Gerasimov's article (from his speech) see Mark Galeotti's Wordpress blog 'In Moscow's Shadows'. Though much discussed since, Galeotti and Charles Bartles have written particularly good analyses. See Mark Galeotti, 'I'm sorry for creating the "Gerasimov doctrine"', *Foreign Policy*, 5 March 2018; Charles K. Bartles, 'Getting Gerasimov right', *Military Review*, January–February 2016.

21 For Putin's approach to television in Russia see Arkady Ostrovsky (2015), *The Invention of Russia: The Journey from Gorbachev's Freedom to Putin's War*, London: Atlantic; Tina Burrett (2010), *Television and Presidential Power in Putin's Russia*, Abingdon: Routledge. For Putin's approach to internet companies post-2011 see Sanovich (2017); Nikolay Kononov, 'The Kremlin's social media takeover', *New York Times*, 10 March 2014.

22 The entire archive of Kristina Potupchik's emails can be found at potupchik. com.

23 Charles Clover (2016), *Black Wind, White Snow: The Rise of Russia's New Nationalism*, New Haven, CT: Yale University Press. For descriptions of the

Nashi summer camps see Julia Ioffe, 'Russia's nationalist summer camp', *New Yorker*, 16 August 2010; Anna Nemtsova, 'Kremlin's extremist youth camp in Russia', *Daily Beast*, 10 August 2011; Luke Harding, 'Welcome to Putin's summer camp', *Guardian*, 24 July 2008.

24 As quoted in the excellent paper by Julie Fedor and Rolf Fredheim (2017), '"We Need More Clips about Putin, and Lots of Them": Russia's State-Commissioned Online Visual Culture', *Nationalities Papers*, 45:2, 161–81.

25 'Controversial Nashi spokesperson quits', *Moscow Times*, 28 June 2012.

26 Aleksandra Garmazhapova, 'Gde zhivut trolli. I kto ikh kormit' ['Where the trolls live. And who feeds them'], *Novaya Gazeta*, 7 September 2013; Max Seddon, 'Documents show how Russia's troll army hit America', *Buzzfeed*, 2 June 2014. See also 2015 articles on the St Petersburg agency by Adrian Chen (*New York Times*), Shaun Walker (*Guardian*) and Alec Luhn (*Guardian*).

27 Alex Stamos, 'An update on information operations on Facebook', Facebook Newsroom, 6 September 2017.

28 Footage of this is currently still available on YouTube and at Facebook, see 'berkut, polonenuy', Fari Ahad/Facebook, 23 January 2014, https://www.youtube.com/watch?v=z0zD3pOG-Tk (accessed 21 May 2018).

29 For Berkut see, for example, 'Ukraine's Berkut police: what makes them special?', BBC News, 26 February 2014; for incorporation of Berkut into Russian interior ministry see Vladimir Kolokoltsev, 'Russian interior bodies created in Crimea and Sevastopol', TASS, 25 March 2014. CyberBerkut posts sourced via the Wayback Machine internet archive.

30 Adam Hulcoop, John Scott-Railton, Peter Tanchak, Matt Brooks and Ron Deibert, 'Tainted leaks: disinformation and phishing with a Russian nexus', Citizen Lab, 25 May 2017.

31 Lauren Carroll, 'Are the Clinton WikiLeaks emails doctored, or are they authentic?', *Politifact*, 23 October 2016; Willsher and Henley, 'Emmanuel Macron's campaign hacked'.

32 See posts by the Digital Forensic Research Lab on Medium.com, notably Ben Nimmo and Donara Barojan, 'Kremlin and alt-right share "Nazi" narrative', *Medium*, 18 August 2017. See also Isaac Arnsdorf, 'Pro-Russian bots take up the right-wing cause after Charlottesville', *ProPublica*, 23 August 2017.

33 Joseph Cox, 'I bought a Russian bot army for under \$100', *Daily Beast*, 13 September 2017.

34 Alessandro Bessi and Emilio Ferrara (2016), 'Social Bots Distort the 2016 US Presidential Election Online Discussion', *First Monday*, 21:11.

35 Even though the 'Gerasimov doctrine' does not exist, according to Mark Galeotti, who coined the term, it has come to be associated with a new approach to warfare that includes the weaponized use of information.

36 Samantha Bradshaw and Philip N. Howard (2017), 'Troops, Trolls and Troublemakers: A Global Inventory of Organized Social Media Manipulation', Working Paper 2017.12, Computational Propaganda Research Project, University of Oxford; John Reed, 'Vietnam army reveals 10,000-strong cyber warfare unit', *Financial Times*, 26 December 2017; Peter Salisbury, 'The fake-news hack that nearly started a war this summer was designed for one man: Donald Trump', *Quartz*, 20 October 2017.

Chapter 4: The Facebook Elections

1 Julio C. Teehankee and Mark R. Thompson (2016), 'Electing a Strongman', *Journal of Democracy*, 27:4, 125–34.

2 Figures for time spent on social media from 'Digital in 2017', We Are Social, 24 January 2017, https://wearesocial.com/special-reports/digital-in-2017-global-overview (accessed 14 June 2018, figures up to January 2017), Statista (https://www.statista.com) and Internet World Stats (https://www.internetworldstats.com).

3 The most informative reporting of the campaign was by *Rappler* and includes an interview with Nic Gabunada, who ran Duterte's social media team. See Jodesz Gavilan, 'Duterte's P10M social media campaign: organic, volunteer-driven', *Rappler*, 1 June 2016. See also Julio C. Teehankee and Mark R. Thompson (2016), 'Electing a Strongman', *Journal of Democracy*, 27:4, 125–34.

4 For Duterte's appeal for calm see 'Duterte to supporters: be civil, intelligent, decent, compassionate', *Rappler*, 13 March 2016; for a report of the threats see '"Sana ma-rape ka": netizens bully anti-Duterte voter', *Rappler*, 7 April 2016. Duterte's assassination warning to journalists was widely reported; see Simon Lewis, 'Duterte says journalists in the Philippines are "not exempted from assassination"', *Time*, 1 June 2016.

5 For good context on Beppe Grillo's rise see Jamie Bartlett, Caterina Froio, Mark Littler and Duncan McDonnell (2013), *New Political Actors in Europe: Beppe Grillo and the M5S*, London: Demos; for the 2013 Czech election see Ann a Matušková and Wadim Strielkowski (2014), 'Technology Applications in Czech Presidential Elections of 2013: A Story of Social Networks',

Mediterranean Journal of Social Sciences, 5:21; for Hungary see, amongst other coverage, 'If Facebook "likes" were votes, the far-right Jobbik would be the largest Hungarian party', Observationalism blog, 15 February 2014; for *New York Times* quote see editorial 'Argentina's transformative election', 26 November 2015.

6 In addition to news reports on Malaysia see James Gomez (2014), 'Social Media Impact on Malaysia's 13th General Election', *Asia Pacific Media Educator* 24:1, 95–105. Public opinion poll figures for the Scottish referendum from YouGov; see 'Q&A: Scottish independence row', BBC News, 17 January 2012.

7 For early political experiments on Facebook see Jeff Gulati and Christine B. Williams, *Social Media in the 2010 Congressional Elections*, SSRN, 23 April 2011; Kaye D. Sweetser and Ruthann Weaver Lariscy (2008), 'Candidates Make Good Friends: An Analysis of Candidates' Uses of Facebook', *International Journal of Strategic Communication*, 2:3, 175–98.

8 Ellen McGirt, 'How Chris Hughes helped launch Facebook and the Barack Obama campaign', *Fast Company*, 1 April 2009.

9 Aaron Smith and Lee Rainie, 'The Internet and the 2008 Election', Pew Internet and American Life Project, 15 June 2008.

10 For analyses of social media and the 2008 Obama campaign see Derrick L. Cogburn and Fatima K. Espinoza-Vasquez (2011), 'From Networked Nominee to Networked Nation: Examining the Impact of Web 2.0 and Social Media on Political Participation and Civic Engagement in the 2008 Obama Campaign', *Journal of Political Marketing*, 10:1, 189–213; Thomas J. Johnson and David D. Perlmutter (2009–10), 'Introduction: The Facebook Election', *Mass Communication and Society*, 13:5, 554–9; Emily Metzgar and Albert Maruggi (2009), 'Social Media and the 2008 US Presidential Election', *Journal of New Communications Research*, 4:1, 141–65; Jessica Vitak, Andrew Smock, Paul Zube, Caleb Carr, Cliff Lampe and Nicole Ellison (2009), '"Poking" People to Participate: Facebook and Political Participation in the 2008 Election', International Communication Association; Julia K. Woolley, Anthony M. Limperos and Mary Beth Oliver (2009–10), 'The 2008 Presidential Election, 2.0: A Content Analysis of User-Generated Political Facebook Groups', *Mass Communication and Society*, 13:5, 631–52.

11 Gulati and Williams (2011).

12 Aaron Smith, 'The Internet and Campaign 2010', Pew Research Center, 17 March 2011; Aaron Smith, 'Why Americans Use Social Media', Pew Research Center, 14 November 2011.

13 See Cristian Vaccari and Rasmus Kleis Nielsen (2013), 'What Drives Politicians' Online Popularity? An Analysis of the 2010 US Midterm Elections', *Journal of Information Technology & Politics*, 10:2, 208–22.

14 Smith, 'Why Americans Use Social Media'.

15 Facebook statistics and services from Statista; from Miguel Helft, 'Facebook makes headway around the world', *New York Times*, 7 July 2010; from David Kirkpatrick (2011), *The Facebook Effect: The Real Inside Story of Mark Zuckerberg and the World's Fastest-Growing Company*, London: Virgin; and from contemporary news reports.

16 Zeynep Tufekci (2017), *Twitter and Tear Gas: The Power and Fragility of Networked Protest*, New Haven, CT, and London: Yale University Press.

17 Facebook statistics from Facebook Newsroom announcements: 'One billion people on Facebook', 12 October 2012 (plus 'One billion – key metrics', available at https://fbnewsroomus.files.wordpress.com/2012/10/facebook-1billionstats.pdf (accessed 22 May 2018); 'Facebook year in review 2012', 12 December 2012; '2013 year in review', 9 December 2013; '2014 year in review', 9 December 2014). For India and Brazil see Cotton Delo, 'By 2017 India to boast the most Facebook users – by far', *AdAge*, 9 May 2013; PTI, '112 million Facebook users in India, second largest user base after US', *India Today*, 17 December 2014; 'Latin America loves Facebook', *eMarketer*, 2 March 2016. For Indonesia see Lily Kuo, 'Indonesia's presidential race is being fought with Facebook updates and "happy" sing-alongs', *Quartz*, 6 June 2014. For the US see Facebook and MacArthur Research Network on Youth and Participatory Politics (https://ypp.dmlcentral.net).

18 Katie Benner, 'Facebook can tell you what to expect in the voting booth', *New York Times*, 28 October 2016.

19 Max Grömping (2014), '"Echo Chambers": Partisan Facebook Groups during the 2014 Thai Election', *Asia Pacific Media Educator*, 24:1, 39–59.

20 Wolfram Schaffar (2016), 'New Social Media and Politics in Thailand: The Emergence of Fascist Vigilante Groups on Facebook', *Austrian Journal of South-East Asian Studies*, 9:2, 215–33.

21 Antonio García Martínez (2017), *Chaos Monkeys: Mayhem and Mania inside the Silicon Valley Money Machine*, London: Ebury Press.

22 See Emil Protalinski, 'Facebook starts displaying ads in the News Feed', *ZDNet*, 10 January 2012.

23 See Josh Constine, 'Facebook lets businesses plug in CRM email addresses to target customers with hyper-relevant ads', *TechCrunch*, 20 September 2012.

24 See 'Updates to custom audiences targeting tool', Facebook Newsroom, 27 February 2013.

25 See David Cohen, 'UPDATED: Facebook officially launches Lookalike Audiences', *AdWeek*, 19 March 2013.

26 Harold Lasswell (1927), *Propaganda Technique in the World War*, New York: Alfred A. Knopf.

27 Hynek Jeřábek (2001), 'Paul Lazarsfeld: The Founder of Modern Empirical Sociology – A Research Biography', *International Journal of Public Opinion Research*, 13:3, 229–44.

28 Paul F. Lazarsfeld, Bernard Berelson and Hazel Gaudet (1948), *The People's Choice: How the Voter Makes Up His Mind in a Presidential Campaign*, 2nd edition, New York: Columbia University Press.

29 Michael Scherer, 'Friended: how the Obama campaign connected with young voters', *Time*, 20 November 2012.

30 Ed Pilkington and Amanda Michel, 'Obama, Facebook and the power of friendship: the 2012 data election', *Guardian*, 17 February 2012.

31 Craig Elder, interview with author, 4 December 2017.

32 Tim Ross has a much fuller and more detailed description of the Conservatives' campaign in *Why the Tories Won: The Inside Story of the 2015 Election* (2015), London: Biteback.

33 See Martin Moore (2016), 'Facebook, the Conservatives and the Risk to Fair and Open Elections in the UK', *Political Quarterly*, 87:3, 424–30.

34 Dominic Cummings has written about the strategy of Vote Leave at length on his personal blog (https://dominiccummings.com). The figures referenced are from Cummings.

35 See 'On the EU referendum', Dominic Cummings's Blog.

36 See Chandni Vatvani, 'How President Jokowi uses social media to click with people', Channel NewsAsia, 28 March 2017.

37 Robert M. Bond, Christopher J. Fariss, Jason J. Jones, Adam D. I. Kramer, Cameron Marlow, Jaime E. Settle and James H. Fowler (2012), 'A 61-Million-Person Experiment in Social Influence and Political Mobilization', *Nature*, 489, 295–8.

38 Alan S. Gerber, Donald P. Green and Christopher W. Larimer (2008), 'Social Pressure and Voter Turnout: Evidence from a Large-Scale Field Experiment', *American Political Science Review*, 102:1, 33–48; Alan S. Gerber, Gregory A. Huber, David Doherty, Conor M. Dowling and Costas Panagopoulos (2013), 'Big Five Personality Traits and Responses to

Persuasive Appeals: Results from Voter Turnout Experiments', *Political Behavior*, 35:4, 687–728.

39 Katherine Haenschen (2016), 'Social Pressure on Social Media: Using Facebook Status Updates to Increase Voter Turnout', *Journal of Communication*, 66:4, 542–63.

40 For figures on turnout see Niraj Chokshi, 'Facebook helped drive a voter registration surge, election officials say', *New York Times*, 12 October 2016; Sharon Gaudin, 'Thanks to Facebook, voter registrations surge', *Computerworld*, 14 October 2016. For the three million extra voters see David Cowling, 'General election 2017: the mystery of the three million "extra" voters', BBC News, 17 May 2017.

41 For references to figures see Alyaa Azha, 'Social media crucial in election campaign', *Free Malaysia Today*, 19 April 2013; Kuo, 'Indonesia's presidential race'; Statista; and *Reuters Institute Digital News Report 2016*, Reuters Institute for the Study of Journalism. For Elder's comments see 'Craig Elder – The Role of Digital in the Conservatives Election Campaign', Campaigning Summit/YouTube, 18 June 2015, https://www.youtube.com/watch?v=i-BPRArB5gg (accessed 22 May 2018). For *Bloomberg*'s report see Sarah Frier, 'Facebook and Twitter contend with their role in Trump's victory', *Bloomberg*, 9 November 2016.

42 Joshua Green and Sasha Issenberg, "Inside the Trump bunker, with days to go", *Bloomberg*, 27 October 2016.

43 It is not possible to correlate votes and voters but Democratic turnout overall was much lower than previously, notably in key battleground states, and amongst black voters. See David Plouffe, 'David Plouffe: What I got wrong about the election', *New York Times*, 11 November 2016; Bernard L. Fraga, Brian Schaffner, Jesse Rhodes and Sean McElwee, 'Why did Trump win? More whites – and fewer blacks – actually voted', *Washington Post*, 8 May 2017.

44 Josh Roberts, 'Instant Articles now open to all publishers', Facebook Media, 12 April 2016.

45 See, amongst the many articles about Russian ads on Facebook, Matt Reynolds, 'This is what you need to know about those Russian Facebook ads', *Wired*, 2 November 2017.

46 See Samidh Chakrabarti, 'Hard questions: what effect does social media have on democracy?', Facebook Newsroom, 22 January 2018.

47 Mark Zuckerberg, Facebook post, 20 May 2017, www.facebook.com/zuck/posts/10103737049349941 (accessed 14 June 2018).

Chapter 5: Anarchy in the Googlesphere

1 For video see 'Senator Al Franken questions Facebook VP about political ads purchased with foreign currency', C-SPAN, 31 October 2017, https://www.c-span.org/video/?c4688912/senator-al-franken-questions-facebook-vp-political-ads-purchased-foreign-currency (accessed 30 May 2018).

2 Martin Kihn, 'Why ad tech is more complicated than Wall Street', Gartner, 4 December 2014.

3 See Yuyu Chen, 'Programmatic 101: Marketers turn to vendors for ad tech lessons', *Digiday*, 10 May 2017.

4 Bob Hoffman (2017), *BadMen: How Advertising Went from a Minor Menace to a Major Menace*, San Francisco: Type A Group. For an issue that has become central to the functioning of the digital sphere, ad tech is surprisingly under-researched. In addition to Hoffman's book there is Joseph Turow (2011), *The Daily You: How the New Advertising Industry is Defining Your Identity and Your Worth*, New Haven: Yale University Press; and Mike Smith (2015), *Targeted: How Technology is Revolutionizing Advertising and the Way Companies Reach Consumers*, New York: Amacom. More are emerging, but beyond these one has to use reports (which are often proprietary), statements and information from companies themselves, industry journals (most notably *Digiday*) and news articles (including investigations by *ProPublica*). There are also a clutch of very useful blogs and posts by experts, most notably Stratechery by Ben Thompson, Doc Searls, Augustine Fou and Danny Sullivan (before joining Google).

5 For assertions of a duopoly see, for example, Reuters, 'Why Google and Facebook prove the digital ad market is a duopoly', *Fortune*, 28 July 2017; for a helpful breakdown of Google ad revenue see Eric Rosenberg, 'The business of Google', *Investopedia*, 13 November 2017; and for Facebook see Rakesh Sharma, 'How does Facebook make money?' *Investopedia*, 25 April 2018.

6 Sergey Brin and Lawrence Page (1998), 'The Anatomy of a Large-Scale Hypertextual Web Search Engine', Stanford University, available at http://ilpubs.stanford.edu:8090/361/1/1998-8.pdf (accessed 30 May 2018).

7 From Ken Auletta (2009), *Googled: The End of the World as We Know It*, New York: Penguin Press. The various biographies about Google each describe aspects of its development of digital advertising, mostly in positive terms. In addition to Auletta (2009) see John Battelle (2006), *The Search: How Google and Its Rivals Rewrote the Rules of Business and Transformed Our Culture*, rev.

ed., London: Nicholas Brealey; and Steven Levy (2011), *In the Plex: How Google Thinks, Works, and Shapes Our Lives*, New York: Simon & Schuster.

8 See Eytan Elbaz, 'Ten years later: lessons from the Applied Semantics' Google acquisition', *AllThingsD*, 22 April 2013.

9 See Brian Morrissey, 'Today in history: Google buys Applied Semantics', *Digiday*, 23 April 2013.

10 Edwin Bartlett (1845), *Guano, Its Origin, Properties and Uses*, New York: Wiley & Putnam.

11 There is a healthy range of material about guano and its uses, dating back to Bartlett (1845), and including David R. Montgomery (2007), *Dirt: The Erosion of Civilizations*, Berkeley: University of California Press; W. M. Mathew (1970), 'Peru and the British Guano Market, 1840–1870', *Economic History Review*, 23:1, 112–28; Matthew Wills, 'Are we entering a new golden age of guano?', *JStor Daily*, 4 May 2016; and David Armitage, 'From guano to Guantánamo', *Times Literary Supplement*, 4 December 2013. For a much fuller account see Gregory T. Cushman (2013), *Guano and the Opening of the Pacific World: A Global Ecological History*, New York: Cambridge University Press.

12 For a good description of the Macedonian news factory see Samanth Subramanian, 'Inside the Macedonian fake-news complex', *Wired*, 15 February 2017.

13 Sir Martin Sorrell, quoted in Alan Rusbridger, 'Does Journalism Exist?', 2010 Hugh Cudlipp Lecture, transcript at https://www.theguardian.com/media/2010/jan/25/cudlipp-lecture-alan-rusbridger (accessed 30 May 2018).

14 David Sidor (2004), *The Click: A Memoir and Lessons Learned during the Great Internet Boom*, Lincoln, NE: iUniverse.

15 See Jessica E. Vascellaro, 'Google agonizes on privacy as ad world vaults ahead', *Wall Street Journal*, 10 August 2010.

16 Quoted in Auletta (2009).

17 Edmund Lee, 'Google's Invite Media founders: Why we decided not to start the next Facebook', *AdAge*, 4 April 2011.

18 See Nicholas Carlson, 'Meet the 24-year-old who just sold a $70 million company to Google', *Business Insider*, 2 June 2010; David Kaplan, 'Google and Invite Media: one year later, DSP looks to global expansion', *Gigaom*, 7 June 2011.

19 Peter Kafka, 'Google's final price tag for Invite Media: $81 million', *AllThingsD*, 9 June 2010.

20 'The DoubleClick Ad Exchange: growing the display advertising pie for everyone', Google official blog, 17 September 2009.

21 For a report see Lara O'Reilly, 'Google's DoubleClick ad server went down, costing publishers globally "$1 million an hour" in lost revenue', *Business Insider*, 12 November 2014.

22 Figures and quotes on ad fraud from Google official blog.

23 Mike Shields, 'The ad exchange quality issue', *Digiday*, 2 August 2011.

24 See, for example, 'Google user data to be merged across all sites under contentious plan', *Guardian*, 25 January 2012; and response from the Information Commissioner's Office, 'Google to change privacy policy after ICO investigation', 30 January 2015.

25 John McDermott, 'Google takes its tracking into the real world', *Digiday*, 6 November 2013.

26 See Kashmir Hill, 'Facebook will use your browsing and apps history for ads (despite saying it wouldn't 3 years ago)', *Forbes*, 13 June 2014.

27 For an analysis of the Facebook model see 'Inside Facebook's ad machine', Enders Analysis, April 2016; and 'Programmatic advertising in the mobile era: direct marketing success and beyond', Enders Analysis, March 2016.

28 See Steven Engelhardt and Arvind Narayanan (2016), 'Online Tracking: A 1-Million-Site Measurement and Analysis', *CCS 2016: Proceedings of the 2016 ACM SIGSAC Conference on Computer and Communications Security*; Tom Simonite, 'Largest study of online tracking proves Google really is watching us all', *MIT Technology Review*, 18 May 2016.

29 Julia Angwin, 'Google has quietly dropped ban on personally identifiable web tracking', *ProPublica*, 21 October 2016.

30 Daniel Kreiss and Shannon C. McGregor (2018), 'Technology Firms Shape Political Communication: The Work of Microsoft, Facebook, Twitter, and Google with Campaigns during the 2016 US Presidential Cycle', *Political Communication*, 35:2, 155–77.

31 Charlie Warzel, 'Trump fundraiser: Facebook employee was our "MVP"', *Buzzfeed*, 12 November 2016.

32 Ben Elgin and Vernon Silver, 'Facebook and Google helped anti-refugee campaign in swing states', *Bloomberg*, 18 October 2017.

33 Claire Allbright, 'A Russian Facebook page organized a protest in Texas. A different Russian page launched the counterprotest', *Texas Tribune*, 1 November 2017.

34 See 'The Methbot Operation', White Ops, www.whiteops.com/methbot for full description.

35 Jennifer Valentino-DeVries, Jeff Larson and Julia Angwin, 'Facebook allowed political ads that were actually scams and malware', *ProPublica*, 5 December 2017.

36 Lucia Moses, 'Does programmatic advertising have an alt-right problem?', *Digiday*, 17 November 2016.

37 Jonathan Albright, 'Who hacked the election? Ad tech did. Through "fake news", identity resolution and hyper-personalization', *Medium*, 31 July 2017.

38 Kate Stanford, 'How Political Ads and Video Content Influence Voter Opinion', Think with Google, March 2016.

39 Based on count of trackers by Ghostery in May 2018.

40 Dipayan Ghosh and Ben Scott, '#DigitalDeceit: The Technologies Behind Precision Propaganda on the Internet', New America Foundation, January 2018.

Chapter 6: The Unbearable Lightness of Twitter

1 'Rania Ibrahim's Snapchat/FB Live from Inside the Grenfell London Tower Fire. With Subtitles', Faz Naz/YouTube, 15 June 2017, https://www.youtube.com/watch?v=e0SP7PV0Avk (accessed 30 May 2018).

2 Mark Rice-Oxley, 'Grenfell: the 72 victims, their lives, loves and losses', *Guardian*, 14 May 2018; 'Grenfell Tower Inquiry: Names of all 72 victims read out', BBC News, 31 May 2018.

3 Kensington and Chelsea Foundation, @KandCfoundation, Twitter, 15 June 2017, https://twitter.com/KandCfoundation/status/875282231278919680 (accessed 30 May 2018).

4 'Grenfell Tower fire: how Twitter users united against the tragedy', *The Week*, 15 June 2017.

5 Sam Sholli, '"You come when people die!" Jon Snow "mobbed" for coverage of Grenfell Tower disaster', *Express*, 18 June 2017; 'Angry resident confronts Channel 4's Jon Snow over Grenfell Tower coverage', LBC, 15 June 2017.

6 See Gemma Newby, 'Why no-one heard the Grenfell blogger's warnings', BBC News, 24 November 2017.

7 For more on news coverage see Freddy Mayhew, 'Journalists missed concerns raised by Grenfell residents' blog – but specialist mag sounded alarm on tower block fire safety', *Press Gazette*, 21 June 2017; Dominic Ponsford,

'Grenfell Tower fire disaster suggests more journalism is needed in London – not less', *Press Gazette*, 21 June 2017.

8 'KCTMO – Playing with fire!', Grenfell Action Group blog, 20 November 2016.

9 Jon Snow, 'The Best and Worst of Times', James MacTaggart Memorial Lecture, Edinburgh TV Festival, 23 August 2017.

10 Dhiraj Murthy (2011), 'Twitter: microphone for the masses?', *Media, Culture and Society*, 33:5, 779–89; @abdur, 'Top Twitter trends of 2009', Twitter blog, 15 December 2009; 'Twitter responds to the Japanese disaster', Pew Research Center, 17 March 2011.

11 In addition to *Hatching Twitter* (2013), London: Sceptre, see Nick Bilton, 'All is fair in love and Twitter', *New York Times*, 9 October 2013.

12 Referenced in Noah Arceneaux and Amy Schmitz Weiss (2010), 'Seems Stupid until You Try It: Press Coverage of Twitter, 2006–9', *New Media and Society*, 12:8, 1262–79.

13 Clive Thompson, 'Clive Thompson on how Twitter creates a social sixth sense', *Wired*, 26 June 2007.

14 Steve Hodson, 'Twitter is not a micro-blogging tool', *Mashable*, 18 July 2008.

15 Jessica E. Vascellaro, 'Twitter trips on its rapid growth', *Wall Street Journal*, 26 May 2009; @kevinweil, 'Measuring tweets', Twitter blog, 22 February 2010.

16 Paul Farhi (2009), 'The Twitter Explosion', *American Journalism Review*, April/May.

17 George Washington University and Cision, '2009 Social Media & Online Usage Study', December 2009.

18 Alfred Hermida (2010), 'Twittering the News. The Emergence of Ambient Journalism', *Journalism Practice,* 4:3, 297–308.

19 Alan Rusbridger, 'The Splintering of the Fourth Estate', Andrew Olle Media Lecture, Sydney, 19 November 2010; transcript published in the *Guardian*, 19 November 2010.

20 Quoted in Stephen R. Barnard (2016), '"Tweet or Be Sacked": Twitter and the New Elements of Journalistic Practice', *Journalism*, 17:2, 190–207.

21 Marcel Broersma and Todd Graham (2013), 'Twitter as a News Source: How Dutch and British Newspapers Used Tweets in Their News Coverage 2007–2011', *Journalism Practice*, 7:4, 446–64.

22 Biz Stone, 'What's Happening?', Twitter blog, 19 November 2009.

23 Project for Excellence in Journalism, *State of the News Media 2006: An Annual Report on American Journalism*, available at http://assets.pewresearch.

org.s3.amazonaws.com/files/journalism/State-of-the-News-Media-Report-2006-FINAL.pdf (accessed 31 May 2018).

24 See consecutive *State of the News Media* reports; plus Felix Richter, 'The decline of newspaper advertising continues', Statista, 7 September 2012.

25 Steven Waldman, 'The Information Needs of Communities: The Changing Media Landscape in a Broadband Age', FCC, July 2011.

26 Leonard Downie Jr and Michael Schudson (2009), 'The Reconstruction of American Journalism', *Columbia Journalism Review*, November/December.

27 Jennifer Dorroh (2009), 'Statehouse Exodus', *American Journalism Review*, April/May.

28 Margaret Simons, 'Journalism faces a crisis worldwide – we might be entering a new dark age', *Guardian*, 15 April 2017.

29 Based on estimates by industry journal *Press Gazette*.

30 Working Party on the Information Economy, 'The Evolution of News and the Internet', OECD, 11 June 2010.

31 Dominic Ponsford, 'How the rise of online ads has prompted a 70 per cent cut in journalist numbers at big UK regional dailies', *Press Gazette*, 24 January 2017.

32 Andy Williams, 'Stop press? Crisis in Welsh newspapers and what to do about it', Radical Wales, 10 October 2011.

33 Kate Starbird, Dharma Dailey, Ann Hayward Walker, Thomas L. Leschine, Robert Pavia and Ann Bostrom (2015), 'Social Media, Public Participation, and the 2010 BP Deepwater Horizon Oil Spill', *Human and Ecological Risk Assessment*, 21:3, 605–30.

34 Referenced in Alfred Hermida, Seth C. Lewis and Rodrigo Zamith (2014), 'Sourcing the Arab Spring: A Case Study of Andy Carvin's Sources on Twitter During the Tunisian and Egyptian Revolutions', *Journal of Computer Mediated Communication*, 19:3, 479–99.

35 Paul Farhi, 'NPR's Andy Carvin, tweeting the Middle East', *Washington Post*, 12 April 2011.

36 Craig Silverman, 'Is this the world's best Twitter account?', *Columbia Journalism Review*, 8 April 2011.

37 See Farida Vis (2013), 'Twitter as a Reporting Tool for Breaking News: Journalists Tweeting the 2011 UK Riots', *Digital Journalism*, 1:1, 27–47.

38 Hermida et al. (2014); Vis (2013).

39 For more see Bahareh Rahmanzadeh Heravi and Natalie Harrower (2016), 'Twitter Journalism in Ireland: Sourcing and Trust in the Age of Social

Media', *Information, Communication and Society*, 19:9, 1194–1213; Barnard (2016); John H. Parmelee (2013), 'Political Journalists and Twitter: Influences on Norms and Practices', *Journal of Media Practice*, 14:4, 291–305; and Arthur D. Santana and Toby Hopp (2016), 'Tapping into a New Stream of (Personal) Data: Assessing Journalists' Different Use of Social Media', *Journalism and Mass Communication Quarterly*, 93:2, 383–408.

40 Marcel Broersma and Todd Graham (2016), 'Tipping the Balance of Power, Social Media and the Transformation of Political Journalism', in Axel Bruns, Gunn Enli, Eli Skogerbø, Anders Olof Larsson and Christian Christensen (eds), *The Routledge Companion to Social Media and Politics*, Abingdon: Routledge.

41 See Mary Madden, 'State of Social Media: 2011', Pew Research Center, 14 December 2011.

42 'Social Networking Popular across Globe', Pew Research Center, 12 December 2012.

43 *Reuters Institute Digital News Report 2013*, Reuters Institute for the Study of Journalism.

44 Emily Guskin, 'How do you use Facebook and Twitter for news?', Pew Research Center, 7 November 2013.

45 Twitter Inc., 'One hundred million voices', Twitter blog, 8 September 2011.

46 'In changing news landscape, even television is vulnerable', Pew Research Center, 27 September 2012.

47 See Iryna Pentina and Monideepa Tarafda (2014), 'From "Information" to "Knowing": Exploring the Role of Social Media in Contemporary News Consumption', *Computers in Human Behavior*, 35, 211–23.

48 Andreas Jungherr (2016), 'Twitter Use in Election Campaigns: A Systematic Literature Review', *Journal of Information Technology and Politics*, 13:1, 72–91.

49 Tom Rosenstiel, Amy Mitchell, Kristen Purcell and Lee Rainie, 'How people learn about their local community', Pew Research Center, 26 September 2011.

50 Gay Alcorn, 'Australia's journalism is in mortal danger. Politicians should join the fight to save it', *Guardian*, 3 May 2017.

51 For a full description of the situation in Canada see *The Shattered Mirror: News, Democracy and Trust in the Digital Age* (2017), Ottawa: Public Policy Forum.

52 Ramón Salaverría and Beatriz Gómez Baceiredo (2018), *Spain – Media Landscape*, European Journalism Centre; *Reuters Institute Digital News Report 2017*, Reuters Institute for the Study of Journalism.

53 Julia Cagé (2016), *Saving the Media: Capitalism, Crowdfunding, and Democracy*, Cambridge, MA: Belknap Press.

54 Minutes of EFJ annual meeting, Bucharest, Romania, 18–19 May 2017.

55 Gordon Ramsay and Martin Moore, *Monopolising Local News: Is There an Emerging Democratic Deficit in the UK due to the Decline of Local Newspapers?*, Centre for the Study of Media, Communication and Power, King's College London, May 2016.

56 Esther Addley, 'The 10 top news stories of 2014 on theguardian.com', *Guardian*, 26 December 2014.

57 See 'Survey: people aren't news reading; they're "news snacking"', *AdWeek*, 25 June 2013.

58 Philipp Müller, Pascal Schneiders and Svenja Schäfer (2016), 'Appetizer or Main Dish? Explaining the Use of Facebook News Posts as a Substitute for Other News Sources', *Computers in Human Behavior*, 65, 431–41; Logan Molyneux (2018), 'Mobile News Consumption: A Habit of Snacking', *Digital Journalism*, 6:5, 634–50.

59 See Elina L. Niño, 'Deciphering the mysterious decline of honey bees', *The Conversation*, 24 May 2016.

60 Rasmus Kleis Nielsen (2015), 'Local Newspapers as Keystone Media: The Increased Importance of Diminished Newspapers for Local Political Information Environments', in Rasmus Kleis Nielsen (ed.), *Local Journalism: The Decline of Newspapers and the Rise of Digital Media*, London: I. B. Tauris.

61 The findings on the *Port Talbot Guardian* and Rachel Howells's research are from Howells's PhD dissertation and from an interview and conversations with the author.

62 Rachel Howells, email exchange with author.

63 Matthew Clayfield, 'The little blue bird has flown: how Twitter lost its value as a news source', *Guardian*, 13 June 2017.

64 See Nitasha Tiku and Casey Newton, 'Twitter CEO: "We suck at dealing with abuse"', *The Verge*, 4 February 2015.

65 Twitter Inc., 'Progress on addressing online abuse', Twitter blog, 15 November 2016.

66 Douglas Guilbeault and Sam Woolley, 'How Twitter bots are shaping the election', *The Atlantic*, 1 November 2016.

67 Graham Vyse, 'Can journalists live without Twitter?', *New Republic*, 26 June 2017.

68 See Liana B. Baker, 'Twitter CEO calls company "people's news network"', *Reuters*, 11 October 2016.

69 *American Views: Trust, Media and Democracy*, Gallup/Knight Foundation, January 2018.

70 See Philip M. Napoli, Sarah Stonbely, Kathleen McCollough and Bryce Renninger, 'Assessing the Health of Local Journalism Ecosystems: A Comparative Analysis of Three New Jersey Communities', Rutgers School of Communication and Information, June 2015.

71 Ramsay and Moore (2016).

72 Based on news reports and on email correspondence with *Athens Live* (AthensLive.gr). According to *Athens Live* the two remaining newspapers in the area, the *ThessNews* and *Typos* of Thessaloniki, employ only a handful of people, and have low circulation and minimal interaction with the city. See Panagiotis Mandatzis, 'Daily newspapers in Thessaloniki are dying', *AthensLive*, 21 December 2017; Lambrini Papadopoulou, 'Greece's second city faces life without major local daily', IPI, 5 December 2017.

73 See William Turvill, 'Local councils now employ at least 3,400 comms staff – more than double the total for central government', *Press Gazette*, 10 April 2015; William Turvill, 'UK police forces spend more than £36m a year on PR and communications', *Press Gazette*, 1 May 2015.

74 Juliet Eilperin, 'Here's how the first president of the social media age has chosen to connect with Americans', *Washington Post*, 26 May 2015.

75 Annika Bergström and Maria Jervelycke Belfrage (2018), 'News in Social Media: Incidental Consumption and the Role of Opinion Leaders', *Digital Journalism*, 6:5, 583–98.

76 Peter Oborne and Tom Roberts (2017), *How Trump Thinks: His Tweets and the Birth of a New Political Language*, London: Head of Zeus.

77 Joyojeet Pal (2015), 'Banalities Turned Viral: Narendra Modi and the Political Tweet', *Television and New Media*, 16:4, 378–87.

78 Shakuntala Rao (2018), 'Making of Selfie Nationalism: Narendra Modi, the Paradigm Shift to Social Media Governance, and Crisis of Democracy', *Journal of Communication Inquiry*, 42:2, 166–83.

Chapter 7: Platform Democracy

1 'Amazon, Berkshire Hathaway and JPMorgan Chase & Co. to partner on US employee healthcare', Business Wire, 30 January 2018.

2 Nick Wingfield, Katie Thomas and Reed Abelson, 'Amazon, Berkshire Hathaway and JPMorgan team up to try to disrupt health care', *New York Times*, 30 January 2018.

3 Derek Thompson, 'Amazon, Berkshire Hathaway, and JPMorgan are going to fix health care – somehow', *The Atlantic*, 30 January 2018.

4 David Crow, 'Amazon, Berkshire and JPMorgan join forces to shake up healthcare', *Financial Times*, 30 January 2018.

5 Clinton Leaf, 'Amazon–JPMorgan–Berkshire Hathaway: what their new health venture really means', *Fortune*, 31 January 2018.

6 Amitai Etzioni, 'An open letter to Jeff Bezos – you are needed to disrupt the health care sector', *Quartz*, 29 September 2017.

7 'Amazon Web Services, American Heart Association partner on precision cardiovascular medicine', *Beckers Health IT & CIO Report*, 12 July 2016.

8 Eugene Kim and Christina Farr, 'Amazon has a secret health tech team called 1492 working on medical records, virtual doc visits', CNBC, 26 July 2017.

9 Bob Herman, 'Amazon reportedly talking to pharmacy benefit managers', *Axios*, 20 September 2017.

10 David Rowan, 'DeepMind: inside Google's super-brain', *Wired*, 22 June 2015.

11 Memorandum of understanding, referenced and linked to from Julia Powles and Hal Hodson (2017), 'Google DeepMind and healthcare in an age of algorithms', *Health and Technology*, 7:4, 351–67.

12 See 'DeepMind Health at NHS Expo 2016 – Delivering the Benefits of a Digital NHS', DeepMind/YouTube, 8 September 2016, https://youtu.be/L2oWqbpXZiI (accessed 31 May 2018).

13 See Verily website (https://verily.com) and various reports including Jessica Hamzelou, 'Google's new project will gather health data from 10,000 people', *New Scientist*, 24 April 2017; and Jo Best, 'Project Baseline: Alphabet's five-year plan to map the entire journey of human health', *ZDNet*, 31 January 2018.

14 'Apple is going after the health care industry, starting with personal health data', CBInsights Research Briefs, 20 September 2017.

15 See Apple ResearchKit, CareKit and HealthKit websites (https://developer.apple.com/researchkit/, https://developer.apple.com/carekit/, https://developer.apple.com/healthkit/); and Tim Cook keynote speech, September 2017, referenced in 'Apple is going after the health care industry, starting with personal health data', CBInsights Research Briefs, 20 September 2017.

16 Diane Coyle (2018), 'Platform Dominance: The Shortcomings of Antitrust Policy', in Martin Moore and Damian Tambini (eds), *Digital Dominance: The Power of Google, Amazon, Facebook, and Apple*, New York: Oxford University Press.

17 For more see the Cancer Genomics Cloud (www.cancergenomicscloud. org), the Cancer Genome Atlas at AWS and the National Institutes of Health (NIH) (https://cancergenome.nih.gov/).

18 Brian M. Bot et al. (2016), 'The mPower Study, Parkinson Disease Mobile Data Collected Using ResearchKit', *Scientific Data* 3, article no. 160011.

19 See 'Apple is going after the health care industry'.

20 For report see Aliya Ram, 'DeepMind develops AI to diagnose eye diseases', *Financial Times*, 4 February 2018.

21 Powles and Hodson (2017).

22 'Aetna to transform members' consumer health experience using iPhone, iPad and Apple Watch', Aetna, 27 September 2016.

23 Casey Newton, 'Inside Facebook's plan to build a better school', *The Verge*, 3 September 2015.

24 Natasha Singer, 'The Silicon Valley billionaires remaking America's schools', *New York Times*, 6 June 2017; Natasha Singer and Mike Isaac, 'Facebook helps develop software that puts students in charge of their lesson plans', *New York Times*, 9 August 2016.

25 'Who we are – mission', Summit Public Schools website, summitps.org/ whoweare/mission (accessed 31 May 2018).

26 Nichole Dobo, 'Despite its high-tech profile, Summit charter network makes teachers, not computers, the heart of personalized learning', *Hechinger Report*, 1 March 2016.

27 Chris Weller, 'There's a teaching method tech billionaires love – here's how teachers are learning it', *Business Insider*, 1 September 2017.

28 David Marley, 'Mark Zuckerberg and his plan for a personalized learning revolution', *Times Educational Supplement*, 19 January 2017.

29 Mark Zuckerberg, 'A letter to our daughter', Facebook, 1 December 2015.

30 'CZI takes over building Summit Learning Platform', *EdSurge*, 13 March 2017.

31 Bill Gates, 'I love this cutting-edge school design', GatesNotes, 22 August 2016.

32 Singer, 'The Silicon Valley billionaires remaking America's schools'.

33 Issie Lapowsky, 'Inside the school Silicon Valley thinks will save education', *Wired*, 4 May 2015.

34 Natasha Singer, 'How Google took over the classroom', *New York Times*, 13 May 2017.

35 Joanna Allhands, 'Why use Google Classroom? Here's what you need to know', *azcentral*, 9 October 2017.

36 John F. Pane, Elizabeth D. Steiner, Matthew D. Baird, Laura S. Hamilton and Joseph D. Pane, *Informing Progress: Insights on Personalized Learning Implementation and Effects*, RAND Corporation, July 2017.

37 Monica Bulger, 'Personalized Learning: The Conversations We're Not Having', Working Paper, Data & Society, 22 July 2016.

38 Faith Boninger, Alex Molnar and Kevin Murray, *Asleep at the Switch: Schoolhouse Commercialism, Student Privacy, and the Failure of Policymaking*, National Education Policy Center, August 2017.

39 Leonie Haimson, 'Parents rebel against Summit/Facebook/Chan-Zuckerberg online learning platform', Parent Coalition for Student Privacy, 31 August 2017.

40 'Privacy Center', Summit Learning website, https://www.summitlearning. org/privacy-center (accessed 1 June 2018).

41 Deborah Lupton and Ben Williamson (2017), 'The Datafied Child: The Dataveillance of Children and Implications for Their Rights', *New Media & Society*, 19:5, 780–94.

42 Emma Hinchliffe, 'Lyft just came out with its biggest innovation yet: buses', *Mashable*, 29 March 2017.

43 Spencer Woodman, 'Welcome to Uberville', *The Verge*, 1 September 2016.

44 Laura Bliss, 'A bus-shunning Texas town's big leap to microtransit', *CityLab*, 20 November 2017; Hanna Creger, 'Uber and Lyft's effort to disrupt public transportation will hurt the environment and screw the poor', *AlterNet*, 26 August 2017.

45 Cliff Kuang, 'An exclusive look at Airbnb's first foray into urban planning', *Co.Design*, 2 August 2016.

46 Andrew Ferguson, 'The rise of big data policing', *TechCrunch*, 22 October 2017.

47 Alex Bozikovic, 'Google's Sidewalk Labs signs deal for "smart city" makeover of Toronto's waterfront', *Globe and Mail*, 17 October 2017.

48 Sidewalk Labs, RFP submission, 17 October 2017, available at https://side-walktoronto.ca/wp-content/uploads/2018/05/Sidewalk-Labs-Vision-Sections-of-RFP-Submission.pdf (accessed 1 June 2018).

49 'TfL works with Waze and Eurotunnel to prevent Blackwall Tunnel closures', Transport for London, 8 December 2017.

50 Ken Auletta (2009), *Googled: The End of the World as We Know It*, New York: Penguin Press.

51 Peter Thiel (2014), *Zero to One: Notes on Startups, or How to Build the Future*, New York: Crown Business.

52 Bernard Crick (1962, revised edition 1964), *In Defence of Politics*, Harmondsworth: Penguin.

53 George Orwell, 'Freedom and happiness', *Tribune*, 4 January 1946, in Peter Davison (ed.) (2001), *Orwell and Politics*, London: Penguin.

Chapter 8: Surveillance Democracy

1 For report see Amruta Byatnal, 'Tembhli becomes first Aadhar village in India', *The Hindu*, 29 September 2010.

2 Dina Gerdeman, 'India's ambitious national identification program', *Working Knowledge*, Harvard Business School, 30 April 2012.

3 Amiya Bhatia and Jacqueline Bhabha (2017), 'India's Aadhaar Scheme and the Promise of Inclusive Social Protection', *Oxford Development Studies*, 45:1, 64–79.

4 Pranesh Prakash, 'Aadhaar marks a fundamental shift in citizen-state relations: from "We the People" to "We the Government"', *Hindustan Times*, 3 April 2017.

5 Kiran Jonnalagadda, 'A rant on Aadhaar', Kārana, *Medium*, 6 December 2016.

6 Rachna Khaira, 'Rs 500, 10 minutes, and you have access to billion Aadhaar details', *The Tribune*, 4 January 2018.

7 Shekhar Gupta, 'God, please save India from our upper class Aadhaarophobics', *ThePrint*, 9 January 2018.

8 Sally Engle Merry (2011), 'Measuring the World: Indicators, Human Rights, and Global Governance', *Current Anthropology*, 52:S3, S83–S95.

9 Harriet Swain, 'The suspect Romeo', interview with Timothy Garton Ash, *Times Higher Education*, 11 July 1997.

10 R. Ramakumar, 'What the UID conceals', *The Hindu*, 21 October 2010.

11 Nandan Nilekani, 'Ideas for India's future', TED Talk, May 2009. See also Nandan Nilekani (2009), *Imagining India: Ideas for the New Century*, London: Allen Lane; and Nandan Nilekani and Viral Shah (2016), *Rebooting India: Realizing a Billion Aspirations*, London: Allen Lane.

12 Nandan Nilekani, 'Unique Biometric ID: Creating a Large Scale Digital Ecosystem Using the Aadhaar Experience', South Asia Institute Mahindra Lecture, Harvard University, 3 November 2014.

13 Pranav Dixit, 'India's national ID program may be turning the country into a surveillance state', *Buzzfeed*, 4 April 2017.

14 Anjali Bhardwaj and Amrita Johri, 'Aadhaar: when the poor get left out', Hindu Centre for Politics and Public Policy, 18 January 2018.

15 Anumeha Yadav, 'In Rajasthan, there is "unrest at the ration shop" because of error-ridden Aadhaar', *Scroll.in*, 2 April 2016.

16 Menaka Rao, 'Why Aadhaar is prompting HIV positive people to drop out of treatment programmes across India', *Scroll.in*, 17 November 2017.

17 From TrustID website, www.trustid.in/about-us (accessed 1 June 2018); and 'Matrimonial frauds – Beware!', TrustID blog, 24 June 2016.

18 Pratap Bhanu Mehta, 'Big Brother is winning', *Indian Express*, 8 February 2017.

19 Adarsh Ramanujan, 'Right to privacy: SC judgment raises serious questions about Aadhaar', *Financial Express*, 5 September 2017.

20 See Amber Sinha, 'Should Aadhaar be mandatory?', *Deccan Herald*, 9 December 2017.

21 PTI, 'There's an orchestrated campaign to malign Aadhaar: Nandan Nilekani', *Indian Express*, 11 January 2018.

22 ET Now video, available on Facebook at https://www.facebook.com/etnow/videos/1471268036248071/ (accessed 1 June 2018).

23 R. Sriram, 'View: What privacy setback? Aadhaar may have just sealed Modi's victory in 2019', *Economic Times*, 28 August 2017.

24 See Linda Poon, 'Singapore, City of Sensors', *CityLab*, 21 April 2017.

25 Matt Hamblen, 'Singapore's "city brain" project is groundbreaking – but what about privacy?', *Computerworld*, 12 December 2016.

26 Aaron Souppouris, 'Singapore is striving to be the world's first "smart city"', *Engadget*, 3 November 2016.

27 Singapore Housing and Development Board, 'My Smart HDB Home @ Yuhua', videos available on YouTube.

28 See Siau Ming En, 'Tele-rehab option for physiotherapy to be rolled out at 14 institutions', *Today* (Singapore), 5 May 2017.

29 PM Lee Hsien Loong, National Day Rally speech, 20 August 2017, Institute of Technical Education College Central. Transcript and video available at 'National Day Rally 2017', Prime Minister's Office website, http://www.pmo.gov.sg/national-day-rally-2017 (accessed 1 June 2018).

30 Shane Harris, 'The Social Laboratory', *Foreign Policy*, 29 July 2014.

31 Ezra Ho (2017), 'Smart Subjects for a Smart Nation? Governing (Smart) mentalities in Singapore', *Urban Studies*, 54:13, 3101–18.

32 'Freedom of the Press 2014 – Singapore', Freedom House.

33 'Singapore: Events of 2017', *World Report 2018*, Human Rights Watch.

34 Elgin Toh, 'AGC initiates contempt of court case against Li Shengwu', *Straits Times*, 14 November 2017.

35 'Lee Kuan Yew's Singapore: an astonishing record', *The Economist*, 22 March 2015.

36 Paul Guyer (2000), *Kant on Freedom, Law, and Happiness*, Cambridge: Cambridge University Press.

37 Masashi Crete-Nishihata, Lotus Ruan, Jakub Dalek and Jeffrey Knockel, 'Managing the message: what you can't say about the 19th National Communist Party Congress on WeChat', Citizen Lab, 6 November 2017.

38 Gary King, Jennifer Pan and Margaret E. Roberts (2013), 'How Censorship in China Allows Government Criticism but Silences Collective Expression', *American Political Science Review*, 107:2, 326–43.

39 Peter Lorentzen (2014), 'China's Strategic Censorship', *American Journal of Political Science*, 58:2, 402–14.

40 Gary King, Jennifer Pan and Margaret E. Roberts (2017), 'How the Chinese Government Fabricates Social Media Posts for Strategic Distraction, Not Engaged Argument', *American Political Science Review*, 111:3, 484–501.

41 Margaret Roberts (2014), 'Fear, Friction, and Flooding: Methods of Online Information Control', PhD dissertation, Harvard University; see also Margaret E. Roberts, 'Testimony before the US–China Economic and Security Review Commission: Hearing on China's Information Controls, Global Media Influence, and Cyber Warfare Strategy', 4 May 2017.

42 Lo Shih-hung, 'How Apple is paving the way to a "cloud dictatorship" in China', *Global Voices*, 10 February 2018.

43 'Alibaba Partners Chinese Govt to Trial Blockchain in Healthcare', CCN, 22 August 2017.

44 Meng Jing, 'Baidu offers facial recognition technology to help Beijing airport streamline boarding, traffic', *South China Morning Post*, 24 August 2017.

45 Liza Lin and Josh Chin, 'China's tech giants have a second job: helping Beijing spy on its people', *Wall Street Journal*, 30 November 2017.

46 'State Council Notice Concerning Issuance of the Planning Outline for the Construction of a Social Credit System (2014–2020)', posted by Rogier Creemers on China Copyright and Media blog, 14 June 2014.

47 Eva Xiao, 'Tencent's new credit system to use payments, social data', *Tech in Asia*, 31 January 2018.

48 Mara Hvistendahl, 'Inside China's vast new experiment in social ranking', *Wired*, 14 December 2017.

49 DH News Service, 'Philippines shows interest in Aadhaar', *Deccan Herald*, 25 January 2018.

50 Jayadevan PK, 'India's latest export: 20 countries interested in Aadhaar, India Stack', *Factor Daily*, 10 January 2018.

51 Meera Srinivasan, 'Sri Lanka is keen to introduce an Aadhaar-like initiative', *The Hindu*, 21 December 2017.

52 Reuters staff, 'Thailand to roll out biometric checks for SIM cards nation-wide', Reuters, 6 November 2017.

53 'The winners of the "Le Monde" Smart-Cities 2017 Global Innovation Awards', *Le Monde*, 31 May 2017.

54 'About the Prize', Lee Kuan Yew World City Prize website, https://www.leekuanyewworldcityprize.com.sg/about/about-the-prize (accessed 4 June 2018).

55 Karishma Vaswani, 'Tomorrow's Cities: Singapore's plans for a smart nation', BBC News, 21 April 2017.

56 Ralf Dahrendorf, 'The rise and fall of meritocracy', *Project Syndicate*, 13 April 2005.

57 Yadav, 'In Rajasthan, there is "unrest at the ration shop"'.

58 Jathan Sadowski and Frank Pasquale (2015), 'The Spectrum of Control: A Social Theory of the Smart City', *First Monday*, 20:7 (original emphasis).

59 Radheshyam Jadhav, 'First Indian to get Aadhaar card & her village are truly "cashless"', *Times of India*, 29 December 2016.

Chapter 9: Democracy Rehacked

1 Emmanuel Macron, speech in Athens, 7 September 2017, transcript at 'European Union – Speech by the President of the French Republic (Athens, 7 September 2017)', France Diplomatie, https://www.diplomatie.gouv.fr/en/french-foreign-policy/european-union/events/article/european-union-speech-by-the-president-of-the-french-republic-athens-07-09-17 (accessed 4 June 2018).

2 Claudia Chwalisz and David Van Reybrouck, 'Macron's sham democracy', *Politico*, 12 February 2018.

3   Richard Wike, Katie Simmons, Bruce Stokes and Janell Fetterolf, 'Many Unhappy with Current Political Systems', in *Globally, Broad Support for Representative Democracy*, Pew Research Center, 16 October 2017.

4   Roberto Stefan Foa and Yascha Mounk (2016), 'The Danger of Deconsolidation: The Democratic Disconnect', *Journal of Democracy*, 27:3, 5–17.

5   Paolo Gerbaudo (2017), *The Mask and the Flag: Populism, Citizenism and Global Protest*, London: C. Hurst.

6   Manuel Castells (2013), *Communication Power*, 2nd ed., Oxford: Oxford University Press.

7   Simon Tormey (2015), *The End of Representative Politics*, Cambridge: Polity Press.

8   John Keane, 'The End of Representative Politics?', *The Conversation*, 19 May 2015.

9   David Van Reybrouck (2016), *Against Elections: The Case for Democracy*, London: Bodley Head.

10   Jason Brennan (2016), *Against Democracy*, Princeton: Princeton University Press.

11   Ricardo de Querol, 'Zygmunt Bauman: "Social media are a trap"', *El País*, 25 January 2016.

12   See Mélida Jiménez, 'Is democracy in a worldwide decline? Nope. Here's our data', *Washington Post*, 15 November 2017.

13   International IDEA (2017), *The Global State of Democracy: Exploring Democracy's Resilience*, Stockholm: International IDEA.

14   See 'Guards at the Gate: The Expanding State Control over the Internet in Iran', Center for Human Rights in Iran, January 2018.

15   See 'Sudan to unleash cyber jihadists', BBC News, 23 March 2011.

16   See 'Freedom on the Net 2014: Sudan' and 'Freedom on the Net 2015: Sudan', Freedom House.

17   Nga Pham, 'Vietnam admits deploying bloggers to support government', BBC News, 12 January 2013.

18   Excerpts from the emails can be found at Efe Kerem Sozeri, 'RedHack leaks reveal the rise of Turkey's pro-government Twitter trolls', *Daily Dot*, 30 September 2016.

19   Gerbaudo (2017).

20   See various accounts including Sally McGrane, 'Icelander's campaign is a joke, until he's elected', *New York Times*, 25 June 2010, in addition to archived pages of the Best Party and its policies at the Wayback Machine internet archive (at bestiflokkurinn.is).

21 See Dana Bash, 'Trump taps Brad Parscale to run his 2020 re-election campaign', CNN, 1 March 2018.

22 Theresa May, speech at World Economic Forum Annual Meeting, 25 January 2018. Video available at World Economic Forum website (https://www.weforum.org).

23 See, for example, Tony Romm, 'President Trump wants a "sweeping transformation" of government tech, he says at a White House meeting with execs', *Recode*, 19 June 2017.

24 For an excellent assessment of digital democracy initiatives around the globe see Julie Simon, Theo Bass, Victoria Boelman and Geoff Mulgan, 'Digital Democracy: The Tools for Transforming Political Engagement', NESTA, February 2017.

25 'Pauline Véron: "le budget participatif de Paris aurait aussi pu être thématique"', lesbudgetsparticipatifs.fr, 22 November 2017.

26 Further information at Paris Budget Participatif (https://budgetparticipatif.paris.fr/bp/).

27 Brian Wampler and Mike Touchton, 'Brazil let its citizens make decisions about city budgets. Here's what happened', *Washington Post*, 22 January 2014.

28 See 'Better Reykjavik', citizens.is, https://www.citizens.is/portfolio_page/better_reykjavik/ (accessed 4 June 2018).

29 See the World Values Surveys 2011 to 2014.

30 Macon Phillips, 'A good problem to have: raising the signature threshold for White House petitions', White House blog, 3 October 2011; and Macon Phillips, 'Why we're raising the signature threshold for We the People', White House blog, 15 January 2013.

31 Paul Hitlin, '"We the People": five years of online petitions', Pew Research Center, 28 December 2016.

32 J.A. 'Deport Justin Bieber and revoke his Green Card', created 23 January 2014, We the People, White House.

33 Harald Mahrer and Robert Krimmer (2005), 'Towards the Enhancement of E-Democracy: Identifying the Notion of the "Middleman Paradox"', *Information Systems Journal*, 15:1, 27–42.

34 Christopher H. Achen and Larry M. Bartels (2016), *Democracy for Realists: Why Elections Do Not Produce Responsive Government*, Princeton: Princeton University Press.

35 Alexis de Tocqueville (1994 edition), *Democracy in America*, Everyman's Library, London: David Campbell Publishers Ltd.

36 Kevin Roose and Sheera Frankel, 'Mark Zuckerberg's reckoning: "This is a major trust issue"', *New York Times*, 21 March 2018.

37 See May, speech at World Economic Forum Annual Meeting; and Anushka Asthana, 'Theresa May calls on tech firms to lead fight against online extremism', *Guardian*, 25 May 2017.

38 See Noé Jacomet, 'How the g0v movement is forking the Taiwanese government', Open Source Politics, *Medium*, 13 April 2017.

39 Audrey Tang, 'Uber responds to vTaiwan's coherent blended volition', pol.is blog, *Medium*, 23 May 2016.

40 Quoted in Max Rashbrooke, 'How Taiwan is inoculating itself against the Uber "virus"', *CityMetric*, 8 February 2017.

41 Edward White, 'INTERVIEW: Taiwan's "Digital" Minister, Audrey Tang (Part 2)', *News Lens*, 3 November 2016.

42 'Estonia and Iceland – what we share', Ministry of Foreign Affairs, Republic of Estonia, 23 October 2009.

43 Helen Margetts and Andre Naumann, 'Government as a Platform: What Can Estonia Show the World?', Oxford Internet Institute, University of Oxford, February 2017.

44 Daniel Vaarik (2015), 'Where Stuff Happens First. White Paper on Estonia's Digital Ideology', available at https://www.mkm.ee/sites/default/files/digitalideology_final.pdf (accessed 5 June 2018).

45 BDA, think tank of the president of Estonia. Cited in Margetts and Naumann, 'Government as a Platform'.

INDEX